DAN BANA

Also by Stanhope White:

DESCENT FROM THE HILLS

Stanhope White

DAN BANA

The Memoirs of a
Nigerian Official

H

JAMES H. HEINEMAN, INC. · NEW YORK

Published in the United States of America by
JAMES H. HEINEMAN, INC.
60 East 42nd Street
New York, New York 10017

Library of Congress Catalog Card Number: 67–11679

British publisher: Cassell and Company Ltd
Printed in Great Britain and bound in the United States of
America

To Margaret
who also preferred bush,
and to
the people of Northern Nigeria

For forms of government let fools contest;
Whate'er is best administer'd is best.

Pope

Preface

In September 1965 I wrote to my old friend, Sir Abubakar Tafawa Balewa, Prime Minister of Nigeria, telling him of this book. I wrote:

Since I returned to England I have been asked on many occasions to give talks about Nigeria; I have always been dismayed at the ignorance of the British people about your country, but delighted at the interest shown when the pill of knowledge is hidden in the sugar of personal reminiscence. Indeed, my experience is that British audiences are most receptive and I feel that I may have done something to foster good relations between Nigeria and Great Britain.

With the idea of reaching an even wider audience, I have written a book which has been accepted for publication by Cassells. In it I have described the more interesting and amusing incidents in my career as Assistant District Officer and District Officer in Bornu, Benue, Kano and Sokoto provinces. In the introduction and in the last chapter I have touched on some of the problems that you face and some of the mistakes that we made. . . .

Could you consider writing a short foreword for it?

The reply to this letter appears overleaf; but the march of events culminating in the assassinations of the night of 14–15 January meant that Sir Abubakar was never to write the foreword.

It may be held that no book about Nigeria under British rule has any relevance to the position today. But no matter what fate may overtake those who rule Nigeria from now on, the ordinary mass of the Nigerian people remains the same. We who served Nigeria may have had doubts about the wisdom of the steps taken to give Independence; we may have had terrible fears for the future; but nothing can destroy our love for her peoples or our fervent hopes for their future.

If our fears are realized, Sir Abubakar and Sir Ahmadu Bello, the Sardauna of Sokoto and Prime Minister of Northern Nigeria, will have died in vain.

CABINET OFFICE,
LAGOS,
NIGERIA.

PPS.27   17th September, 1965.

Dear Mr. White,

    My Private Secretary has just brought to my notice
a copy of your letter which was earlier addressed to me.
I am sorry that the first letter did not reach me.

    I am glad to know that you have written a book
about my country as a result of your many years service
in Northern Nigeria. I am sure that such a book will be
of great help not only to the people of Nigeria but to
others who have not yet had the opportunity of visiting
this country.

    I am looking forward to receiving a copy of the
Printers' Proof when this is ready, and it will be my
pleasure to write a Foreword.

        With best wishes.

                    Yours sincerely,

                    Abubakar Tafawa Balewa
                    Prime Minister of the Federal
                    Republic of Nigeria.

Mr. Stanhope White,
8 Church Road,
Old Felixstowe,
SUFFOLK.

Contents

CONTENTS

Illustrations

Acknowledgements

I would like to thank the Ministry of Information, Lagos, for permission to reproduce many of the photographs in this book, taken by their photographer Francis Uher. Thanks are also due to Sir Alan Herbert for permission to quote from his poem 'Exploitation'. Readers of the old *West African Review*, now alas no more, may recognize parts of Chapters 6 and 17, which originally appeared in that periodical.

A special note of thanks should go to my old colleague Mr. F. W. Parsons, now of the London School of African and Oriental Languages, for his explanation of the meaning of my nickname of 'Dan Bana'. The Hausa language is one of many subtle inflections and shades of meaning; the principal meaning of 'Dan Bana' is 'he who is up to date'.

To what extent this is a compliment is for the reader to decide.

Introduction

In his recent book *A Start in Freedom* the author, then Sir Hugh Foot, writes that when introducing himself to American audiences he tells them that they are looking at a member of a vanishing race, for Colonial Governors will soon be as dead as the dodo. The Colonial Administrative Service, from which most Governors came, is already dead, and the Empire it served is no more.

There has always been almost complete ignorance in this country of the colonies for which it had assumed responsibility, and little apparent desire to learn. Now they are mostly independent, but independence has not brought economic self-sufficiency. Instead, there are more and more demands for help which, if they are not met by us, will be met by the Communist countries. These demands are resented by the British taxpayer, who seems to have so many problems of his own to solve; he meets students from these countries filling places at our universities badly needed by ourselves, who angrily claim that they have every right to expect such help as it is but small recompense for many years of exploitation. We receive OXFAM appeals for starving children, yet we see pictures of vast sports grounds and official palaces costing hundreds of thousands of pounds in the countries where such children live. Ignorance must be dispelled on both sides; sympathy and understanding must take its place, for we are all members of one world community.

In Africa the newly independent states are not old political entities with strong internal racial and administrative ties, freed after a short period of alien, European rule to resume their halted progress. Instead, most are chunks of the earth's surface arbitrarily made into political units as the statesmen of Europe drew straight lines and arcs on almost blank maps of the continent at conferences in Brussels and Berlin eighty years and more ago, in successful efforts to avert war between themselves over the division of this unknown territory.

It is therefore no wonder that, from time to time, we read of murder and rape stemming from tribal and religious hatreds kept in check when Europe ruled. These hatreds are often much fiercer than that between white and black of which so much is written, but of which we in Nigeria knew nothing.

The problems that the governments of these countries face are many; transcending them all is the appalling problem of the population explosion brought into being by death control. If it is not solved its effects will equal those of a nuclear war, and indeed may be the cause of such a catastrophe, for the mushroom crowd holds as great a menace as the mushroom cloud. The new governments, almost submerged by their rapidly increasing populations, are as hopeless in their efforts at forward progress as was the Red Queen; no matter how great their forward strides may be, they stand still. But we are all—black and white, brown and yellow—citizens of one planet from which there can be no flight when populations or bombs explode. The problems of our former colonies are no longer our direct responsibility, but as members of one of the richer units in the world community we must still help.

Ignorance must be dispelled on both sides. Yet those who speak of Scots and Welsh, English and Russian, who reject the concept of 'European' but talk of 'African', do great harm. Africa, like Europe, is a continent; we in Europe are basically of one race; in Africa there are many: Hamites, Bantu, Nilotics, Semites, Negroes and others. There is greater ethnological difference between an Ibo of Eastern Nigeria and a Shuwa Arab of the North than there is between the Arab and ourselves. Before 1900 there was not, even legally speaking, any such thing as a Nigerian; we must pray that the term can come in time to have real meaning.

Compared with many parts of Africa, Nigeria appears steady as a rock; if it were to fail and fall apart the outlook for Africa and her diverse peoples would be grim.

This book is not an attempt to consider these daunting problems or to suggest facile solutions for them; nor is it a learned study of the part played by the Colonial Administrative Service in the history of Africa in the first half of this century. It is only a personal record of eighteen years' service to the people of Northern Nigeria, and of friendships with men of many tribes:

ex-slaves and emirs, horse-boys and premiers, pagans and descendants of the Prophet. In eighteen years, of necessity, I often came into direct contact with some of these problems; some should have been solved before we handed over responsibility. It should have been a prerequisite for independence that others, particularly those of the ridiculous frontiers and divided peoples, should have been submitted to international scrutiny and rectification.

Contact with these problems means that they must appear in the pages that follow; perhaps, like Mr Stiggins's 'moral pocket-handkerchiefs', this book will instruct as well as amuse, and thus do something to better understanding between the two countries.

What were we like, we members of the Colonial Administrative Service? Ignorant, gin-swigging, unshaven remittance-men of whom Britain was well rid, spending more time in the arms of our Tondeleyos than in prosaic work? Or tropical-suited and -helmeted, mere Civil Servants removed from the dusty corridors of Whitehall to the magic of tropic seas and skies, to polo and racing and exclusive white clubs, where obsequious 'boys' waited on our smallest whim? Did we really know our territories and their peoples and their problems, or were they merely subject matter in files which paused momentarily on our desks *en route* from the 'In' to the 'Out' tray?

There is a recent study of the service by Professor Heussler of Syracuse University who, as an American, is not prejudiced in our favour. In *Yesterday's Rulers* he records much to admire and much to serve as a model both to his own country and to the United Nations in their relations with the underdeveloped countries; he laments that no place was found for us in the various Agencies of the United Nations, where our knowledge of Africa and our love of and respect for her peoples could have been used for the benefit of the world community. He writes of the way the majority of us preferred to work in 'bush', as those parts remote from the benefits of civilization are called, and of our amused contempt for those of our fellows desk-bound in the various Secretariats, and for the members of the Home Civil Service in the Colonial Office, working with paper, not men. He quotes a letter from one such District Officer: 'For my sins I have been posted to the Secretariat, to half-sexed work for which I have no training and no inclination.'

We in the Provincial Administration had little time for those who worked at the centre; they, exasperated beyond measure when their paper-work was held up through the non-appearance of some return, would scathingly refer to us as 'Bush D.O.s'. I was the writer of that private letter, unaware when it was written that it would be kept, filed and released for quotation fifteen years later. Sir Hugh Foot speaks for those who worked at the centre; I for the Bush D.O., without whose efforts the 'start in freedom' could never have occurred.

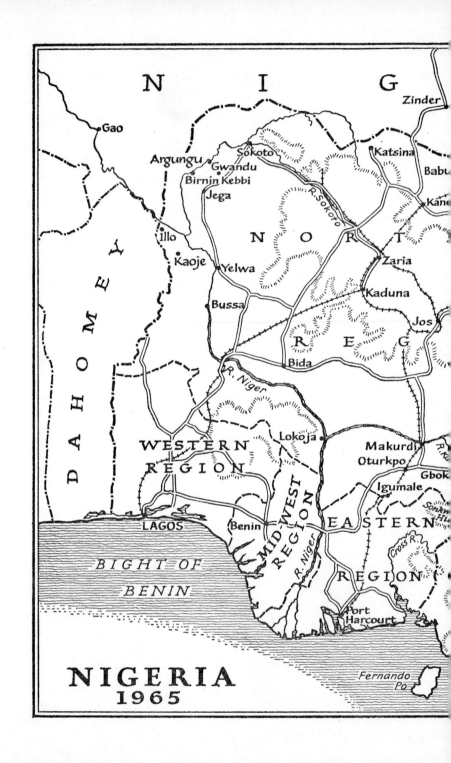

NIGERIA
1965

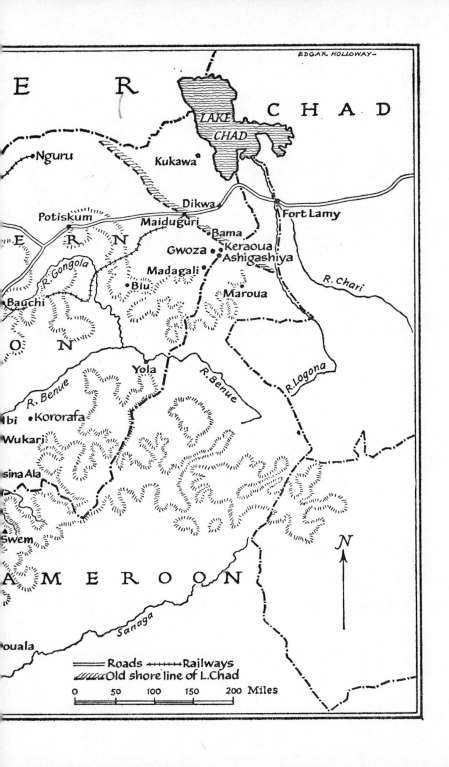

EDGAR HOLLOWAY—

E R · Nguru · Kukawa C H A D

LAKE CHAD

· Dikwa

Potiskum · Maiduguri · Fort Lamy

E R N · Bama

· Gwoza · Keraoua

Madagali · Ashigashiya

R. Gongola · Biu · Maroua R. Chari

Bauchi

O N

Yola R. Benue R. Logona

R. Benue

bi · Kororafa

Wukari

sina Ala

Swem

N

A M E R O O N

Sanaga

ouala

Roads ┼┼┼┼ Railways

Old shore line of L. Chad

0   50   100   150   200 Miles

PART ONE

Bornu

CHAPTER ONE

The Market at Maiduguri

The heat of the sun, as ever in these border lands of the Sahara, was, even at ten in the morning, almost too great to bear, but under the shade of the lines of great fig trees, planted by the first administrative officers when they moved the Capital of Bornu from Kukawa in the swamplands of Chad to a new site on the ridge which marked the lake's ancient shoreline, it was like riding in the nave of some great, green cathedral. A little to my rear rode Arab, the Resident's Chief Messenger and Interpreter. He was mounted on a skinny brown stallion, riding deep in an old French cavalry saddle too large for the horse; his legs hung down well below its belly and he gripped the small brass Shuwa stirrups—for they are too small to allow the whole of the foot to be placed in them—with each big toe. Like many more Arabs, even though they came from diverse parts of Africa, he preferred these to the more usual huge shovel-shaped stirrups used by the Kanuri and throughout Hausaland, through which the whole foot could slip—sometimes with fatal results when a rider fell in a ceremonial charge and his skull was broken between pounding hooves and the way beneath when neither stirrup-leather nor girth broke.

The connection between the lands on either side of the great desert is of immeasurable antiquity, perhaps never broken except when the sands covered the border lands in the drier parts of the cycles of climatic change. At one time Mourzouk and other towns of the Fezzan fell within the Bornu Empire and even after the loss of these to the Turkish conquerors of North Africa, a colony of Tripolitan Arabs had lived at the Bornu Court and acted as intermediaries between the ruling powers on either side of the Sahara desert. Until the coming of the European, this colony had been largely engaged as agents for the caravans which crossed the desert each year with thousands of slaves, of whom many left their bodies to become sun-dried and mummified, horrible testimony for years of man's inhumanity to man, until mercifully

3

covered at last by the drifting sands. These slaves were purchased with the proceeds of the trade goods from Europe brought on the southward-bound caravans, from the members of the Bornu nobility who each year organized raids against the countries of the Kirdi or Pagans in the hills and swamps of the south. Of this colony, now peaceful traders in wares other than human bodies, and living on the edge of the great market, Arab was a leading and highly respected member.

The two miles of alternating aching heat and restful shade which lay between the European station and the new African town of 'Yelwa' or 'Yerwa', 'The place of plenty', were soon covered. We had heard the noise of the great *Kasuku Leteninbe*, or Monday Market, as we mounted, a noise chiefly of many voices blended by distance into a hum like that of some great hive. As we reached its edge, the noise, the smells, the heat and the flies were almost overpowering. Few who have not experienced it can have any conception of the pertinacity of flies to stick to the mouth or the corners of the eyes or the nostrils or the armpits—anywhere in fact that they can obtain some slight degree of moisture. We were assailed on all sides.

The centre of the market consisted of brick and cement stalls raised a foot or so above ground level, roofed with corrugated-iron sheets; farther out were smaller stalls in long rows consisting of a low bank of mud bricks sheltered by a thatched roof carried on supports three or four feet high. On the periphery of these were still others, consisting of little more than a plaited grass mat thrown over four upright sticks, to give some little shade from the scorching sun, for with the growth of the town the market had far outgrown that originally built under avenues of figs, planted as bare stakes to give great shade these thirty or so years later.

The market was thronged by perhaps eight or ten thousand people, a *mélange* of tribes, races and religions from the segment of Africa running from the Mediterranean to the Bight of Benin, of whom the northernmost were the Tripolitan Arabs. These were as light-skinned as I—or even lighter, for they shunned the sun— and they wore tight white trousers, short, shirt-like gowns of striped white cotton, waistcoats of brown or red serge decked out with black embroidery, and low red fezes or white skull-caps.

4

Their greetings were long and in Arabic, which Arab translated into Hausa for me, and they bade us enter the shade of their shops to drink small cups of black, sweet, Turkish coffee. These shops, open to the market's milling throng, were filled with trade goods from Europe; behind them were the noisome warehouses packed with goatskins, cattle hides, gum arabic, corn and ground-nuts. From the roof of each shop hung lines carrying folded lengths of white shirting with large blue trade-marks on each, marks conservatively bought year after year despite the fact that all were heavy with fuller's earth and other dressings to make the cotton appear—until washed—as best linen. Lengths of cheap cotton prints, some few velvets, tins of kerosene, packets of bis-cuits, jars of a well-known vapour rub, whose English manu-facturers, wondering at their enormous sales in this one part of Africa, were not to know that to their customers a jar of what they called 'Mr Lethem' bore the honoured name and therefore the warranty of one of the early and greatly respected Residents of Bornu. Cheap scents with labels showing large-breasted maidens, the face—but not the bosom—concealed as with all true Moslems, cheap writing-paper, skull-caps, soap and bars of iron loaded the shelves. Many of the shops were presided over—in the absence of the Master of the House, haggling round the back over the purchase of dried goatskins—by sluttish-looking black women magnificent in robes of bright prints, the concubines or junior wives of the Tripolitans, whose senior wives, presumably as white as themselves, were never allowed from the strict secrecy of the harem.

We left our horses in the care of the Arab who had given us coffee and, with Arab leading, made our way through the market. This was my first visit and formed part of my general education and introduction to Bornu. My Hausa was of little use in this crowd and the English language of even less value; Arab and I conversed largely in Hausa with from time to time an English word. As we made our way through the crowds he was greeted by many in either Arabic or Kanuri, for it was of these two races that the market throng was chiefly composed; it was in one or other of these languages that he addressed a stall-holder when I put questions to him.

There is a great difference between the members of these two races, despite the fact that the Kanuri claim an origin in the Arabian Peninsula; the Shuwa, whilst often tall, are always slightly built whilst the Kanuri are a fine, muscular race with rather flat faces showing no doubt the admixture of negroid blood from their long residence in these parts. Most of the men wore plain indigo-dyed blue gown and trousers, with yard-wide hats of plaited grass which shaded not only their faces but, as the sun at midday was almost vertically overhead, their bodies in addition. Many carried tall spears with large leaf-shaped blades; not as mere ornament or from custom but because of the many highway robbers who infested the roads of Bornu, a legacy of the troubled times of the last fifty years of the nineteenth century. On the edge of the market was the place to which the firewood-carriers brought their wares, staggering in with bent legs under enormous loads balanced on a pad on their heads and with the skin on either side of the scalp ruckled by the weight into many folds. For nine or ten miles around Maiduguri most of the tree cover had been stripped to supply the needs of the town and a start was being made on the growth of quick-growing neems with seeds from India, to replace the lost cover and to provide fuel for the future. These hewers of wood—and drawers of water for many of the households in the town—were in most cases Pagans from the Gwoza Hills away to the south whose ancestors had been captured from time to time in slave-raids to perform the same menial tasks that these, their descendants, performed willingly. At home they went naked but when they ventured forth, protected by the peace that the European had brought, to earn the two shillings which each compound must pay as tax each year, they donned a few shreds of tattered rags, or leather aprons to conceal their nakedness. Not for modesty's sake, for in the markets at the foot of their hills, as I was soon to see, they went naked unconcerned in front of the equally unconcerned clothed Fulani and Shuwa and Kanuri women. But here, in Maiduguri, they were in a tiny minority and cover was needed less to hide their genitals as such than to disguise the fact that amongst the circumcised Moslems they were uncircumcised Pagan. With dirt-stained bodies and unkempt hair, with little knowledge of any language but their own, they kept themselves to themselves, working for threepence or sixpence a day, eating poor foods and sleeping on mats under

6

the trees or under the empty stalls of the market at night, until they had accumulated enough to pay the tax at home and to buy some few small luxuries.

In the great crowd were other races, many also of Pagan origin, but who went clothed at home, or at least partially so; some from the plains which lie between the Kanuri and Shuwa country and the hills of the Gwoza Pagans, to whom they were probably related ethnologically; others who were of distinct racial groups—stocky, well-built pocket Hercules, the Sara, Banana and Musgu from the swamps of the Chari and Logona, the great northward-flowing rivers which entered Chad away to the southeast.

Over all hung a light cloud of dust; everywhere were strong smells; everywhere flies; scarcely a whisper of a breeze stirred the air as we made our circuit. Many of the stalls were stocked with the same European goods which we had seen in the shops of the Tripolitans—cloth, thread, fezes and so on. One or two sold nothing but imported brass basins of various sizes which enjoyed great popularity amongst the Shuwa women who decorated the inner 'rooms' of their houses with row after row of them, thus both storing and displaying their wealth at one and the same time. There were sellers of red peppers and of wild red rice from the Chad swamps; of natron, a very impure salt from the oasis of Bilma far to the north of Chad whence it was brought once a year in great caravans of perhaps ten thousand camels. (On leave eighteen months or so later, I saw a Paul Robeson film of which I remember nothing except my astonishment at seeing, tucked away in the ersatz Hollywood nonsense, a series of authentic shots of the great salt-caravan.) European salt was also on sale; this was obtained in blocks from the European stores, crushed to powder, mixed with flour and a little water, then baked in moulds under hot ashes to give hard cakes which could be sawn into fragments of all sizes, down to those retailed for a few *aninis* a time—an *anini* being the tenth of a penny.

As well as firewood, other commodities had their own special areas on the periphery of the main market; at one place were great heaps of Guinea corn carried to market in huge hide bags across the backs of oxen; most of the corn was of the white variety known as *masakwa*, laboriously planted by hand in the

7

rich black soil around Chad as the waters shrank with the coming of the dry season. At another point were animals for sale: horses, donkeys, camels, sheep, goats and cattle. Most of the horses were poor jaded brutes with great, open saddle-sores, almost too worn out to flick away the swarms of moisture-seeking flies sucking around their eyes. The camels, too, often showed even greater sores on their emaciated humps, sometimes with maggots squirming over the exposed and stinking flesh, whilst the patient donkeys called to mind Sam Weller's comment that no one had ever seen a happy donkey in this world. The cattle on the other hand were often plump and in good condition, with great humps, bursting with fat, hanging sideways over their bodies.

The condition of the animals in the market was under the surveillance of a *Mallam* or junior employee of the Veterinary Department, who either treated the animal on the spot or ordered it away to the animal dispensary where it could be put out of its misery or kept until healed. There was no such happy release for the pathetic remnants of humanity who begged piteously for help: blind men and women, sometimes two or three in whining crocodiles, each with begging-bowl in one hand, the other clutching the end of a stick held by the one in front, calling for the alms which God had ordained that the Faithful must give. Burnt-out lepers with no fingers or toes; grotesquely deformed men and women, some with twig-like legs swinging themselves rapidly through the crowd on little wooden shoes held in either hand; a few lunatics, often completely naked and covered in filth, with slobbering jaws and expressions less intelligent than those of the animals nearby.

Farther on was the market for dried fish from Chad where great, brown, strongly smelling bundles showed a few fins and heads to bear testimony to their piscine origin. Next the meat stalls, cement slabs with a good supply of water but with great masses of horrible bottle-green flies settling on the meat. Nearby were the sellers of cooked meat with their little mounds of sand and ash, perhaps a yard across, on which they kindled afresh each day small fires of charcoal and cornstalk. They squatted cutting goat-meat into small lumps and skewering these on foot-long lengths of cane; these were smeared with a mixture of groundnut-oil and powdered nuts and then set upright in the mound of sand to cook around the fire.

Beyond these again were the dye-pits, five or six feet deep like the pots in which the robbers hide in *Chu Chin Chow*; these too with their own distinctive, repulsive smell, a compound of rotting indigo and the cow-manure with which it was mixed—whether to release the dye from the leaves or to act as mordant to the cloth I know not. Each dyer had a long ten-foot pole with crossed staves tied to one end; this he plunged into each noisome pit and stirred the evil-smelling, bubbling contents. Some squatted on the rim of their pit wringing out the clothes which had been dyed; their arms were green-blue from many years' exposure to their wares. Under large trees were the men who took the dried cloths and beat into each one powdered antimony to give a deep blue, shiny lustre; grey-bearded wearers of their products would from time to time carefully wipe their beards on the sleeves of their gleaming gowns to get the blue-bearded appearance admired from Dakar to Baghdad.

Under more trees on the edge of the market were the weavers busy at their looms, and in neighbouring streets others preparing their warps from bobbins of cotton spun by women in villages nearer the Lake where cotton was grown. Up and down they walked, guiding the thread from the bobbins through a loop at the end of a light cane, round stakes thrust into the sandy road. When the warp was prepared, it was carefully transferred to the loom to be woven into narrow four-inch-wide strips many feet long. Their looms were placed under the trees for shade, and if no tree was available a light shelter was constructed to protect the bent head of the weaver from the cruel heat as he threw the shuttle from hand to hand. Round each big toe were looped the strings which alternately raised and lowered the two parts of the warp; this stretched beyond the loom to end coiled in a weighted calabash; as the woven strip grew it was wound round itself to grow at last to resemble a coiled hose-pipe on a fire-engine. The amount each man wove each day was marked by the track of the calabash in the sand as it was drawn forward with each pass of the shuttle. Its speed and appearance gave it the weavers' name of 'the tortoise'.

In addition to the usual currency of Nigeria—brass shillings and nickel pennies, halfpennies and tenths of a penny, these all with holes through their middle to facilitate stringing—the Maria Theresa dollar and French and Italian silver coins were to be seen, whilst the rolls of narrow cloth, known as *gabaga*, were also acceptable currency. After careful examination of the fineness of the weaving a bargain would be struck at so many fathoms of cloth; the seller and buyer squatted on the ground facing each other, the fathom's length apart. The buyer would carefully place the end of his *gabaga* under one big toe and then roll the hose-pipe like a reel to the seller; the latter would similarly clasp the end of the agreed length under a big toe and return the reel. As the lengths mounted, the onlooker could see that the buyer reduced each one by perhaps a quarter of an inch; at the other end, the seller similarly added to each length by drawing that end a little closer towards him; when all was measured each was happy in the thought that he had gained or saved perhaps six inches in all. The tension of alternate fathoms was similarly varied, in that the buyer of the goods pulled the fathom as tight as possible to stretch it by perhaps half an inch, whilst the seller rolled his length out gently and with no tension to ensure that in this way he got a similar amount.

Late arrivals came striding in, their gowns girded up the better to allow them to step out, across their shoulders a stick or spear over which both hands were hung with the arms hanging down each side. Little cavalcades of Fulani women carrying cala-bashes of milk in which floated small pats of good yellow butter came chattering into the market; Shuwa women riding on the rumps of cattle holding before them the loads that they hoped to sell; stout Kanuri matrons, their hair gathered helmet-like on their heads, with tribal marks deep cut in each cheek, a red or green button in one pierced nostril, a small glass charm tied to the hair above the forehead, its shape said to commemorate the period when the Berber peoples were Christian.

Heat, dirt, smells, flies, noise; sweat and disease; misery and avarice; yet a scene repeated countless times during the next eighteen years, in many parts of Nigeria, of which I never tired. The medicine-men with their dried frogs and hornbill heads, seeds, spices and Heaven knows what else; the learned *Mallams* who wrote a verse of the Koran on a piece of paper, which was then folded and sewn into a piece of leather as a charm to hang from wrist or elbow (I was long known as the 'European of the Charm' when in jest I purchased one to help me catch those evading payment of the cattle-tax); the barbers squatting in front of their clients, shaving face or head, stropping locally made razors on the palms of their hands. An oft-repeated joke, guaranteed to reduce to laughter all but he who sat with his back towards me as he was being shorn, was to attract the attention of the barber, and to motion silently that he draw the razor across the throat thrust out towards him.

Under more great trees was the butter market where sat the Shuwa and Fulani women with their wares. The Fulani were more aquiline of feature than the Shuwa, many of whom had the wide nostrils which showed the admixture of negroid blood. The hair of the Fulani generally hung in long black plaits, gleaming from the application of melted butter; the Shuwa had short hair often powdered with red pepper. Many of both races had babies asleep on their backs or seated between their mothers' legs, sucking at pendulous breasts swinging above them. Many of the younger girls had magnificent figures, their firm, arrogant breasts exposed as they sat, their clothes around their loins. Arab looked at me as we turned away.

'If the Master of the House wishes to have a Fulani or Shuwa virgin, it can be arranged,' he told me; as we returned slowly to the Government Station he expounded the local attitude to such matters. This was a man's world in which women played but a small part. All men, no matter what the colour of their skin, were the same at heart; it was natural to want a woman, above all to want a virgin. Some white men differed from the black in that they had nothing to do with women other than their true white-skinned wives, but others took concubines for a few months or a few years and none thought either ill or well of them. Few children were born of such unions though one later Assistant District Officer was said to have his own cousin as his steward boy. In nearby Dikwa, where I was soon to go, the Germans had been in charge for a dozen years, the French for two and the British for twenty; of British offspring there were none, of Germans but few, but several junior members of the Native Administration were said to have French blood in their veins and French brains in their heads.

11

We mounted the ridge and came into the full heat of the early afternoon; nothing stirred except the shimmer of the heat-haze over the white road; it was nearly three, the hour when exhausted nature demanded rest from the eternal heat and glare; the station slept. We parted: Arab to return to the Residency to ponder over the questions of this latest European; I to my cement box to rest and to read some Hausa, to emerge an hour or so before dusk for polo or a ride.

CHAPTER TWO

The Bornu Empire

It was in August 1936 that I first saw Bornu. I was not a complete stranger to Africa, for I had been with the Egyptian Desert Survey and with Leakey, hunting for earliest man, in East Africa, where my name has been given to one of the sites in the fabulous Olduvai Gorge. In Kenya and Tanganyika we worked on a shoestring; those members of the Colonial Administrative Service whom we met, we regarded with awe; they trekked with campbeds and large tents, crockery and water-filters; two of us shared a tent, we slept on the ground, ate off enamel plates and drank liquid mud as it came from the water-hole, merely boiling it to kill the certain infection it contained. Boiling could not remove the taste of animal urine and at times we only knew whether we drank soup or tea, coffee or water, by the container in front of us.

Now I was a member of that Service, but posted to Northern Nigeria as I had refused to serve in Kenya, where it seemed to me that our colonization of the White Highlands was based on injustice or error that must lead at last to conflict with the Kikuyu when they sought to repossess their lands, taken from them, as they saw it, by force and guile. East Africa had an almost perfect climate, and the Administrative Service lived amongst some of the most fantastically beautiful country in the world, often amongst herds of tens of thousands of head of game. I had rejected such bounties for the colourless savannah and swamps of Bornu.

A fortnight by sea from Liverpool to Lagos, hearing, not for the last time, the old Coaster song, first sung when this was 'The White Man's Grave':

> The West Coast in the best coast,
> It's the best coast of all;
> In Nigeria they're very superior ...

Superiority it was said, increased as we travelled down the coast.

In Northern Nigeria were the most superior, men who rode and played polo.

Forty-eight hours by train to Jos, then 356 miles by lorry to Maiduguri, capital town of the Province of Bornu. Nineteen-thirty-six was the first year in which the road was open during the whole of the rains, so, unlike my predecessors, I had to trek no part of the way. With me were two boys found for me in Lagos, my household appliances, food and drink for a year, saddlery, camping equipment, shot-gun and all the rest of the paraphernalia advised by the Colonial Office and willingly supplied by the firms of tropical outfitters. We received no kit allowance so had to hypothecate a large part of our monthly salary to pay for the equipment without which we could not do our work. Everything was packed in loads weighing not more than sixty pounds for head-loading on trek. We had signed contracts as cadets which bound us not to get married for three years, so that we could serve in stations where no white woman could live.

After three days by lorry, I was put in a small cement box euphemistically called a rest-house, given a meal by a wireless officer who had been a fortnight in the country, and from 7 till 9 a.m. next day initiated into the mysteries of being Assistant District Officer in charge of the Provincial Office, or A.D.O.O. as I was known to all; then home to breakfast, and at 10 a.m. my predecessor handed over and left me to carry on the business of government. I looked at my first files with distaste. During my probationary year at Cambridge after returning from Kenya, I had been taught the Hausa language, and Colonial History, and Accounts, and Law, and many other things, but nothing about files or offices.

I had learnt something of the history and organization of Nigeria: how from the mid-1870's it had been administered in theory by the Royal Niger Company, a monopolistic trading organization expected to pay for the cost of administration and defence from the profits stemming from its monopoly of trade. Little progress had been possible away from the shelter of the Company's steamers on the great rivers, and in the 1890's Britain and France nearly went to war over Fashoda in the Sudan, and Nikki and other places along the border of Dahomey and what was to become Nigeria. On 1 January 1900, the Charter had been abrogated; with great reluctance Great Britain assumed responsibility for the government of the area, and made the legendary Lugard her first Governor of Northern Nigeria.

To rule this vast country, Lugard had divided it into Provinces, each in charge of a Resident with Assistant Residents below him. In a short time, the system was modified to allow each Province to be divided into Divisions, each in charge of a District Officer, with the Resident responsible for the Divisions in his Province. The Resident lived at the town of the principal Emir or Chief and each District Headquarters was generally at the town of some less important ruler. Lastly came the Assistant District Officers, some filling headquarters posts such as that I now occupied, or subordinate to a District Officer, supervising Treasuries or Prisons or spending most of their time on tour, riding or walking round the more inaccessible parts of the country, settling disputes, assessing areas for tax, checking the counting of nomadic cattle for the cattle-tax and so on.

The organization of Bornu was typical of all the Provinces in the North. The Province was larger than Scotland with a population a little over a million; it contained the Emirates of Bornu (larger than Wales), Dikwa, Biu, Fika and Bedde; the first three formed Divisions by themselves and the two last were joined in a fourth. The Administrative Staff consisted of a Resident, four District Officers and perhaps five A.D.O.s; one main road passable at all times of the year, the last ten miles of the railway from Kano; the whole of the central part of the Province, an area bigger than Wales, as flat as a billiard-table, without a stone on its surface, where one could suffer from claustrophobia in the rains when the corn grew above a mounted man's head and from agoraphobia in the dry when only a few thorns broke the shimmering heat-haze.

The camel and horse were the chief means of transport, with oxen used by the Shuwa particularly in the rainy season in the swamps around Lake Chad, where their split hooves gave better foothold in the belly-deep mud and water than the single hoof of the horse. The temperature in the dry season up to 124° shade —if any could be found—and, perhaps more importantly from the point of view of the traveller, 160° sun. For perhaps a fortnight or so in January as low as 40° with, in the north-east where the dunes of the Sahara commenced, a slight frost one night in four years or so.

Ten Administrative Officers; and at Maiduguri, at that time, two doctors, a nursing sister, a sanitary inspector, a vet, an engineer and three foremen of works, two of whom were building the aerodrome, and two officers and three British N.C.O.s of a company of the 5th Battalion of the Nigeria Regiment, stationed here for internal security. Half a dozen European employees of trading firms and one bank completed the little community. At the other Divisional Headquarters there was no one apart from the D.O. and perhaps his wife, but at Nguru, at railhead in the far north-east, looking westwards to Kano rather than eastwards to Maiduguri, were an A.D.O. and five or six more traders.

Not a large establishment for all that had to be done, and with no cost to the British taxpayer, for the Nigerian budget of about £6,000,000 per annum paid for everything, not only in Bornu but in all the rest of the country. Government on the cheap, but good government, with most of the Europeans imbued with what is called the missionary spirit, and—though all would have mocked this suggestion—with an *esprit de corps* in their service to Nigeria and a certain pride in living under conditions, often grumbled at to be sure, which by any standard were hard.

Even in Maiduguri there were few amenities. Water drawn by hand from wells many fathoms deep; three or four electric lights in each house from dusk until midnight; 'permanent houses' of brick and cement with tin roofs, as opposed to 'temporary houses' of mud walls and thatch in which lived our clerical staff. One of the first refrigerators, driven by kerosene, and two battery-powered wirelesses. The greatest amenity was shade, particularly when the Indian neems flourished and turned aching sand roads into bowers of deep, cool shade. Six polo fields of hard sun-baked sand, used in rotation as the surface crumbled; a cement tennis court; good duck shooting at the end of the rains. This was the haven of rest for which we A.D.O.s yearned as we trekked from village to village.

My day started with the sun at six; at the office from seven till nine, shouting a greeting as one passed to the wives still abed drinking their tea where they had slept in the cool of their garden; breakfast from nine till ten, then more office till two-thirty or

16

three; lunch, a Hausa lesson, perhaps polo, tennis, a walk or a ride; then in the cool of the evening several would sit outside yarning over a drink; sometimes a small dinner-party. Once a fortnight an English mail arrived with the latest papers and letters already three weeks old.

Bornu was once the name of all the country surrounding Lake Chad and, although scarcely heard of in this country, was then a mighty empire which stretched far to the west and south, and across the Sahara to the Fezzan in southern Libya. To be from Bornu is, in Nigeria, akin to being descended from one who came over with the Conqueror in this country, or from one of the Pilgrim Fathers in the States. Whilst largely unknown today, Bornu, on the west of the lake, and Kanem, the country on its eastern shore, appear on some of the earliest European maps of Africa. Indeed, unless destroyed in the Spanish Civil War, the day-to-day diary of one of the old Moorish Universities in Spain is said to have recorded in about the eleventh century the arrival 'from our sister establishment at Timbuktu, of Professor So-and-so, and in his suite Maina Idrisu . . .' Maina is an old Bornu title approximating to Prince, so whilst William's ladies recorded history in their tapestry, the civilized parts of the Western world recorded what was probably the first visitor from Bornu to Europe.

Lake Chad is something of a mystery: it is fresh, very shallow, and receives most of its annual increment from the Chari and Logona, rivers rising far to the south. In the same way as the polar ice advanced or retreated over these islands during the great Ice Ages, so desert and wetter conditions alternated in this part of Africa; indeed the variations were probably interrelated; an advance of ice into southern Europe coinciding with a green Sahara and a greater Chad; when the ice retreated, the rains failed in Africa, the sands of an early Sahara blew where hippopotami had previously disported, and Chad shrank or even disappeared for a time. In this country the geologist traces the path of the ancient glaciers from the boulder clay and erratics they left behind; in Nigeria, old sand dunes piled against the south-western faces of the hills about the tenth to twelfth degrees of north latitude mark a not far distant desert era.

Eighty or so miles away from the western shore of the present lake, running from south-east to north-west, is a long, low ridge of sand, hundreds of miles long, known as the Dar-el-Jimeil or the Camel-back. West of this ridge, Bornu is a sandy plain with a few river courses which carry water for a few months during the rains; east of the ridge, the country is a mud flat, flooded in the rains, baked hard in the dry season with great cracks in which a horse can break a leg. In Lake Chad itself is a swarm of islands; in the mud flats, every village is on a low mound which excavation shows to be formed of white, wind-blown desert sand; these mounds and the swarm of islands in Chad are all old dunes formed in some desert era, later surrounded by a much greater lake, the western shore of which was the Dar-el-Jimeil ridge. Today, we are in an intermediate phase; almost desert for eight months in the year, almost lake for four. Were anything to occur on the head-waters of the two great rivers, the Chari and Logona, to divert their water to the River Benue—as may be happening—the result would be a return of the desert to most of Bornu and the other countries around the lake.

The variation between the sandy plains of the west and the great mud flats of the east is reflected in the vegetation and wild-life of the two areas and in the ways of life of their human in-habitants. Much of the present lake is a vast papyrus swamp, with channels cleared through it from island to island along which the Budduma propel their craft, half boats, half rafts made of papyrus, a form of transport only found elsewhere in Africa on the lakes of Abyssinia. Hippos and manatees and an abounding fish-life are to be found in the lake—also biting flies, mosquitoes, and the hundreds of millions of small birds which in huge flocks strip the cornfields in the middle of the dry season. In the tall reeds on the edges of the lake lives a herd of elephant, isolated from their fellows elsewhere in Africa for many years; on the sandy plains of the west live ostrich and the graceful *dama* gazelle. On the islands live the Budduma, little known to the inhabitants on the western shore, probably descendants of some of the people who formerly ruled all this part of the world, driven to their present refuge by the influx of strangers from the north-east.

West of the Dar-el-Jimeil live the Kanuri people, and the wandering cattle-owning Fulani nomads, found across Africa from the hinterland of Sierra Leone to the Sudan; on the village mounds in the area between the waters of the lake and the ridge, where deep wells give water the year round, live other Kanuri. On others, where water cannot be found in the dry season, live the Shuwa Arabs, owners of vast herds of cattle, the westernmost of the Baggara Arabs who formed the backbone of the armies of the Mahdi and Khalifa which conquered the Sudan and killed Gordon; a few pass the dry season at water-holes in western Bornu, but the majority spend it in great swamps south of the lake, particularly one called Kutelaha. Before most of the Arabs leave on their annual migration after water, they plant out by hand thousands of acres of a special type of Guinea corn on which no rain ever falls, but whose roots keep pace with the level of the falling water table. In January the harvest is taken in by the young men and women who stay behind when the rest of the village leaves, and is buried in great holes dug in the sands of the old dead dunes. So great is the harvest, despite the locust-like birds, an old man told me, that if the rains failed one year in every ten in western Bornu he could make enough profit that year from his vast hidden granaries to see him through the next decade until the rains again failed.

In all three areas—sandy plains, mud flats and swampy lake—cattle are kept; but of three amazingly distinct types, each adapted to its habitat and largely incapable of living in that of either of the other two. The Fulani in the open country of the west, who arrived perhaps three hundred years ago, have herds of red cattle with long, thin horns similar to the animals kept as semi-sacred by the Ankole and Watutsi of other parts of Africa. These horns, perhaps four feet long, mean that the animals can never be penned in shelter. They must therefore be kept away from the biting flies of the lake in open country on the western plains. The Shuwa have a short-horned breed, many of them with horns dangling on either side of the face, swinging as the animal walks; these can be penned during the hours of daylight in the great *tum-tums* as the Shuwa houses are called. The semi-aquatic Budduma need an animal that can swim from island to island and avoid most of its tormentors by lying almost submerged in the lake; their animals therefore have huge feet, with widely splayed hooves to get through the mud, and enormous horns often three feet or more in diameter, filled with hollow air-spaces, and forming natural

19

Mae Wests to support the animals on their swims. Which came first, the chicken or the egg; which came first, the environment or the animal?

For many thousands of years, therefore, the wide plains of Bornu and the area of the lake have seen great variations between desert and water. To the south-west are the mountains of the Cameroons and the central mountain area of Nigeria, with long peninsulas of mountains sticking like the fingers of a glove into the plains of Chad. We may never know the full history of the lands around the lake, but the mountains have been inhabited for long periods of time, as lying on the surface I have found both palæolithic and neolithic stone axes. In the Dikwa Division these mountains rise perhaps 3,000 feet above the plains at their feet, or to about 5,000 feet above sea-level, naked, harsh and forbidding in the dry season, green and beautiful in the rains when the clear air allows one to see distant peaks, sixty or more miles away.

At some distant epoch these mountains were terraced with a system of stone walls to hold up the earth on which the inhabitants of the mountains could grow their crops. Parts of the hills consist of areas of huge boulders thrown together in indescribable confusion, with individual boulders as big as large houses. Elsewhere the terrace walls have been built up like the stone walls in northern England; where the slopes are gentle the terraces are perhaps one or two stones high; in many parts they extend vertically for a thousand or even two thousand feet, and in those parts where the slope is severe, individual walls may be ten feet or more high to support a terrace only a few inches wide, on which only two rows of corn can grow. The present inhabitants say that their ancestors found the terraces when they came to the hills and it is obvious that the work in this relatively small area is that of centuries. This terrace system is not peculiar to this part of Africa, for it extends across much of the continent along the eleventh parallel of north latitude, into Arabia, and north to Sinai and the Lebanon. Is it too far-fetched to wonder if there is any connection between the builders of these stone walls and the first inhabitants of Egypt, spreading northwards when a relaxation of the desert allowed movement to the north? Certainly the earliest of the pyramids—that of Sakkara—rises in steps in the form of a terraced hill, similar to so many of those in the Gwoza area;

perhaps in memory of the ancestors and a way of life left far away to the south?

Be that as it may, the mountains of the south and the islands of Chad, hidden behind their impenetrable shield of papyrus, were the places of refuge to which the earliest inhabitants of this area of whom we have any records fled as new waves of immigrants came into what is now Nigeria from the north-east.

In the Moslem parts of Nigeria there are written records of considerable antiquity, as well as verbal records of historical events in the last two thousand years; large numbers of completely illiterate peasants have a very wide knowledge of their history, far beyond that which most Europeans have of theirs. Not so many years ago, in Kano, the great trading metropolis of the lands south of the Sahara Desert, there was a man who could recite the history of that city for the past thousand years; this feat was the more remarkable as he did not learn a string of dates on which to build his history, but instead knew what happened 'so many years ago', so that every year he had to revise his knowledge and bring it one year forward; he was not an isolated example but perhaps the most remarkable.

The Arabic alphabet was introduced into Northern Nigeria several centuries ago, and there are in existence, if not the original documents, at least several ancient copies of earlier histories. After allowing for errors and the introduction of alien matter from time to time, it is a remarkable fact that for a large part of what only a century ago was called by us 'Darkest Africa' there is a great deal of accurate record and tradition stretching back to periods before the Romans invaded these islands, an era of which most Europeans know little or nothing.

In Bornu, traditions go back to a period about two thousand years before the start of the Moslem era, that is to about 1500 B.C., and the following periods prior to the British Administration can be recognized:

1500 B.C. – A.D. 500
A.D. 500 – A.D. 942
A.D. 942 – A.D. 1250
A.D. 1250 – A.D. 1808
A.D. 1808 – A.D. 1902

In the first of these, the whole of the area, and possibly the whole of Africa south of the Sahara, was occupied by Negro tribes, remnants of which are to be found today in the hills to the south of Bornu. In about A.D. 500 these more primitive people were ousted from the plains of Bornu by another race of Negroes called the Sau or So who left behind them many still-existing towns and a series of deserted sites which were probably occupied for many years, as they stand as mounds above the level of the plains of the country. In these Sau towns are to be found very large baked earthenware pots sometimes six feet high and with walls an inch or more thick, which have been dug up from time to time. They have been identified as storage vessels for corn or water, but are more probably funerary jars in which notables were interred. To still later immigrants, the Kanuri, these huge pots were equated with their own water-pots which the women take to the village well, and not unnaturally Kanuri folk-lore has made the Sau into a race of giants. One such story tells of a Sau hunter covering a distance of about a hundred miles in a few giant strides while he carried in either hand the elephants he had killed.

The Sau drove their predecessors into the hills of the south and then, in about 942, there arrived a new wave of immigrants from the north-east, the Jukons and their related peoples who later founded another mighty empire, that of Kororafa, away on the River Benue. They remained in Bornu for about two hundred to three hundred years, and do not appear to have driven out the Sau or completely assimilated them, for when in the middle of the thirteenth century the next wave of invaders, the Kanuri, began to move into the country to the west of Lake Chad from the lands on the eastern shore, they found many towns still inhabited by the Sau. The Jukons disappeared completely from Bornu; but in many of the towns of the swampland round the lake, the people describe themselves as Kanuri, but add that they are descendants of the Sau. Their biggest settlements were at Ndifu and Ngala, and at the latter place, near the southern shore of Chad, on the roof of the house of the chief man of the town, there was, and perhaps still is, a collection of stones shaped by man which were reputed to have magical powers. The nearest outcrop of rock is some eighty miles or so away, at Wasa, where there are two large, isolated, rocky hills sticking up from the flat plains of Chad. A local tradition is that it was on one of these that the Ark came to rest, and that the name of Bornu is more correctly Dar Nuhu or the Land of Noah.

The whole area, despite the present Moslem religion of its inhabitants, is full of pagan customs, the origin and meaning of which have long been forgotten. At one village when a new village head is appointed, he is placed in a certain room of the ancestral house of the village head, and walled up therein for a period of seven days, except for a small hole near the roof through which milk is passed to him. At the end of this period, a hole is broken through at one particular place in the wall of the room, and he is then drawn head-first through it. To my explanation of this as a typical ceremonial rebirth with the chosen man spending the magical period of seven days in the womb before crawling head-first into the new world of village headship the then village head listened in disdainful silence, whilst around us the villagers laughed in unbelieving derision.

In about A.D. 1250 the Jukons in turn were pushed away to the south-west by the first of the immigrant Kanuri. The Kanuri's own traditions go back to prehistoric times when they, a white race, lived in Arabia; from there they crossed to Africa, and, in the lands between the Nile and Lake Chad, intermarried with local Negroes. The Hausa word for the Kanuri is *Beri-beri*, a name akin to that of their relations, the Berbers of North Africa, who have retained their white skins as their travels north of the Sahara did not bring them into contact with Negro peoples. The retreat of the Jukon led to a resurgence of the power of the Sau and they appear to have claimed ownership once more of the Bornu plain. During the next two hundred years, more and more Kanuri moved westwards until, at last, one of their most famous rulers, Mai Ali Dunanami, bought land from the Sau on which to build a new capital.

The history of this purchase is a delightful folk-tale. The Sau chief sold as much land 'as could be surrounded by a bullock hide'; the wily Kanuri took a hide and had a thin sliver of thing cut off, round and round the hide until it was consumed; he was then able to enclose with the thong an area with a circumference of several miles where he built his famous capital of Birnin N'gazargamo in the west of Bornu not far from the present railhead at

Nguru. A great earthen wall was built to protect the capital and inside were palaces and public buildings constructed of burnt brick of which many fragments of wall still stand to this day; they were built at a time when in most of East Anglia houses were being built in wattle and daub.

Kanuri records of their rulers go back to the time when they still lived in Arabia; written records exist of the chief events in the history of this new capital from 1488 until 1808 when it was destroyed by the Fulani, and as with our own history in the same period these records are of constant wars with the surrounding peoples. In about 1660, Birni—as it is generally called in Bornu—was invested on the north side by an army of Tuareg from the fastnesses of the Sahara, and on the south by an army from the Jukon capital of Kororafa. A great gloom descended on the inhabitants, broken by the laughter of one man who was hastily taken before his chief. On being asked what he had to laugh about when all others were plunged in despair, the cheerful one said that it had occurred to him that as neither the Tuareg nor the Jukon were yet aware of the others' presence, it should be possible for Bornu to combine with one to defeat the other, and then the defeat of the late ally should be possible. The plan was put into effect and, with the Tuareg on their side, the Bornu hosts drove the Jukons from the scene. When the issue was still in the balance the Bornu ruler prayed for divine help, lightning struck the ground and flames ran towards the Jukon camp. In turn the Jukon leader pleaded for divine intercession and this time the heavens opened and rains quenched the flames. But all to no avail; at the end of the day the Bornu army remained master of the field whilst to south and north fled the remnants of the two invading armies.

Friendly relations with the Jukon were soon reopened and an ambassador from Bornu resided at the Jukon capital until the arrival of the British Administration. It is said that the first Bornu ambassador travelled the many hundreds of weary miles carrying with him live coals in a bed of cotton, and delivered the still glowing embers and the unharmed cotton to show the authenticity of his credentials. Not to be outdone the Jukon ambassador, in his turn, left his capital carrying water from the Benue in a woven grass basket and delivered every drop at Birni.

At the beginning of the nineteenth century occurred the *Jihad* or Holy War of the immigrant Fulani under the great leader Uthman dan Fodio, founder of the Sokoto dynasty, against the Hausa rulers of the western part of what is now Northern Nigeria, which was almost completely successful. The great trading city of Kano appealed for help to Bornu, which had been from time to time its overlord; this was given but nothing could stop the victorious advance of the Fulani, and they took their revenge for the help given to Kano by capturing and sacking Birni in 1808. This disaster occurred at a time when the rulers of Bornu had become soft and effete with their relatively untroubled occupation of the land. In his difficulty, the Bornu *Mai*, or King, appealed for help to a certain learned *Mallam*, Muhammed el Amin el Kanemi, who was to pass into history as Shehu Lamino. This man was a descendant of a line of learned Sheikhs, and he gave help in the first instance in literary form by writing a series of open letters to the Fulani leader, Shehu Uthman dan Fodio, showing how heinous was the crime of waging a Holy War not on the ungodly, but on the faithful Moslems of Bornu. As has happened on many later occasions, no notice was taken of this attempt at appeasement, so Shehu Lamino called for help from the Shuwa Arabs, who had first arrived in Bornu about the beginning of the seventeenth century and who had been reinforced over the years by later arrivals. Fighting between the Hausa and Fulani on the one hand, and the Kanuri and Shuwa on the other, continued for many years. The days of the *Mais* of Bornu were numbered; whilst Shehu Lamino never took the title of Shehu or leader in his lifetime, he was in all but name the real ruler of the land; by 1846 his descendants finally established themselves in name as well as in fact as the rulers of Bornu and the family of the *Mais* became of no account.

The first European entry into Bornu of which we have certain knowledge took place when the British explorers Clapperton, Oudney and Denham arrived across the desert from Tripoli in the 1820's, to be followed in 1850 by the German Barth who was employed by the British Government, and then by other explorers at intervals until the turn of the century.

In 1893 Bornu was invaded from the east by a horde of Arabs and Sudanese led by Rabeh, the foster-son of Zubeir Pasha, fleeing from the Khalifa in the Sudan; this force was well armed with rifles and cannon and was able to make an inferior kind of gunpowder when supplies ran short. On their westward advance from the Nile they had conquered each little state in turn, looting and collecting a vast number of women before moving on. When the then Shehu of Bornu heard of the arrival of these desperadoes on his border he sent an army of 3,000 men to deal with them, an army which fled on the first volley from Rabeh's men, hundreds being killed. With a force of 1,500 riflemen and 500 horse armed with spears, and two small cannon, Rabeh advanced into Bornu. Shehu Hashim, with a new army of 6,000, attacked Rabeh at Ngala, but with no better success, and the remnants of the Bornu forces fled northwards to Kukawa, to which place the capital had been moved after the sack of Birni. Another skirmish took place here with the same result and Kukawa in turn was looted and sacked. The unfortunate Hashim was next murdered by his relative Kiari, who declared himself the Shehu of Bornu, and advanced on Rabeh with another large and hastily collected army. At first fortune appeared to favour the new Shehu; Rabeh gave battle with only 700 men who were soon driven back and the Kanuri army in their turn looted his camp and vast harem. But the retreat was only a ruse, and under cover of darkness Rabeh returned to the attack. This time there was no mistake; the Kanuri fled and Shehu Kiari was captured. He was brought before Rabeh, who complimented him on being a brave but foolish man, asking how he thought Bornu could resist a seasoned band of fighting men who had fought their way across Africa. Kiari replied to the effect that this was no time to talk: 'Had I captured you, you would have been dead at the hands of my slaves ere now,' he said. Rabeh, saying that he would not hang so brave a man, ordered one of his slaves to cut Kiari's throat; with two of his brothers, Kiari was killed in the same way as a sheep is slaughtered, and I have spoken with men who claimed to have been present.

Rabeh next withdrew to Dikwa which he made his capital, and where he lived for the next seven years, with his band of ruffians and vast numbers of captured women. Many are the tales that are told of him; on one occasion it is said that as he passed through the market-place a Shuwa woman seized his gown and prayed for

his help. 'O great one,' she cried, 'help this your miserable servant; behold yon miscreant *askar* of yours, he has taken and
drunk my milk without paying for it.' Rabeh called the man,
who denied having touched the milk; but the woman persisted.
'Woman,' said this latter-day Solomon, 'you say that he has but
now drunk your milk; if so it is still within him; I shall have his
belly cut open. If the milk is there I shall pay you for it myself; if it
is not I shall have you cut into small pieces as slowly as possible;
choose: shall he be cut or left?' The woman was adamant, the
man was seized and there and then slit open; the evidence satisfactorily seen, he was put out of his misery and the woman received
her halfpenny.

In 1899 there arrived in the vicinity of the lake a large French
column, commanded by that Lamy after whom Fort Lamy is
named, which in the next year had several brushes with Rabeh,
eventually killing him at the battle of Kusseri in 1900, and, a
couple of years later, crossing into what had in theory become
German territory and advancing deep into what was on the maps
Nigeria, they killed his son, Fadl-Allah. This marked not only the
end of Rabeh's rule, but also the end of Bornu as a single kingdom, and its division among the British, Germans and French.

The arrival of the European powers in Bornu could not have
occurred, from the point of view of the unfortunate peasantry, at a
more opportune time. The countries around Chad had been
ravaged from end to end by Rabeh and his men; but quite apart
from the impact of this latest raider from the east, the Bornu
Empire itself had never enjoyed peace from the time of the Fulani
Jihad, as after the end of the rule of the *Mais* and their replacement by the descendants of Shehu Lamino these in turn had
fallen to quarrelling among themselves.

Before Fadl-Allah had been killed, he had met a representative
of Lugard—who had raised the Union Jack over Northern
Nigeria at Lokoja on 1 January 1900—in the person of Major
McClintock. McClintock had recommended that the new administration should recognize Fadl-Allah as the ruler of Bornu,
despite the fact that he was only the son of a military adventurer
with no real title. With the death of Fadl-Allah the way was open
to reinstate either a descendant of the *Mais* or one of Lamino's
family. The French followed the latter course in respect of that

part of the country concentrated on Dikwa, and when the Germans appeared to claim this area they replaced him with another.

It was only after 1918 that any finality appeared when under British rule two Chiefs of the Kanuri were recognized: one, the Shehu of Bornu with his capital at Maiduguri—an artificial town created by the British—and the other the Emir of Dikwa in the Mandated Territory, which, because of the Mandate, could not be reunited with Bornu as history demanded. The rather delicate relationship between the two areas was, the Nigerian government hoped, accepted by the local peasantry who would recognize the consummate skill of the British Administration from the fact that whilst in Bornu the ancestral title of Shehu was recognized, in Dikwa we used the alien one of Emir. In English the distinction was perhaps valid; in Hausa both titles became 'Sarki', in Kanuri both became 'Shehu' and in Arabic both 'Sheikh'. As the number of English-speakers amongst the peasantry was nil, the distinction was not perhaps appreciated to the degree that those in the Secretariats imagined.

In 1936, the Shehu of Bornu was the ancient Umar, Sanda Kura, who had been proclaimed Shehu by the French at Zinder in 1900 and deposed by them at Dikwa the following year. He became Shehu of British Bornu in 1922 and was succeeded on his death in 1937 by the then Emir of Dikwa, another Umar, Sanda Kiarimi (son of the Kiari whose throat was cut by Rabeh's orders), who still rules.

The Kanuri are a fine people of magnificent physique, justly proud of their ancient lineage. The first Nigerian Governor of Northern Nigeria is Sir Ibrahim Kashim, a son of Bornu whose perfect English was notable when he taught in the Middle School in Maiduguri. There was less social intercourse between the European members of the Administration and the Shehu and his Councillors than was the case elsewhere, as the Shehu spoke neither Hausa nor English and we spoke no Kanuri; but three times a week some half-dozen Europeans and some of the younger Kanuri played polo together.

In 1937, before he was translated to Bornu, Shehu Umar Kiarimi, as Emir of Dikwa, was told by the then District Officer that one of the armed guards on the main roads was getting too old for his duty. The roads of Bornu, as a result of the disturbed

28

condition of the country in the latter half of the nineteenth century, had many robbers upon them, and in Dikwa there were half a dozen posts manned by men armed with old rifles who maintained patrols. The man in question owned that he was about ninety years of age; obviously in any self-respecting organization he must be replaced as too old for the post, and the job of protecting a road against highway robbers, entailing long hours in the saddle, was scarcely perhaps the best place in which to pass one's declining years. But the Emir was adamant. 'He cannot be replaced in this manner; he was Rabeh's mightiest leader in battle; he killed a score of men with his own right arm; his name is feared throughout the land. If he is replaced by some young stripling known to none, the road will be closed by highwaymen.' Tradition had its place, and its way.

As Shehu of Bornu, Umar Kiarimi has seen great economic development and at last the railway has been built to Maiduguri. The Kanuri are a proud and very capable race who live in a harsh environment; they are looked up to by most of the inhabitants of the Northern Region because of their mighty past, and they are held in very great respect by many of the inhabitants of the rest of Nigeria and the surrounding countries. They will, I think, play an ever more important part in the history of their country and indeed of the world, and if oil should one day be found in the great plain of Bornu around Lake Chad, their future will be bright.

CHAPTER THREE

Ghosts

Sergeant Bukar Maroua, one of the messengers at Maiduguri, was a Fulani from Maroua, across in the Cameroons. Almost a thousand miles from the centre at Sokoto, this area had been brought into the Empire of Uthman dan Fodio by one of his flag-bearers in the *Jihad* or Holy War of the early nineteenth century. As this fact was unknown to, or ignored as of no importance by, the statesmen of Europe when they carved up Africa, Maroua had became part of the German Cameroons, and then, after 1918, part of the French Mandate. Like many another, Bukar had been conscripted into the German forces, and, after the end of the fighting at Mora, had joined the Nigeria Regiment and fought against his former rulers in Tanganyika. As with many others of his race from this part of the world he had little of the outward appearance of a Fulani. Maroua lay amongst the hills of the Northern Cameroons: hills raided for slaves, many of whom, being tiny children, were kept in the town to be converted to Islam, and, if girls, to become concubines or even the wives of the master of the house. This constant intermixture with negroid blood had the inevitable result on the physique of the Maroua Fulani: they approximated more and more to the stoutly built, square-faced Pagans, while retaining their original language, religion and pride of race.

Bukar had enjoyed his war and, like many others, loved nothing better than to tell long stories of the campaign in East Africa. As we reached the point of battle, his eyes would brighten and he would start to smile—'and just then our Sergeant, Hussaini Kukawa, was hit in the leg and rolled on the ground bellowing with pain'. It was long before he could continue—the memory of the occasion brought great gusts of laughter and tears to his eyes. We never did reach the end of the tale of when Corporal Moma Yerwa was killed in action.

Shortly before I left Maiduguri for Dikwa, with Bukar Maroua

in mounted attendance and Kamkura my horse-boy walking behind, we visited a spot half a mile from the nearest European
house where a number of cattle had been collected after purchase
by the Veterinary Officer for issue in due course to mixed farmers
to draw small ploughs. They were all short-horned animals as
these alone could be stalled to provide the dung that was part of
their duty, and they were destined for Kano, for as yet no Agricultural Officer had been posted to Bornu, and no attempt yet
made to instruct our farmers in such better methods.

The thirty or so animals were penned inside a rough fence of
thorns, less to protect them from outside interference than to prevent them straying at night or running away back to the herd
from which they came. They were in the charge of a Hausa employee of the Kano Native Administration and a couple of youths,
and their trek of three hundred miles to a new life would soon
begin. As we approached the older man came forward to greet us.

'*Zaki, sanu sanu,*' he said. 'Lion, greetings.'

'*Sanu mai shanu,*' I replied. 'And to thee, O Master of the
Cattle.'

'Thou art well?'

'Only well; and thou? and the cattle? are they well?'

'We are well, but we shall be glad to leave this spot; it is be-
witched. For there are ghosts here and the animals have been
disturbed. Last night they were panicked and it is but now that we
have collected them again. One of my boys is still away looking
for the last animal which has not yet been found. If we find it not,
I shall come to ask you to beat the wire and tell my European in
Kano that we have lost one of his beasts.'

Bukar Maroua nodded his head sagely.

'Verily the place is haunted, of that we are all aware. Seest thou
there a baobab with a tamarind growing in its bosom, and there
another embracing a like tree. Know ye not, ye men of Kano, that
such pairs of trees are ever the abode of spirits?'

The other nodded his head in turn.

'Ye speak truth, O wise one; of that fact all the world is aware.
But as these are the ghosts of white men, I thought they would
not trouble us.'

I looked from one to another; Kamkura came to my assistance.

'Master of the House, you have often seen two trees growing

intertwined; yonder, see, is a silk cotton and a tamarind, and near our house a baobab and a silk cotton; rarely does a tamarind grow with a baobab; it is forbidden by the powers of the afterworld, and when it occurs it is because Satan has prepared a house in this wise for his followers.'

'Thus it is,' said Bukar, 'but these ghosts are not followers of Satan but two white men who died here many years ago. Near here was their house; see—yonder you can trace the outline of its walls,' and I followed his finger to where a slight rectangular eminence showed where once a mud-walled house had stood. 'It was a Government house and two of Lugard's men lived therein; but they died and now they and their boys and their horses all live in those trees.'

'They must be a bit crowded,' I said, but my flippancy was reproved by Kamkura.

'It is true, Master of the House; all here know of the fact and we were amazed when these animals were penned here.'

'It was not my doing,' said the cattle-drover, 'but the European who oversees the cattle told me to come here and laughed at my fears. I have been almost a month and each night I have heard the ghosts—though seen them not. I hear them descend from their trees and they speak in your language. One calls to the other "Sarve" and I hear the ping, ping as they play with balls the game that I have seen outside the house of drinking in Kano. They laugh and the other calls "Sarve" in his turn and again I hear the sound of the balls beating on the ground. This goes on for perhaps an hour, then each night they call "Boy" and I hear a horse neigh and then two sets of hooves cantering down the road. But never have I seen horse nor rider nor boys. After a little time there is the sound of galloping hooves returning and my cattle have heard them and have stopped chewing the cud to listen. We hear the boys run from the house and a voice calls "Pass bath", and then silence falls and the cattle resume their chewing; they cannot see over the thorns and they think that these are real men that they hear, but we three know differently.'

His two assistants had drawn near and nodded their heads in agreement.

'Thus it has been each night since we first came, but the ghosts have never disturbed us until last night.'

'And then O Master of Cattle, what differed from the play of previous nights?' asked Bukar; 'if your cattle have thought until then that these were in truth Europeans from the lines, why did they flee last night?"

'Lion,' said the herder, 'I wish not to offend the spirits but last eve they spoke unwisely. Last night as always we heard them play their game and depart on their ride; we heard the sound of their hooves as they returned but instead of calling their boys to take their horses, they came over here; we could hear the panting of their steeds and the jingle of their bridles as they stood looking at these animals. I swear by Almighty God that they stood where you now stand and yet they left no hoof- nor foot-mark in the sands. I prayed that they would leave as is their wont, and I cursed their boys for being late to take their horses. It is ever the way of those who serve the European to be not there when called. But to my horror I was addressed by one of the ghosts; I near fainted when he spoke in Hausa.'

Had this been Ireland he would, I felt, have been crossing himself and telling his beads by now.

'And what said he?' asked Kamkura.

'Verily he spake to me in the pure Hausa of Kano. "Greetings," he cried, "greetings, O thou with the cattle; thou hast a fine herd; yonder bull will reach a great price at the cattle mart at Goniri." I answered not—for who would speak with the shades —nor dare I tell him that these were not for sale but for the European of the Farms at Kano to give to those who farm with the plough.

'Then the other spake. "Tell me, O thou of the cattle, have the owners of these cows paid their *Jangali* this year? Hast thou the paper of receipt to show that the tax has been paid in full?" And at the word *Jangali*, my animals fled, for as thou knowest, O White Man, the Fulani and the Shuwa train their animals to flee at the sound of the word that they may not be counted. They fled and we followed—glad to leave this place and its ghosts until the light of dawn returned. They fled and we have found all but one; when that is back we leave, for we shall not stay to be counted for tax by ghosts.'

'Verily, you speak true,' agreed Bukar. 'We will speak to the European of the cattle and tell him thy tale. It would be well to move to near the place where the sky canoes come to earth, for there is much grazing at Pompomari.'

'We have told him, and leave when the heat of the day has left the sky.'

We turned and on our way back Bukar Maroua instructed me in the ways of ghosts.

'It is ever thus,' he said. 'When a man dies far from his tribe he is chained to the place of his death until Judgement Day. Thus it is that every white man who dies here remains in his old haunts; the ghosts of black men are generally malign and do harm for they are amongst strangers far from their own kin and they are afraid and like all frightened men strike at others. Thus it will be with the spirits of our men who died in East Africa, far from their native home amongst the spirits of the men who in life fought to kill them. But the ghosts of the white men differ. You came not here with fear and hate in your hearts for the peoples of this land, but to help us and to bring peace; and those who die remain chained to the land they once served.'

'Verily,' came from Kamkura as he trudged behind, 'it is true; for who would harm in death that which he cherished in life. Hast thou visited Gujiba, Bukar? They say in the town that there the ghost of a colour-sergeant walks each night.'

'It is true; each night he walks. And only a few moons ago at the start of this rainy season he near killed the Resident. It fell in this way. It was at Gujiba that the French killed Fadl-Allah and it was there that, when they first came, the British established a Resident and placed a company of troops with him. In those days there was much trouble in the land and, as they feared attack, they built a strong fort down in the valley below the town near to the water supply. And there they lived, an officer and two white sergeants and a Resident and a company of troops. Corporal Hassan Damagaram of the Native Administration police was with them at this time and knows the history of the place. But the low site was unhealthy and there was much sickness and in the second year one of the sergeants died. It is said that he came off parade in the heat of the morning into the hut where he lived; he removed his equipment and flung it into the corner of the room; he shouted "Boy" and fell to the ground and when they came to him he was dead.

34

'He was buried without the fort and the Government erected an iron cross to mark the spot as is their wont. Another sergeant came and took over his hut, but on the second afternoon after his arrival he left the hut and refused to return; all heard that as he lay resting the dead man walked in, took off his equipment, called for his boy, and died. And the other sergeant tried the hut—for the white men laughed at their companion—but he too heard these things. So the officer burnt that hut to the ground and built another. But in a short time it was known that the spirit had moved too.'

'But why,' I asked, 'should the ghost move? Why if he suffered in life to the moment of his death, should he repeat his sufferings each day?'

'I know not, for who can explain the world of the spirits? But this I know, for I have looked : nowhere near Gujiba is a baobab clasping a tamarind to its bosom. Nowhere to which a spirit might flee. As therefore they destroyed his home and he had no spirit home to go to, the ghost must move to another.'

'Truly so,' came from near the tail of my horse.

'And indeed in due course the troops left and a new Residency was built on the ridge near the town. It is known to all in Gujiba that in a short time the sergeant had followed and occupied the guest-house, for being but a sergeant he dare not disturb the representative of the Governor, the Resident himself.'

'Of course not,' came from my tail.

'Again the years went by and the Residency was moved elsewhere and the house became a rest-house; the guest house was no longer wanted so the thatch was taken off and the walls left to crumble. Hassan Dumboa, I know him well, was made the Sarkin Barriki, and he tells me that as keeper of the rest-house he has of an afternoon waited for some European who has been delayed, and he has heard the ghost enter and die. And this now in what once was the Resident's own bedroom. It was for this reason that our own Resident was nearly killed this year; I know for I was with him and heard the shot. But it was not the ghost but this selfsame European of cattle who laughed at the fears of the herder behind us. It fell this way.

'The Resident and I were on trek to Biu by car but on our return the heavens opened and the road became a river. We were perhaps ten miles from Gujiba and the country is unpopulated. The car was stuck, there was nothing we could do; so we took a few things and set out for Gujiba hoping to return on the morrow with men to pull the car from the mud. So the steward boy took the Resident's bed, and he himself a water-bottle and a haversack with some food, and I my own load and that of the steward; and as we marched through the mud and the blackness, the steward fell behind and I had to assist him with his load. So the Resident went on ahead of us.

'Unknown to us, to the north of Gujiba a similar thing had happened and the Veterinary Officer too had left his car storm-bound, and made his way on foot to the rest-house with his boys. Their way lay through the town, so the rest-house keeper joined them, but on arrival his steward boy refused to sleep at the rest-house and Hassan Dumboa testified to the truth of the story that the steward told his master. But he laughed, and they erected his bed, and left him for the town.

'And in due course, with our Resident far ahead, we too arrived. It was near midnight and the night as black as the mouth of hell. The Resident entered the rest-house and I heard him throw his haversack down and call "Boy", and at once there was a shot and a European ran past me for the town calling out in the language of the white men.'

Bukar Maroua, his voice almost lost in his tears of laughter, was near falling from his horse.

'Think of it, my friend Kamkura, there was the European of the cattle almost killing the Resident as he thought it was the ghost, and then causing the townsfolk to flee to the shelter of the bush, for as he fled through the town he shouted that the evil spirit followed at his heels. Master, it was late next day before we had learnt the truth and got the people back to their houses.'

'What trouble he has caused, that colour-sergeant. Cannot the Europeans lay his ghost?' asked Kamkura.

I shook my head.

'I know not; perhaps one day we can get a missionary from Garkida to pass that way and say a prayer over his grave.'

I had already heard the tale. It was a very subdued Veterinary Officer who had had to explain to his Resident next day that he had shot at him in error, having taken him for a ghost.

'Why the devil you want to shoot at a ghost, I know not,' snorted the Resident. 'Poor old Macnamara has never harmed anyone. I've heard him not once but a dozen times. All he wants to do is to die in peace, not be shot at. And in any case, you ought to know that you can't shoot a ghost.'

A year or two later I visited the grave. It lies at the foot of a great baobab into the bark of which had first been cut the name, rank and date of death of Colour-Sergeant Macnamara; later a standard issue iron cross had been erected. May his soul rest in peace.

Many years later, in the Gwandu Division, I selected the town of Mungadi for development. We drove wide streets through it and built a school and dispensary. Outside the town was a small hillock covered with impenetrable thorns on which I decided to build a rest-house.

'It is of course the abode of spirits, but in them you do not believe,' said the wise old Emir. 'Build there; it will be an experiment and you shall tell us if indeed there are spirits or not.'

So the rest-house was built and then came the great day when with my wife and boys I slept there for the first time. Came the dawn and with it my messenger from the little town below to tell us that few had slept that night. A vigil had been kept by all, men, women and children in the fearful hope that they might glimpse the powers of the night as they carried off the impious and interfering European.

'Thou art well?' asked the Emir as we greeted him and his Council before he ceremonially opened the school and dispensary. 'As I told you,' turning to his Council, 'I believed not that old wives' tale.' He stifled a yawn, and behind him the Magajin Rafi and the Galadima, his two principal Councillors, wiped their heavy eyes.

'Thus you said; nor did we,' they said.

CHAPTER FOUR

The Gwoza Hills

I spent four months in charge of the Provincial Office, learning under the guidance of the Resident and Mr Mason, the Treasury Clerk, how to deal with such matters as the annual estimates and the annual accounts, to maintain the temporary buildings and to pay station and market labour. I learnt to type with two fingers so that I might deal with those secret matters which no clerk must see. I learnt to minute and to find precedents; I learnt that it was better to rely on memory than on the file-index, so that even today 'File No. 1022B, Maiduguri New Lay-out' is for ever etched on my memory. I learnt something of the problems of government by seeing all inward and outward mail, between the Resident and his District Officers and between him and the Chief Commissioner, as he was then called, at the Head-quarters of the North in far-off Kaduna.

Mr Mason was, like three of his fellows, from the Gold Coast; two of the others were from what is now the Western Region, and the sixth was an Ibo. Mr Mason had come to Bornu as a young man in 1910, and a couple of years later had become Collector of Customs. Owing, said a harsh court, to his dishonesty (owing, said Mr Mason, to false witnesses), he had been found guilty of misappropriating some of the Customs Dues, and sent to prison. In 1914 the staff shortage was such that he was welcomed back, restored to the establishment and, in time, rewarded with a pension, which, alas, he did not live to draw for more than a year. Together he and I controlled the expenditure of Government funds; he did the work; he prepared the vouchers; I signed them where he told me. My compound was always spotless; his temporary housing was always being whitewashed or rethatched.

Next I had a little over a month in Bornu Division; then I was moved to Dikwa Division, where I was to become the touring officer in charge of the Unsettled Pagan District of Gwoza. But first I travelled the fifty miles or so to Dikwa itself by an ancient lorry; in the rainy season the journey took three days.

Dikwa was even more desert-like in appearance than Maid-uguri; the main square was a mass of white, swirling sand dominated by the mud fort built by Rabeh. Across the square were the Central Offices and the prison, and soon after my arrival we were called from our early-morning tea by shouts in the square. Issuing forth in our pyjamas, my District Officer and I found that the Chief Warder, a large and portly gentleman like so many middle-aged Kanuri, had emerged from the prison on hearing the call to prayer; he performed the necessary ablutions and then spread his prayer-mat on his favourite spot outside the wall of his prison; as he advanced onto this, to his astonishment the ground opened and he was precipitated on to something that squirmed and screamed. In his first fright the Chief Warder sprang out of the hole that had opened below him and shouting that he had narrowly escaped from the clutching hands of the Devil himself he rushed back into the prison. His shouts aroused the town; others rushed to his aid; one, more daring than the rest, peered into the hole and luckily recognized the half-dead would-be escapee, almost suffocated with the sand that had poured down on to him, almost crushed by the generous proportions of the Chief Warder. Reassured that his worst fears were groundless, the latter now opened up the cells of his charges and from one of them there was a hole leading down and under the outer wall. The occupants of this cell were sound asleep, though a little sandy in places and a little breathless.

Dikwa was another of the old Sau towns built on a dead sand dune and may indeed have been inhabited from a very distant epoch. It had been made the capital of his empire by Rabeh before his death at Kusseri, a few miles to the east, in 1900. After his death the French occupied the town for a couple of years before handing over to the Germans, who fled in 1914 leaving it to be reoccupied by the French. In 1919 it was finally handed over to the British and became the headquarters of the Division; today it is but a shadow of its former state, for in 1940 it was decided that the headquarters must be moved from this sandhill in the swamp to the town of Bama, forty miles away to the south-west on the Dar-el-Jimeil ridge. But this was still in the future.

After my short stay in Dikwa, I left in an old Albion lorry capable at full speed of about fifteen miles an hour, down from the mound on which Dikwa was built, across the great mud flat of the plain round Chad, to Bama on the Dar-el-Jimeil ridge; from here my route lay along the ridge to the village of the same name, then away for ten or fifteen miles to where the man I was to relieve was building a new station.

Soon after leaving Dikwa we could see away to the south in the clear morning air heralding the approach of the rainy season the top of the highest point of the Gwoza or Mandara Hills; this was Mount Zeledufa, first seen by European eyes by Denham in 1823 when he accompanied a slave-raid from Kukawa. Between Bama and Dar-el-Jimeil, a whole vista of mountains filled the horizon to the south, with an isolated one, Kerawa Hill, lying half-way between Dar-el-Jimeil and the new station at Ashigashiya.

A few weeks later, staying in the rest-house at Kerawa, I was surprised by screams and shoutings in the street and emerged to find a wild *sauve-qui-peut* in progress, with everyone bursting from the market like mad things. My first thought was that a great fight had broken out between the hillmen and some of the plains people, but in a short time we learnt that a swarm of bees had descended on the town. We hastily lit smoke fires to protect both ourselves and our horses and in due course heard what had occurred. A woman, carrying a pot of honey on her head and with her child strapped in the usual way on her back, had entered the market; the scent of the honey had penetrated to a nest of wild bees in one of the trees overlooking the market and they had swarmed onto her. The whole market had been attacked and those attending had fled. The unfortunate child had been stung to death, the mother was badly stung, and four horses, tethered so well that they were unable to flee, had also died. No wonder the passage of a flight of bees in Africa is a thing of terror.

Both Kerawa and Ashigashiya were small towns split by the stream which at this point formed the international boundary between British and French Cameroons. In 1914, British and French forces had advanced into the German Cameroons; the campaign had been hard and bitter and the Germans had withdrawn to a prepared fortress on Mora Mountain which could be seen from Ashigashiya, a few miles away to the east.

40

My horse-boy, Kamkura, was a Maroua Fulani, Maroua being the headquarters of the country in which Mora lay, and he had been present as a small boy when the first British foraging party had entered Mora; the Germans, doubtless thinking that this was the advance party of the main body, had fled up the hillside. The small British party in their short stay blew open the strongroom, distributed the contents to the people of the town, and then withdrew. When the Germans learnt what had happened Kamkura told me—and many others corroborated the story—they tied the Chief of Mora and his leading men to posts hastily driven into the ground in front of his house, and shot them, leaving the dead bodies as a warning to the townsfolk not to assist the British in any way.

In due course Mora capitulated and the German garrison was allowed to march out with colours flying. The Cameroons was then divided into two parts, the greater part being left to the French to administer, the smaller to the British, and in due course the two powers received Mandates from the League of Nations for these 'trust territories'. The boundary laid down in 1916 was a provisional one and followed for most of its length natural landmarks such as water-courses and mountain ridges, but no attempt was made to deal with any ethnic problems which should arise from this use of geographical features.

In the Dikwa Division the problems that were thus created were formidable; from the lake southwards to about Dar-el-Jimeil the new boundary cut through country inhabited on both sides by Kanuri and Shuwa Arabs; indeed, the great dry season gathering ground of the Shuwa from all over British (now Nigerian) Bornu and from the former French colonies, the great swamp of Kutelaha, was cut by this boundary. From Dar-el-Jimeil southwards to near Ashigashiya, more Shuwa were to be found on both sides of the boundary, together with members of the Gamergu tribe. South of Ashigashiya, the boundary passed into the Hill Pagan area, and cut across the territory of only one tribe, a people called the Matakum or Wulla.

At some date, probably about 1923, for reasons I was never able to discover, and apparently on the authority of no one but the men on the spot, a local amendment was made in the area where Dikwa Division met the next division in Adamawa Province

41

to the south, and where both met the French. The result was that
the Kuvoko tribe, which had been entirely in British territory, was
now split between British and French whilst all the Wulla except
for two villages passed to the French. In 1938 the powers that be
in Geneva or London or Paris or all three decided that the 1916
provisional boundary must be finally delimited, and any local
anomalies removed. We Administrative Officers were asked to list
those in our areas, and the above sets out the position as I reported
it. The joint Anglo-French Boundary Commission started work
in early 1939, commencing at the sea near Douala, and completed
perhaps 150 miles of its labour; then Herr Hitler ended that;
and as far as I know, the provisional boundary, still less this local
variation, has never been rectified or ratified. Now it lies as a
future source of friction between Nigeria and Cameroons, two
sovereign states.

But that was for the future; my immediate problems were to
take over from the officer I was relieving and to finish the erec-
tion of a new station. My District Officer was seventy or more
miles away to the north; my Resident was a little farther away to
the north-west; my nearest European neighbour would be the
French Officer at Mora, twenty miles or so away, or his fellow
about the same distance away to the south at a place call Mokolo.

The wild and savage hill-tribes, remnants perhaps of greater
nations driven from the plains of Bornu by the Jukon or Kanuri
invasions, had been raided for slaves for as long as their old men
could remember. During their years of occupation, the Germans
had not penetrated into the hills, but had contented themselves
with building roads around them. An early German column,
moving along the western face of the Zeledufa Mountain, had
been attacked by the warriors of two related villages, and many
killed on both sides, including, it was said, at least one white man;
the column had withdrawn carrying its dead and wounded but
leaving behind many loads. One of these, a great iron box, resisted all efforts to open it; it was obviously of great worth; perhaps it was full of the silver Maria Theresa dollars, in general
use on the plains, of which a few had been taken by the hillmen
from the bodies of slave-raiders killed in battle. Eventually a great
fire was built and the box toppled onto it from atop a great rock.
What it contained can only be guessed, but I was later shown the

black marks on the rocks and the great scars on men's bodies made when, with a noise like thunder, the box disintegrated, killing many and wounding many more of those who had pressed close.

The man I was relieving and I came from the same college, so we christened the new station Fort Emma, in part to commemorate it and in part to emulate Fort Rabeh. A long, low, mud-brick house, not yet thatched; boys' houses and horse stables on the crest of a low ridge overlooking the boundary below; the lines for my escort of twenty men had been sited at the foot of the ridge three hundred yards away and the same distance, or a little farther, from the small town of Ashigashiya. Until now, the head-quarters of the Touring Officer and his escort had been at Gwoza, on the other side of the mountains, across a precipitous pass over a thousand feet high, or about twenty miles away round the end of the mountains by a track which could be followed by a lorry. Gwoza had fallen into disrepute; it was plagued with sandflies and the hillmen on the Gwoza side had become more peaceful, whilst those on the Ashigashiya side of the mountains were still as truculent as ever. Gwoza too lay close to the hills, and the little station had to be surrounded with a leopard-proof fence and provided with two traps baited with live goats each evening. In the event Fort Emma was not a success; the ridge was one big white ant-hill whilst the police lines had been sited in a swamp; two years later the station was back in Gwoza, and Fort Emma fell to ruin.

The day after I arrived, word came in the late afternoon that fighting had started between the two villages of Wala and Warrabè, where the German column had been attacked thirty years before. A message was sent over the pass to the District Head of Gwoza, making a rendevous with him on the boundary of the two villages for dawn the next morning. At 2 a.m. we rose, mounted our horses and with a dozen police set off for the scene of the fighting; our boys and the rest of the police would leave at dawn and cross the pass to Gwoza from where my companion would leave for Maiduguri in a couple of days' time.

As dawn approached we reached the rendezvous ahead of the Gwoza party, and I lay down in the cool sand with my head pillowed on my saddle. Dawn came, and with it the others, and we spent the next seven hours moving from point to point trying to get the elders of the two villages together to agree on peace. By midday we had their promises to co-operate and the District Head was satisfied that all danger of a great fight was now passed. Leaving him to arrange the date of a peace ceremony we rode on to Gwoza and to our first meal of the day; but as we finished a messenger galloped in to say that fighting had again started. Back at once with those of our police who had not been with us that morning, and finally back to Gwoza long after dark. The next day I was left on my own and spent several days with Wala and Warrabè getting them to agree to a peace ceremony. It had been a good day's introduction to the life of an A.D.O. in bush.

Denham describes the slave-raid he saw, and there is no doubt that the pattern varied little. The raiders swooped at dawn on those Pagan compounds which lay nearest to the plains; they fired the thatches of the huts, and broke down the walls; children and the younger women were seized and carried off; the rest speared, or their arms and legs broken, before being thrown into the flames. As the war horns blew and the warriors came down from the higher parts of the village, the raiders would withdraw, taking with them their prey and such few goats or sheep, spears and hoes, as they were able to carry off.

A year or two before my arrival, the whole area had been plagued by a man always mounted on a white horse, sometimes accompanied by two or three others. Some child going to draw water from the well before the rest of the village was about, would be accosted by the stranger asking for a drink. As the child approached he would be seized and carried off. It appeared that this man had been responsible for the kidnapping of perhaps a score of children in this way in both British and French territory. One morning, a Pagan left his house early to go hunting and saw a little group of four horsemen approaching over the plains below. He hid and watched; in due course a child appeared and the usual little drama started, but as the Man on the White Horse seized the child, the hillman shot the first of his poisoned arrows into his chest; dropping the child, the man and his companions fled and another arrow found its mark in the leader's back; a short distance only was covered by the flying horse before the rider fell dead; his companions fled and, aroused by the shouts of the first man, a score of warriors poured down the hillside.

My predecessor was in his office in Gwoza when he heard the singing and shouting of a great crowd, dragging what looked like a log behind them at the end of a rope. They came into his compound and most dropped back to allow the leaders room to display their prize. With some difficulty—for many spears had been buried in the corpse during its eight miles dragging—he recognized it as a human body. The tale was soon told, and the hero posed and postured as he showed how he had hidden, how he had shot the first arrow, then the second, how the man had rolled from his saddle; others took up the tale and shook their spears still red with the blood of the dead man. Here was a problem; by rights the hero should be seized and tried for murder; but no matter what the outcome, only harm could result from such a course. My predecessor took out his inquest book, wrote in it such parts of the account as fitted his verdict and brought in one of justifiable homicide against a person or persons unknown. Then rewarding the hero, but warning everyone not to do it again, he arranged for the corpse to be buried. I read the letter of congratulation from the French at the end of the *Cavalier au Cheval Blanc*.

When Rabeh had conquered Bornu, many of the Kanuri had fled to the Fulani of Maroua in the east or Madagali in the south, and the hillmen had pillaged the fugitives. They had killed the men and had carried off a few women to become their wives, and I came to know one woman, naked like the rest, but taller and with the Kanuri face-marks to show her origin.

In the months that followed I visited each village in turn. To climb the hillsides to one on or near the top called for good wind and stout thighs. Climbing up what was in effect a very long and steep staircase, the path wound round huge boulders, but always went up the shortest possible way. Hard work for any but a hill-man, and when one stopped for breath or to wring the sweat out of one's shirt, along would come some old crone with pendulous breasts and a wrinkled stomach, striding upwards as if this was a gentle slope on which old-age pensioners take their ease. Behind me followed Pagan youths carrying my trek loads, for on these hills the professional carriers, who would face the mud of the Chad flats, could not carry their load up the steep incline. As soon therefore as my little caravan had been seen moving towards the hill-foot, twenty or more youths had rushed down to barter with the carriers and earn threepence or so for the climb up the hill.

It had been decided a dozen years before that the hillmen must pay a small, nominal tax of two shillings per compound; not a large sum, but in order that they might get it, work had to be created, in the shape of building roads. A social revolution had thus been initiated as the youths, of necessity, laboured on the roads. Their pay, given with one hand, was taken away with the other for the tax of their household. But with the white man petty traders arrived in the area and the youths soon found that by staying at the road work for a few days longer, they could get more than the tax required, and matches and cigarettes were soon appreciated. Perhaps a little soap followed and then cloth, generally red, to wind round the waist as a thick buckler when the war horns cried. Little by little the younger generation wandered farther and farther afield from their ancestral home.

The young men now met less desirable aspects of civilization—not of our Western civilization, but of that of the peoples of the plains. In the past a woman had been a virgin until she was married and that only after the payment of a very high bride-price. In the past not every man could find the capital to embark on matrimony, so it was not uncommon to find old men still virgin. Now instead of labouring for years to save the bride-price, the youths found that, in the Sodoms of the plains, temporary wives could be found willing to sleep with them for as long as their money lasted. Wages were low: fourpence a day; but a man lived well on a penny a day, and eight days' work paid a year's tax. And these women would take a man for threepence or sixpence. It was not long before venereal disease was common; attempts at rape—previously unknown—followed, then virtuous wives were tempted by sums of money to be unfaithful to their absent husbands. Civilization had at last caught up with the hill-men.

Whilst all the inhabitants of this area are apparently the same or very similar, when one investigates, the position is found to be very different, as each village differs from the next and claims a different descent from some semi-mythical ancestor. Adjacent villages may well speak languages as different one from another as Spanish is from Czech, though there is a lingua franca used in the intercourse between villages and between them and the settled peoples of the plains. A community may number ten thousand souls in all, spread over several thousand feet vertically and a mile or two horizontally, scattered in small collections of huts where live an old man, his sons and their wives, his grandsons and their wives, and a miscellaneous collection of goats, sheep, cows, and hens, surrounded by a thorn fence with a gateway closed each night by a gate covered with similar thorns and fastened on the inside. There might be twenty roofs in one of these little kraals, twenty small intercommunicating huts without a window in the whole collection, each six feet or less in diameter and reached one from another through doorways perhaps eighteen inches high. With children there might be fifty people living in one of these collections of huts, and perhaps four hundred of them made up the 'village', though the kraals are in no way grouped, but scattered over the hillside.

The term 'village' was introduced by us to describe these communities, but actually they would be better described as 'kindreds' as every male in the place claims descent from a common ancestor and can thus, theoretically, state his relationship with any other man in the place. There may also be found one or two households of despised outcasts from other villages, men who have committed the enormity of fratricide—fratricide in its widest sense, the killing of a kinsman. There may be, too, one or two households of aboriginal inhabitants, descendants of even earlier inhabitants of the hills, who have lost all knowledge of their ancestry beyond their difference from the rest of the village; these are generally the holders of sacred mysteries of rain-making or of blessing or cursing the fruitfulness of the earth. Some of the 'villages' are distinct from their neighbours, distinct that is in descent and possibly in language, but having the same customs and ways of living as their neighbours. In some places are two or more kindreds which can trace their descent from brothers, sons of a common ancestor, so that whilst in their relations with one another both villages behave as if completely distinct, on occasion they combine against some third village. A group of related villages is known as a clan.

Marriage is of course outside the kindred; where everybody is related—however distantly—marriage within the community would be incestuous. So village intermarries with village, and the cows, or sometimes the goats, and the women, move from one village to the next. Very rarely do they move to the next but one; to do so is to ask for trouble, for the bride may be waylaid and seized by the men of the intermediate village as she passes through, or may well be stolen on the occasion she goes to visit her relatives. Marriage is always a gamble; one gives good cows and receives back a woman who may or may not bear children, who may run away home (though the cows one has given never do so), or who may bring some disaster on her new home; better get one from next door, and not add to the possible troubles by wandering far afield. So until the coming of the white man, and for many years after, there were many thousands of the hillmen who had never been more than a mile or so from their village boundary, and to whom the very names of villages only ten miles away which they could see from their own doorway were unknown.

The two great events in any year are the ceremonies at the harvest and at sowing time. The nature of each is the same, but the degree of excitement differs. At harvest time, with a crop safely gathered, the villagers decide how much may be used for a village beer feast; the beer is brewed and then for a week or ten days—depending on the size of the harvest—the whole village is drunk; old toothless men and women lay stretched in stupor side by side with children of four and five.

At the time of the spring sowing, the elders look into the now sadly depleted corn-bins, and decide whether or not corn can be spared for another big communal celebration, but of necessity, as supplies of corn are low and the people are wanted on the farms, this is not to be compared with the one at harvest. Weddings see smaller and more restricted feasts and the same applies to funerals; but in the Sodoms and Gomorrahs of the plains there are always to be found places where beer is to be obtained the whole year round. It is at these feast times that fights occur, grievances, real or fancied, are remembered, and village attacks village with the concomitant death roll.

During the rest of the year, the villages are usually quiet, unless, like disturbing a hive, a woman or cattle are stolen, when the whole village swarms to war against the offenders. A death can only be wiped out by another death, or by payment of blood-money, and it is a matter of interest to the anthropologist that the price for a bride or a dead man is the same—five head of cattle in the opulent villages, twenty head of goats in the poorer ones. But woe betide the village that kills a man from a stronger neighbour. As soon as the news is out, the war horns blow and the young men swarm out with their bows and poisoned arrows, their spears and their shields, and the women of the weaker but aggressor village snatch up their children and drive off the goats to the holes among the boulders. Then the young men clash, and the fighting goes on till they tire or one village retreats leaving the other to pillage and loot. Then it is each for himself and the young men are to be seen driving off their loot or carrying it on their backs. But the defeated turn, and get their revenge on the scattered swarms of their enemies. Then it is for the old men to get together and add up the losses: dead men against dead men, stolen cows against stolen cows, kidnapped women and girls against their opposite numbers. The women and girls are returned, the animals eventually end up more or less where they should be, and the dead, if equal numbers have been killed on either side, are wiped off the slate. But if the villages differ in the total of their dead, if the one which has killed most will not make up the difference by handing over cattle, then a blood feud has started which will ebb and flow until the debt has been wiped out in one way or another, either in open fight or by hidden ambush.

It is a man's world. Man is born, for some unknown reason, of woman, and the women, when not unclean after childbirth or at their menstrual periods, prepare the meals for the men; they are useful too, as extra hands on the farms and to carry water. But it is to men that the ancestral secrets have been confided; it is after the first male ancestor that a kindred is named; it is they who decide when and to whom a daughter should be married; it is they who have promulgated the uncleanliness of women at certain periods; and it is they who fight and dance at the feasts and ceremonies of the village. A man too lives in his kindred, but a woman, once she has reached marriageable age, leaves her own and moves to that of her husband where she may or may not be accepted by the rest of her husband's kindred—not just those now living, but the majority of the kindred who have already lived or who have yet to be born. It is a man's world; 'I have four sons,' a man will say, and possibly could not answer correctly if asked for the number of his daughters.

The Germans had never penetrated into the hill area of the Dikwa Division; the French, who held it from 1914 until 1920, on one occasion only; European Administration was only introduced to any degree by British Officers from 1919 onwards. The two Pagan Districts of Gwoza and Ashigashiya formed an 'Unsettled District' where no alien was allowed to enter except with the permission and under the surveillance of the local Administrative Officer. The French found it necessary to make similar arrangements on their side of the boundary, but whereas on the British side the Assistant District Officer had an escort of twenty armed police, his French opposite number had one of a hundred and twenty troops.

From time to time trouble in the hills would necessitate the sending of a 'patrol'—a company of troops of the Nigeria Regiment—to assist the A.D.O. and his police, and one such action against the Wulla Village of Lokperè in the early 1930's left a running sore in the District. The village had refused to pay its tax, so, taking advantage of the presence of a patrol, the then District Officer from Dikwa, with his A.D.O., the latter's police, the company of troops and some thirty-odd carriers visited the village. Knowing what was coming, the inhabitants had cleared out and, armed cap-à-pie, danced and mocked the column from the safety of that part of the village which lay in French territory. Nothing worth taking for tax was found, so in due course the British party set off over the hilltops for home. At one point on their return journey, the carriers, with the District Head of Ashigashiya, a certain Malla Sanda, were sent off home by a path leading directly to their home on the eastern side of the ridge, whilst the troops and police followed another to Gwoza on the west. As soon as the column of troops had wound out of sight, the carriers decided to return to Lokperè to loot, about as mad a plan as was ever devised. They had scarcely scattered amongst the Wulla compounds than the horde of fighting men on the French side of the boundary swarmed over to the British side, armed with poisoned arrows and the murderous weapon of the Wulla, the *daniski*, or handbill. Murderous it was, for as the carriers turned to flee up the terraces to the safety of the troops—now some miles away—each in turn was killed by a blow on the back of the skull. The sole survivor was Malla Sanda who often told me of his terror as he fled, hearing the screams as each of his companions was struck down and killed. At one stage his gown was grasped but luckily it tore and his assailant fell heavily and did not regain his feet. Apart from burning the houses of the principal leaders, no punishment was ever inflicted on the Wulla for this massacre, and the burning of stone-walled huts merely meant the loss of the thatch and some of the corn in the corn stores—most being un-harmed below the burnt crust. It was said that the luckless looters were all beheaded, and their skulls preserved in a hole in the rocks on the French side of the boundary, overlooking the village.

The A.D.O. in charge of the area led a very full life, though one of considerable responsibility and entailing a great amount of hard physical exercise, climbing about the hills. On trek in most parts of the North, mud-walled, grass-thatched rest-houses existed only in the larger towns. Away from these we slept in the mud gate-house of a larger compound or occupied one of the huts of a con-veniently placed house. Hens, goats, perhaps horses, would be taken elsewhere for the night, the floor would be swept, grass mats placed across inconvenient openings, and all was ready. But in the Gwoza Hills we were forbidden to sleep in the Pagan huts because of the danger, so we were told, of leprosy. So we trekked with a heavy tent and its poles, three loads extra to the sum of bed, office box and household loads.

At the start of the rainy season, each torrential downpour would be heralded by a wind- and sand-storm; sometimes these came of an evening, very rarely in the early part of the day, most often at night. I would be awakened by the roar of the wind and the flapping of the tent; my pillow would become gritty beneath the mosquito-net, with the wind-borne sand. I must emerge to tighten the guys, to be joined, if I were lucky, by one of my boys or one of the police escort. Generally however, hermetically sealed from all sound in the Pagan stone-walled huts, they slept as the dead; my shouts for assistance disturbed no one over the roar of the rushing wind.

Knowing what would follow, I would strip off my pyjamas and don raincoat and mosquito-boots as I emerged to wrestle with the guys; suddenly there would come a lull; a monstrous pattering sound, then the gale came again with even greater fury and the heavens dissolved in sheets of driving rain, hitting the face like solid sticks. Armed with a torch, I would sit watching the trickles of water grow to rushing streams across the floor of the tent, lifting everything onto tables and chairs. Then, as the tightening canvas warned of the next stage, I would emerge to circle the tent time and again, loosening little by little the tightening guys. The rain would pour down the neck of my raincoat over my naked body; at times the wind would throw the raincoat over my head. I would curse, and then after a time start to giggle; the lightning flashed, the thunder roared, alone I kept the tent standing.

At last the wind would drop and the rain would change to a steady drumming; the canvas finally shrunk, I could venture inside, strip, rub down and back to bed. With the dawn my boys, incredulous and wary of my rage, vowing they had heard nothing.

Rain and heat; mountain and plain; few of us would have wished to be elsewhere; we loved the life; we loved these hills; we respected their people and felt that were we Pagans, we should oppose any attempts by misguided administrators to bring us down to the more easily administered plains.

A few, a very few, found the physical demands on their constitution too great, coupled as these were with the ever-present likelihood of fighting between the villages, with the resultant arguing and cajoling of primitive minds, to add tiredness of mind to that of body. So a few, a very few, asked to be posted elsewhere; with such were the Secretariats manned.

CHAPTER FIVE

Pagan Administration

Normally when an Administrative Officer was on tour in an Emirate, he was accompanied by a representative of the Emir. The Emir and his Council formed the Native Authority for the area, approximating to some degree to the position of a County Council in this country, and we Administrative Officers were there to guide, advise and help, not to rule; at times the line between advice and direct action became a little blurred. The Emir's rep., as he was always called, was in theory a kind of Inspector for the Native Authority; not, I would hasten to add, on the interfering European, but on the District Heads, to ensure that they were doing as they ought, and carrying out the commands and wishes of the Authority. But with strong District Heads, often younger brothers of the ruler, and sometimes heirs apparent, a weak Emir's rep. could become little more than an extra attendant, responsible for seeing that water and firewood were brought, that one's carriers were fed, and so on.

The A.D.O. was there to advise and cajole; if he got no satisfaction, and his advice and that of his representative were ignored, it was for both to report back to Headquarters, the A.D.O. to the District Officer and his rep. to the Emir. In theory at least; for on one occasion a representative came to see me at dead of night, to plead that I would not ask him to send so many letters to his Emir. He was but a poor man, and he could no longer afford the presents which must accompany each missive. This advising, not ruling, was the distinguishing feature of Lugard's system of administration, known as Indirect Rule, and marked us District Officers as a race apart from the District Commissioners of East Africa, who, at least for many years, ruled and did not advise.

In a purely Pagan area this was not possible, and District Officers still ruled more or less directly, but making every attempt to create and foster Native Authorities from the jumble of family and clan heads to whom the local populations looked for guidance.

'The difference between Indirect and Direct Rule is this,' said one wise Resident. 'With Indirect Rule you show a man how to do a thing and leave him to get on with it. He does nothing or does it wrongly, so you show him again. Eventually you have to replace him with another, and him in turn with a third. Finally, if anything is to be done, you do it yourself. With Direct Rule, the intermediate stages are missing.'

Gwoza and Ashigashiya Districts, within the Dikwa Native Administration area, were a bastard arrangement. The hills had never formed part of the empire of any of the rulers of Bornu, and the plains at their feet had been a no-man's-land between the Kanuri of Bornu, the Fulani of Maroua, and the Fulani of Madagali and Mubi, where each power raided for slaves at will. For no apparent reason, after the end of the First World War, the Pagan villages and the plains surrounding the hills had been divided, some to Gwoza, some to Ashigashiya, and the whole area included with Dikwa.

The first attempts to create District Heads had not been successful. At Gwoza a Kanuri had been installed, who fled when a Pagan attack burned Gwoza to the ground and killed many of its inhabitants. Following him, as the southern parts of Gwoza had been more under Madagali than anyone, the next District Head was a member of the ruling Fulani family from that town. On the eastern side of the mountains another Kanuri had been installed, Malla Sanda, later the sole survivor of the Lokperè massacre.

My Emir's representative—for as a Touring Officer I must have one—was another Kanuri, Wuroma Bundi, a man of tremendous energy and some considerable physical bravery. When Malla Sanda died, he was succeeded by Wuroma and I then urged that, as I was permanently resident in the area, I should have no representative with me, and that the two District Heads must be encouraged to stand on their own feet. This argument was accepted; within a very short time, to my very great regret, Wuroma Bundi died, and I then urged that the two Districts should be combined. The Fulani District Head of Gwoza then became the first head of the combined area, with the old Kanuri title of Galadima, 'Lord of the Land in the West'.

His family was that of the ruling house of Madagali. One member, an elder brother of the Galadima, was hated throughout the land, where his name was synonymous with all that is evil, for he had been a patricide and, several times over, guilty of fratricide. When the Galadima was still a boy, this elder brother had left home and in some way obtained a position of trust with the Germans. To their willing ears he poured out tales that his family was a nest of snakes which should be destroyed root and branch. Backed by a party of German African troops, this man returned to Madagali and all his family were shot down except for the Galadima and another brother also in his teens. These two had fled, and had been unable to return to their home until after the death of their infamous brother.

I, and all other administrative officers who served in the area, regarded the Galadima as a very upright and honest man and he was, to the best of our knowledge, trusted and liked by the Pagans. At this time we were forbidden to shake hands with any Africans other than Emirs as it was said the latter resented such familiarity with their subjects; on one occasion I said to my then Resident that I wished to ignore the order in my relations with the Galadima, but was told that I must not make an exception in view of the trouble it would cause elsewhere.

My two messengers were Moman Biu, a Kanuri ex-soldier, and Yerima Boyi, a younger half-brother on his mother's side to the Galadima. Dikwa was a hotbed of intrigue, and after I had left Gwoza the Galadima was accused of some offence, and removed from office. He then distributed his goods amongst the poor of Gwoza, divorced his wives and sent them to their parents, and set out on pilgrimage to Mecca, saying that he would die at Medina on his return. In due course word arrived that his prophecy had been correct and that after completing the pilgrimage at Mecca he had died and been buried in Medina. He was succeeded as Galadima by Yerima Boyi who in turn fell from grace about the time that Nigeria became independent; he now resides across the border in the Cameroon half of Ashigashiya. Again, most of those who served with him find it hard to believe that he too did not fall a victim to the old Kanuri–Fulani hostility.

Moman Biu was a Kanuri, an ex-sergeant-major of the Nigeria Regiment, trustworthy and amusing but not as intelligent as Yerima Boyi. 'Boyi' means the 'hidden one' for, as all know, at times a child refuses to be born at the given time, and remains hidden in his mother's womb (how else can one explain the fact that virtuous wives sometimes present their proud husbands with fine children soon after their return after an absence of a year or more?). They worked well together and many are the miles we climbed in the mountains or rode over the plains of Dikwa. My horse-boy, Kamkura, was a Maroua Fulani and as we rode I learnt of the histories of Bornu, Maroua and Madagali, and I would tell them of England, Egypt, Iceland and East Africa.

On occasion we would tell Hausa stories of which there are a vast number; they knew them from babyhood; I was learning them with the language, from a collection made by a Major Edgar. Certain of these were great favourites, and, no matter how often told, were greeted with shouts of laughter. Some are Rabelaisian; others the ancestors of the 'Uncle Remus' stories; others are plays upon words. One of the latter is of a Moslem teacher who in a time of famine had taken refuge with a Pagan friend whose corn-bins were full. On the day of his arrival, the bonne-bouche was unfortunately stewed dog, forbidden to a Moslem. 'Do not, my friend,' said the Pagan, 'eat my dog; *Kada ka chi karena.*' 'Oh no, I do not despise this food, I thank you in truth,' replied his guest. *'Aah, aah; ban rena ba, na gode maka dayawa.'* The jest lies in the phrase *karena*; *kare na* means 'my dog'. *Ka rena* means 'that which you despise'. These stories were always relished by the team of regular carriers who gathered at each headquarters, and they too would produce their own versions or new stories as we trekked.

One of my regular carriers at Gwoza had only one hand, the result of an explosion when working as a miner in the tin fields, but on occasion it suited everyone's mood to pretend that he was one of the unfortunates who had suffered this form of mutilation as a punishment, for in the Moslem code the punishment for stealing included the amputation of the hand, and other robust punishments such as scarifying the flesh of the palm and of the fingers and binding the latter firmly down on the former, to grow into a clubbed lump; generally the absence of elementary hygiene must have meant an early death.

Kamkura was a great addict of the game of *darra* and generally won. The version much played in Bornu has something of noughts and crosses about it; the two players sit facing each other, smooth the sandy soil between them and then scoop out a series of depressions to form a square six by six; each then places his fourteen pieces—which consist on one side of stones and fragments of pot, on the other of small sticks or corn-stalks, or the seeds of various trees—taking it in turns to place each one. The object of the game is to form a line of three men when a piece is moved, so that in the initial placing each tries to get pairs of pieces with a vacant hole at one end and a third man on the other side of the empty place, but as with noughts and crosses, in addition to trying to place one's own to allow 'a three' to be formed on the first move, one also tries at the same time to queer the pitch of one's opponent; it is here that the skilful player wins the game before a piece is moved. When all the pieces are in place one player moves —vertically or horizontally but not diagonally—and if he forms a three, he removes from the board any one of his opponent's pieces; the latter moves and does likewise; the game ends when one is either reduced to two men, or one's men are so split that one can no longer form threes, and one's opponent can; on rare occasions a draw occurs. The killing position is to get a line of three men, then a vacant space and two more men at right angles from it. When the end man is moved into the vacant space, it forms a three with this pair and leaves behind a similar pair which the next move remakes into a three, and unless this formation is broken by the opponent the latter loses a man every move, as the other shuttles backwards and forwards. This is greeted by the crowd of onlookers with the phrase '*Ya samu doki*' (He has got a horse'); my efforts rarely ended in success, at any rate against Kamkura, as my placing of the pieces had no guile.

In Maiduguri there were one or two old men who played a form of chess; they had not been taught by Europeans, but had learnt it from their fathers, who in turn had first learnt it either away in the East or from some traveller who had come from there to this once mighty empire in the heart of Africa. I could not play the game, but someone who could described it in one of the *Journals* and our engineer, Tommy Brand, took a cine film showing the players and the board. If the game is still played, it may merit investigation by a member of one of the Nigerian Universities to trace its history and to save it from extinction. When Kamkura got into the position described above which gave him an almost certain win, the onlookers cried, '*Ya samu doki*—he has got a horse'; when the Bornu chess-players saw that the game was won, they wagged their heads and opined, '*As Sheikh mat*—the ruler is dead'. Will '*ya samu doki*' ever enter into international usage as has the phrase 'checkmate'?

An introduced game which became increasingly popular over the years was Ludo, played with lightning speed, and, as always, with as many spectators hanging over the board shouting advice at the tops of their voices as there was room for.

When I first employed Kamkura his wages were five shillings a week, and he received the same amount for Njaro's corn; but the cost of living was so low that Kamkura, his wife and Njaro could all feed well on the latter's corn-money—if anything Njaro got too much to eat and after a day or two's rest from trekking our start the next day would not have disgraced the Calgary rodeo. Like my other horses Njaro was a stallion, not a gelding. On one such occasion his buckings and cavortings were so violent that, in order to take some of the spirit out of him, I gave him his head, and we went hell for leather down a winding path through quite thick bush. Suddenly we hit a soft patch—Njaro taking no notice of the bit—I went over his head, and as I hit the ground I saw him standing on his head vertical in the air before he came crashing down alongside me. He scrambled to his feet and, as he did so, stood on the inside of my bare right arm, cutting and bruising the flesh and marking me for life, but without breaking the bone. Then, with his corn thus satisfactorily shaken down, we rejoined the rest of the party at a more sedate pace; being carried for four days through bush with a broken pelvis—even a broken arm—would not have been pleasant. Kamkura left me in 1945 to return to his beloved Bornu—where he died in 1950—and was succeeded by an old soldier, Garuba Kano. In 1952 Njaro died at Kaduna when he must have been about seventeen years of age and the vet told me that Garuba had thrown an old blanket over the corpse before being led away in tears; I had not dared to attend the burial as I was not far from them myself. The Hereafter will be a poor place if Njaro, Kamkura and Garuba are not there to greet me on my arrival.

From Gwoza I looked across to the small Yamtagè Hills at whose feet there had once been a town used as the point from which slave-raids against the hills were mounted, and later as a stopping place for German caravans between Mora and Madagali. It was for a time the headquarters of a petty chief who was the chief supplier of eunuchs to the court of Bornu. The tale was that anyone in a wide area who wanted to get rid of some troublesome youth would send him to this spot to collect 'the horse with the short tail'; on delivering this message, the bearer was told that the horse had to be made ready for the journey; meanwhile he should eat, and food was brought containing a sleeping draught. The unfortunate messenger awoke from this sleep to find his head and feet fastened in a pillory whilst, indeed, the horse with the short tail was being prepared for the journey. This was not a punishment, of course, but the straightforward means of meeting the market demand for a rare commodity. There were eunuchs in Maiduguri at the outbreak of war, and a few years earlier one Emir had approached his Resident asking if, as castration was now forbidden, some convicted murderer awaiting execution could not be operated upon by a European doctor, thus saving the man's life, punishing him, relieving everyone of the bother of execution, and filling a much needed want.

The only products in the area which had any artistic interest were brass or copper ornaments. In recent years, whenever a piece of Benin art has reached the sale rooms, very high prices have been given for it; the story of Benin, 'The City of Blood', its art treasures, its sack by a British force in 1898 and the scattering of the loot throughout the world, is not part of the story of Northern Nigeria. Many of the treasures are made of brass or bronze, and other figurines of the same material have been found at places in Nigeria south of the two rivers. Little is yet known of their history or where the art of making them by what is known as the 'lost wax' or *cire perdue* process was first learnt, but there are still wandering craftsmen, adepts in this method of casting, to to be found throughout Northern Nigeria, who are presumably in some way connected with those who made the larger figures in the past.

One of these operated throughout the area of Southern Dikwa and the Northern Cameroons and I would meet him from time to time when trekking away from the hills; he became well known to me and I would save any cartridges I fired to add to the stock of his raw material; in return he allowed me to learn his process. His main output was in the form of ornaments for the Marghi women to hang about their loins, and these were chiefly in two forms; the first a rod about two inches long, with a ring at one end and a flattened area at the other, with 'coiled string' ornamentation below the ring and above the base; the second was a small bell-shaped ornament with the outside covered with decoration in the shape of raised lines. He told me that on occasion he had made bits and stirrups, and tobacco pipes, and he claimed that given a model he could copy anything in brass. His raw material was bought in the shape of rods from the canteens of the traders along the Benue river, plus old ornaments that he obtained from time to time, cartridges and indeed any form of waste brass.

The objects to be made were first modelled in bees-wax, and he showed great skill and dexterity in producing them, knowing exactly how to make his wax stiff or workable as required. When he was making his usual stock ornaments he needed seventy-two of the first kind or a hundred and twenty of the second before he cast, and when the requisite number was ready, each was enclosed in wet clay to form a cylindrical or cubic block, which was then set in the sun to dry after an iron spike had been pushed through the clay at one end to make a channel leading to the wax within as the clay hardened in the sun. When it was dry enough to be easily handled, the craftsman took a closely woven mat and proceeded to build a wall of clay about two inches high along the two sides and the base of a rectangle. The little cylinders or cubes were then taken and arranged in lines within the rectangle, the first line with the base of each cylinder touching the clay wall, then a gap a little under half an inch wide; on the other side of the gap was another line of clay cylinders with their holes facing the first, and then a line back to back with these, with their holes facing the opposite way, and so on until the farther wall of the rectangle was reached. When this was complete, along the top of the rectangle was built another wall of wet clay, again a little under half an inch from the end of the line of cylinders, with in its middle a funnel of hard baked clay which had been prepared beforehand. When all had dried a quick inspection was made, to ensure that the little hole leading through each clay cylinder to the wax within was not blocked, then more semi-liquid wax was taken and

60

poured along each of the channels and up to the bottom of the clay funnel. A sheet of clay was now rolled out like pastry and carefully fitted over the rectangle and its contents, and when this too had dried in the sun, the whole was carefully inverted, the bottom side similarly covered with a sheet of wet clay, and the whole again returned to the sun to dry. Whilst this was going on, the craftsman would be preparing more models in wax for his next casting.

The mould and its encircling clay now resembled a filled rubber hot-water-bottle, and when it was thoroughly dry and hard it was taken and placed, with two or three others, in a bed of hot ash with the mouth of the funnel uppermost. They were left to bake for some time, at the end of which each 'hot-water-bottle' had become a hard container and the wax within was molten; each 'hot-water-bottle' was next carefully inverted and the molten wax run out into a calabash for re-use at some future time. The quantity of wax that had run out measured the quantity of brass or copper required to take its place, and this was placed in a previously prepared holder, the shape of a half-grapefruit, made of baked clay; this in turn was placed over the top of the funnel on the 'hot-water-bottle', and cemented to it with more clay. When all the moulds had been similarly prepared, they were taken and inverted in red-hot ashes so that the funnel and the brass inside it were now at the base of each; the fire was blown up with bellows and the heat melted the brass in its holder.

From time to time the craftsman would take hold of one of the 'hot-water-bottles' and shake it to test if the brass were yet molten, for now the critical part of the operation was at hand, and all his time and work might be wasted for, in addition to the heat melting the brass, it had also baked the clay hard, and in the process this had contracted and contained cracks which might allow the molten metal to escape. The more obvious cracks were therefore hastily smeared over from time to time with wet clay which dried and filled them.

Presumably the craftsman knows when all is ready by the feel of the movement of the molten metal, but he claimed that he knew by a peculiar smell; I could never distinguish this and it is probably one of the tricks of the trade to persuade onlookers of the difficulties of the craft and to dissuade them from trying to perform what after all was a relatively simple process. When all was ready, a large calabash of water was taken and placed on one side and a large lump of wet clay on the other. A pair of tongs was now taken and the first of the moulds lifted, rapidly inverted, and its base placed on the ground and held by the tongs in the left hand whilst with the right my friend took a large lump of wet clay; almost at once spouts of molten metal burst from the mould, and were closed by his rapidly pressing wet clay over them; as soon as all were stopped, the mould was taken and placed in the water so that the latter would immediately cool the whole and at the same time percolate into the interstices of the clay and loosen them. In a few minutes the remains of the disintegrating mould were removed from the water and the fragments of adhering clay were knocked away. There now remained a mass of shining brass ornaments with small spurs where the pricked holes had been made, connecting the ornaments to the straight bars of metal which had filled the channels previously packed with wax. The ornaments were broken away, a few deft strokes with a file removed the last protrusions and the metal that had filled the channels was recovered for use again.

In addition to the violent smelling to test when the metal was ready for pouring, gibberish charms were spoken and there was some play with the hands before the final act, in order probably further to persuade the gaping crowd of the difficulty of the craft.

The casting complete, this itinerant craftsman would attend a neighbouring market to sell his newly made ornaments; then away elsewhere casting and selling, making his way, as his raw materials were used up, down to the trading station at Yola on the great waters of the Benue. Restocked, he would make his way back to the north, and emerging from the bush weeks after we had last met at some village fifty or a hundred miles away, I would see him under the trees of another village making his next batch of 'hot-water-bottles'.

'Greetings, O European,' he would cry, 'and hast thou of the cartridges? Bring them and I will teach thee again how to make ornaments of brass.'

CHAPTER SIX

Three Graves

To those at the centre of government, the members of the Secretariats in Nigeria and of the Colonial Office in London, all talk of witchcraft is so much arrant nonsense. Moreover, had they had their way, whenever a District Officer caught a Pagan responsible for homicide—and this we were rarely able to do—the full majesty of the law would have been brought into action. The unfortunate prisoner would have been haled some hundred miles away from his home—and in the case of the older men this meant taking them away from the ten-mile-or-so strip of country in which their entire lives had been passed—and kept in prison for maybe two or three months whilst first a preliminary investigation and then a full trial before a judge were held. The unfortunate witnesses would similarly be torn from their families—if they could be caught—and at the end of it all, it would be seen that the white man, despite his oft vaunted impartiality, had been all the time on the side of the dead man's village, for, instead of consenting to a peace ceremony and the payment of five head of cattle as blood-money, he wanted only the death of the killer. Sometimes it would be seen that the white man merely wanted to take advantage of the situation for, doing nothing about the blood-money, he would keep the killer as his slave for several years. Why should any Pagan consent to be tried for homicide when he could not receive an impartial hearing?

Witchcraft was nearly always malignant, rarely benign. One of the few examples I knew of the latter was perhaps more of the nature of a good-luck charm, a charm which any passer-by could invoke. It consisted of a large round boulder weighing perhaps seventy pounds, and no different from many thousands of other, similar boulders to be found in the bed of every dry water-course running from the foot of the Gwoza Hills. For some reason which I could never ascertain and at some date which was allegedly remote but might well have been very recent, it had been found that good luck came to you if, on your journey along the rough track which ran southwards from Gwoza, you put down your load, lifted the stone and carried it for a few steps in the direction you were going. If too old or too weak or too young to lift it, you rolled it over once or twice. It was to be found anywhere along a stretch of the track about six miles long, the extremities marked by large trees, and when in due course I too stopped and staggered a few paces with it, local opinion applauded my good sense. Imagine my anger when I learnt that a Swiss trader from Maiduguri, who was allowed to pass through the Unsettled District during the dry season on a monthly visit to one of his stores in Madagali in Adamawa Province to the south, had carried off the stone. The indignant deputation which brought me the news added that their young men were threatening to fill the Swiss with poisoned arrows the next time he passed through. Had that happened, then the fat would have been in the fire. Blood would have been demanded; a patrol of troops probably sent; people killed. I left hastily for Maiduguri, told the man what I thought about him and returned triumphantly with the stone; it was dropped in its proper place to the plaudits of a large crowd, and soon disappeared out of sight away to the south. The excuse of the abductor had been that he needed a stone on which to whet his skinning knives and that by chance he had hit on this one.

Witchcraft is anti-social: killing a witch may therefore possibly be not only excusable but indeed a social act performed for the general well-being.

One day when I was living in Ashigashiya news was brought that fighting had broken out and that men had died. The fight had occurred between two villages only about ten miles from my house, but I knew that it would take anything up to a week to get the two sides together, so giving orders to my boys to pack my camp kit and to bring the tent, I prepared to ride off at once with a dozen armed police as escort. Four more would come along with the boys and the carriers who would be in no great danger—the fight was purely an inter-village one and neither I nor my followers would be in any way molested unless I became awkward, as perhaps I must.

News had arrived about midday, so when I took the road an

hour later, with my small escort, the two messengers and the District Head and his men, the sun was cruel.

After about an hour we emerged from the bush into the first farms of the Pagan villages which lay at the foot of the great hills towering above us, and for another hour we wound our way outside the last of the giant thorn fences which ring each village and its farms, planted in the past to stop the charge of slave-raiders on horseback. Finally, we reached the boundaries of the first of the villages which had been involved in the morning's fight and turned along a path with towering wait-a-bit thorn fences on either hand. In a short time we reached the first of the houses and saw the naked women and children rush screaming into the first doorway within reach. There were but few men to be seen, and these were all armed with spears, bows and poisoned arrows, shields and war helmets.

At last we reached the larger house where dwelt the leader of the village, leader in all its activities, temporal and sacred. He it was who acted as chief intermediary between the men of the village now alive and those who had passed on or who were still to come from the land of the shades, when the men on earth needed the help of those other, no longer present, members of the community. He it was who planted the first seed at sowing time, who reaped the first head of corn at harvest; to whom all village disputes were taken for settlement; who acted as intermediary with other villages when a quarrel concerned men of different communities. This important man was now a member of the Native Court which met once a week on market days under the new dispensation of the ever-interfering white man, represented by me.

Under a large white-thorned acacia he sat, old Agapalawa, a man aged possibly sixty-five or seventy, still active, but with an enormous patch which set him apart from the majority of his spare fellows. Around him, naked save for small pieces of goatskin which they had twisted under their buttocks to sit upon, were the elders of the clan and one or two of the middle-aged and younger men, like so many baboons, some smoking and spitting, others with their legs straight out in front of them, idly rubbing their skin or poking at some thorn in their feet. As I approached they rose to their feet and greeted me by shaking their fists in my face. Beyond a fence I could hear the wailing of many women and I guessed that there lay the house of one of the two men killed that morning.

'Greetings,' I said. 'Greetings, Agapalawa. But what is this news that has reached me? What is this news of fighting between you and Ngoshè Kubo? Were you not able to stay your young men when they went to fight? Or was it Ngoshè who first attacked? Where are your young men?'—and I dismounted. Kamkura ran up, took the pony to one side and loosened the girths, while some of the Pagans took the horses of my followers. At a word of command from the sergeant of police, two of his men had stationed themselves behind me, whilst the others went in pairs to each of the gateways leading from the thorn-defended paths into this open space. I seated myself on a rock at the foot of the tree and the District Head and my messengers sat to one side; Agapalawa and his followers sat in front of us; behind came the ever-continuing sound of the wailing women, and from time to time some older men would come and join the little group. I could see the police sitting and kneeling in the welcome shade, drinking water brought to them by naked youths; they had slung their bandoliers across their chests and had slipped one clip of cartridges into their rifles. Old Agapalawa sat there silent for a time, rubbing with a small twig in the dust, one leg tucked under him. Then he pushed the twig into the ground, rubbed his hands together to remove the sand and addressed me.

'White man,' he said. 'What you have heard is true. Those dogs from Ngoshè came and carried off a woman this morning, and when our young men ran to free her two were killed. You can hear where the bodies are being prepared for burial this evening. When the news was brought to me, I remembered your words and ran and stopped our young men before they could follow Ngoshè and before more blood could flow, but the young men are angry, they taunt me and they are gathered on the edge of the village nearest Ngoshè waiting to attack them and kill any that they may. Two have died, two others must die, or blood-money must be paid in their place. Such is our law as you know. Were you not here, were I but twenty years younger, those dogs at Ngoshè would have suffered ere now, and two of theirs had gone to join their ancestors in the shades; two, aye, ten of theirs had died.' A great grunt of agreement went up from his fellows. The District Head looked at me and one of the policemen laughed, for it was well known throughout the area that Ngoshè were mighty in war, whilst Agapalawa's village had been for many years peaceable. But for this the death roll would have been greater; but for this their young men would have been in Ngoshè now, killing and being killed—instead of lurking frightened but yelling taunts, within easy reach of the shelter of their own hedges. This I knew, and Agapalawa and his elders knew that I knew, but the customary gambits must be performed and customary fictions observed. It was now about four in the afternoon and the heat lay like a blanket over the land; there was nothing for it but to go to Ngoshè, about a mile farther along. But first, arrangements must be made for the night, and the young men of Agapalawa's had to be persuaded to withdraw.

'Wuroma Bundi,' I said to the Kanuri District Head of Ashigashiya, 'dare you go ahead of me to Ngoshè and tell them that I follow and would speak to them? I fear if they see me coming all will flee to the shelter of their caves and hides in the hills and we shall not see them again today. If they flee, these cowards here will follow to loot and perhaps burn. The day draws on; we must get sense into their heads before dark. Do you want some of the police to go with you or would the Ngoshè people flee?'

'I will go alone,' he said, 'with some of my followers. They will not attack me. Do you follow but do not cross the wadi which forms the boundary between the two villages. I will return there with my news.' He rose and went off on foot whilst my messengers set about the preparations for the night. The carriers and my boys now arrived and we took possession of three near-by houses which backed on to a small, thorn-ringed field. The tent was pitched; mats were taken to form stables for the horses; grass was brought; parts of the walls round the houses were breached to allow easy passage for our little party, and other entrances were closed with stones and thorns, making a little fortress inside the village. Leaving the sergeant with half the police, I went on foot to the rendezvous, passing *en route* the other house where the women of the village howled and beat themselves whilst the gravediggers made ready for the burial at sunset.

In due course Ngoshè was reached and a scene similar to that in the other village was enacted. Here, however, the meeting with the elders was punctuated with cries of defiance from the young men perched scissor-like on the hillside above us. Kubo, the headman of this unit, was a younger man than old Agapalawa, with a crafty face, and his council of elders was jubilant and truculent. Little could be done with them in this frame of mind. Time and patience, much patience, were going to be needed to stop further bloodshed and get them to agree to a peace ceremony. We sat and argued and I urged the elders to restrain their young men.

'I know you will tell me that you are doing what you can: that may be so. Who knows? Perhaps the young men of Ngoshè no longer respect their elders and give no heed to their advice; perhaps you elders are not trying very hard. I know not. But this I do know; tonight I sleep at Agapalawa's and tomorrow I shall return to speak further with you. If you or any of your men come over the wadi between the two villages, as sure as I sit here, my police will shoot and tomorrow I will burn down some of your houses. By the heavens I swear this, and you know that neither I nor any of the other white men, my predecessors, ever went back on his word. Be warned Kubo and you elders; keep your young men quiet or there will be trouble.'

The night passed off, as always, quietly; for the next three days I moved with the District Head from one village to the other, arguing, cajoling, threatening, pleading, remonstrating, joking, angry, weary, tired of the whole affair and of all Pagans. But at last our efforts began to bear fruit; the abducted woman was handed over and returned to her husband; most of the young men, no longer armed cap-à-pie, now attended the meetings in Ngoshè, and at last the elders on both sides, wearied of our presence which effectively stopped all the normal activities of the villages, began to talk less frequently of further fighting and more of a peace ceremony. On the fourth day, agreement was reached: a peace ceremony would be performed on the morrow, ten head of cattle would be handed over as blood-money for the two dead men and we would be able to leave.

So on the morrow at first dawn, with half a dozen police as escort, I sat on the boundary of the two villages with the District Head and my messengers. On one side of the dried up

Rest-houses—permanent . . .

. . . and strictly temporary

The pageantry of the North—*Salla* at Dikwa

The enemy. Locusts on the move

Sau Burial Pots

Trekking in the rains

Blood must atone for blood . . . two warring villages come to terms,
and a mongrel puppy is the only casualty

Bush

Njaro, the obedient

The Hill of Duku

Shegi, the wild

A Pagan village in the hills

A sugar-cane fleet

water-course sat Kubo and four of his elders, one of them holding
a small, yowling puppy; on the other sat Agapalawa with a similar
retinue but without a puppy. In a short time, Agapalawa stood
up and shouted: 'You there, Kubo, and the men of Ngoshè; you
have spilled our blood. Are you now prepared to repay the debt
and sweeten the earth of the taint that lies on it? Answer Kubo.'
'We are ready; we have brought the blood to repay the debt and
blood to sweeten the earth.'

The two little groups stood and advanced to the middle of the
wadi. The puppy was held and cut slowly in half whilst alive, and
the blood allowed to flow down and sweeten the earth and so
remove the taint of human blood which might harm the harvests
of the two villages. Next the oaths were sworn, by heaven and by
earth, that now all was peace between the two communities. As
each oath was sworn, the elders made weird bird-like cries which
could be heard back in the villages by the young men, thus
warned that all fighting was at an end. And finally, with some
reluctance on the part of Kubo, ten head of cattle were brought
and handed over on the boundary to be driven away by the relatives of the dead men, five to each. Five was the number of cattle
needed to buy a new woman as wife for some man in the family,
and thus bring fresh blood to replace that lost in the fight.

Now all was over and I could return home, secure in the
knowledge that no further fight would occur for some considerable
time.

And so homewards; home to the deep shade of the house, so
different from the hot glare of a tent; home to comfortable chairs
and the knowledge that no hot-head would throw a spear at one of
my charges that night. But in the evening came news that Agapalawa and his elders waited on me.

I came out of the house to find the District Head and my
messengers already there, sitting in the shade of the conference
hut, with Agapalawa in their midst, and I could see from their
faces that something serious had happened. As I approached the
whole meeting rose and came out of the hut, shaking their fists at
me in greeting. We exchanged salutations, then sat down in the
hut on logs of wood which were kept there for such affairs.

'Greeting, Agapalawa,' I said. 'What has brought you here?
Has something happened with regard to the peace ceremony?'—

for I feared that perhaps one of the cows had run home and that Ngoshè had refused to return it. The old man nodded his head.

'White man,' he said, 'great trouble has returned to our village, and I, head of the community, have had to take action which will find no favour in your eyes. You will say that I have sinned; so I have come with my elders to tell you all. Punish me as you think fit; but I tell you that I did right.'

The evening shadows were lengthening, and the flag at the top of the staff flapped idly in a slight breeze. From the stables came the whinnying of my horses as the horse-boys bedded them down for the night. Away over the heads of the little group before me under the eaves of the open hut, I could see the police parading, the men going off duty without their puttees, blankets or rifles; those on duty for the night wearing all their equipment. Agapalawa was silent, bending over scratching in the sand. The District Head was still, leaning forward and watching the old man intently; one of the messengers sat forward, looking down at the ground, the other sat back, watching me.

'After you left us this morning,' said the old man at last, 'we returned to the village and sat in conclave outside my house. There were various matters to be settled and we were sitting there arranging them when a woman called Uhè, wife of one of our men, came unbidden into our midst. "What do you want, woman?" I asked her, and she stood and did not answer for a short time. Then she spoke, and she spoke like one mad. "Old man," she said, "the white man has left and you have received ten head of cattle for the dead men Phurso and Umar. But I tell you it was not the men of Ngoshè who killed them, but I, Uhè of the despised Aganjarè. For years you have treated me with contempt; for years I have been little more than a slave in this village. But now I am revenged; I killed your sons. Oh yes, it was the spears and arrows of Ngoshè that let their life-blood pour out on to the sand; it was their arms which lifted the weapons; but it was I, Uhè, who by my witchcraft made them do it. They died, Phurso and Umar, strong in their youth, but I, the despised one, killed them. And you Dipchari, you Guduf, you Nagadio, you Bubayagu, you Ndahan, and you Yerima, elders of this community, before the new moon rises, you too will all be dead. Killed by me, the despised Uhè." '

The old man paused and looked at the others. As each of the

elders heard his name mentioned he raised his eyes to mine to see what he could make of my expression. All were frightened. The District Head was still, watching the old man intently; the two messengers were also bent forward in an attitude of expectancy. Now the police were dismissed and the night guard on my house marched in single file up the incline towards where we sat. The old man continued: 'What would happen, white man, if she lived? We know; these men here before you would all be dead before the new moon rose. What would be said to me when I joined those who had gone before? I am old. My journey to the shades cannot be long delayed; ere many harvests have come I shall have joined the elders who went before. What will they say to me if these men have joined them before their time? Can I leave the village without the advice of these, the wise heads of those on earth?'

The old man was silent, and I felt the eyes of all on me. 'Eyesri,' came from outside the hut as the guard swung by. The shadows were now long; I could see the smoke rising over the little town from the evening cooking fires. A youth riding a horse bareback rode past the police lines and I heard him shout something to the quarter guard. The old man sat with his head drooping.

'White man; there was only one thing I could do. I killed her and her body is now being buried outside the village.' The District Head sat up and looked at me; the two messengers looked at the old man. He sat there with his eyes cast down.

'You did right, Agapalawa,' said one of the elders, the first of his fellows to speak.

There was a grunt of assent from the others.

'I killed her, white man, and am now here to be punished by you, for I know I have offended against your laws. Do with me what you will; I am old.' The old man was silent.

The evening was far spent, and the time for evening prayer for true Moslems at hand. Behind my house I could see one of my boys washing, preparatory to prayer. A hen came cackling and scratching near him and he shooed it away. Within the shelter all were silent.

'Agapalawa,' I said; and at the sound of my voice he looked at me. The District Head, without changing his position, turned

71

his head towards me. 'Agapalawa, as Father of your kindred you did right'—and there was a little gasp from the nearest elder—'but you have offended against the laws of the white man and you cannot go unpunished. I will not write this down in the book of Government; it will remain known only to us here, but blood has been spilt. Tomorrow you must bring me one cow and I will do with it as the Moslems with their *sadaka*, divide it amongst the poor, diseased and bereaved in the town, Pagan and Moslem.'

I rose and left the meeting. A few minutes afterwards as I sat in my chair outside the house I could see in the half-light a file of figures stepping out for home. First went the portly figure of Agapalwa, no longer burdened with doubt, but brisk and erect. Behind came the elders; I could hear their animated voices as they went home, rejoicing in an understanding white man, one who knew as they that many lives had been saved that day.

The little procession passed; the moon came over the horizon; the heat of the day, the infinite weariness of argument with primitive minds, were all forgotten. I was at peace with the world; Africa, the Dark Continent, lay round me, gleaming in the bright moonlight. I could see the hills towering above the villages I had left that morning.

A dog in the police lines howled at the moon and yelped as someone beat it. I thought of the little group of elders headed by Agapalawa, now nearing home; I thought of the three new graves in his village and of the luckless puppy slaughtered that more men might not die. Africa, unchanged for centuries, was at last in movement; had not Agapalawa come to me in his distress, ready to accept the punishment of the white man? Did I fail the code of the white man? Was I in fact an accomplice after the event to the murder of Uhè? Was it wrong to pander to their fear of witchcraft instead of dealing with them as members of the brave new world they scarcely understood and almost certainly did not want to enter? After all, the wise ones of this world, scarcely twenty years after the death of Uhè and only about six after the death of Agapalawa, decided that the inhabitants of this part of the world were sophisticated enough and well enough informed of the minutiae of international affairs such as boundaries, forms of government and so on, to hold a plebiscite as to whether they

should join the new Republic of the Cameroons or the new
Dominion of Nigeria. I considered that Agapalawa and his elders
should not be tried for murder; others decided that many of those
very elders could decide on the whole future of their people by
placing small pieces of paper in boxes through a slit in the top. Or
perhaps the elders thought that the brown and yellow men who
came for a week or two had taken the place of their white men
and had great witchcraft in these boxes which they placed in every
village?

But this was a World War away; my conscience, despite all that
the wise men of Whitehall might say, was at rest.

CHAPTER SEVEN

The Swamps of Chad

Although stationed at Gwoza, I was the only A.D.O. in the Dikwa Division. When, therefore, the time for the cattle-tax arrived, I had to leave what had become my beloved hills, to trek through the endless swamps of Eastern Dikwa, below the Dar-el-Jimeil ridge, checking the numbers of cattle that the District Heads had shown in their returns to the *Beit-el-Mal*, 'The House of Wealth', as the Native Administration Treasury was known.

At first, in the flat plains stretching from the foot of the hills across to the Dar-el-Jimeil ridge, matters were relatively simple; my professional carriers from Gwoza travelled ten miles or even less each day while I and the horsemen in the party ranged far and wide. But soon we had found all the cattle there were to be found and it remained only to venture into the flooded land around Chad to visit each village perched on its mound a few feet above the level of the surrounding waters.

No longer could my carriers show their prowess by running along singing and whistling, covering the day's stint as quickly as possible in order to have the rest of the day free, to lie around chatting with the villagers, posing as men of the great world to the 'fish that dwell only in the village wells', wenching, and perhaps, when my back was turned, persuading some simple peasant to give them free food on the threat of revealing to me some hitherto hidden peccadillo on which they had stumbled. In the swamps no man could rest his load when weary or run when fresh; all were reduced to the same plodding pace, feeling for footholds below the water and then dragging from the mud the heavy feet.

First therefore we had to double the number of carriers, for in this one part alone of the whole of Nigeria, Government recognized the facts of geography, and reluctantly agreed that to each head-load there must be two men. So the Headman went to Bama and a message was sent to Maiduguri, and in a few days he returned with more carriers from those places. The new men were

74

greeted by my regulars with great shouts of astonishment and hands smashed together with great force.

'Ah, it is Musa? What brings you here? Still seeking for a wife, my old one? Abba Gana, hast thou torn thyself from the arms of the women of Yerwa? What news of Kakagidda?' And far into the night the villagers listened to tales of 'when I was in Fika with the European they called Langa-Langa, he who is "tall and bent over like a sickle"', or of the tidings of war and women in that far land of 'Eesafrica' to which many of the older men had gone in the Great War.

So into the swamps: myself, my two messengers, the Emir's representative, the District Head and three of his followers all on horseback, with Kamkura bringing up the rear on my second horse. Off at dawn through perhaps three or four miles of water and mud to the first village; the cattle counted, on to a second, then a third; and in the early afternoon the last crossing to the village where we would spend the night.

The leading horseman gave his tired brute a series of vicious digs with the points of the shovel-shaped stirrups; his horse lurched forward through the mud for two or three paces, then relapsed into its former, tired, dogged pace. The rest slowly followed: a couple of hundred yards behind, waist-deep in water, each with one hand balancing his load, the other clutching his stick with which to prospect for the hidden holes, came my carriers and their headman; the rear of the procession brought up by the relief carriers who had thankfully handed over to their fellows a few minutes before.

Around us on every side stretched water; to the north it was unbroken to the horizon where at some indeterminate point the flooded plains merged with the waters of the lake itself. To the south it stretched away for a dozen miles or so to where a few trees could be seen in scattered clumps marking the higher ground; beyond, forty miles away, a blue mass marked the top of Mount Zeledufa, the highest of the Gwoza Hills. Behind us to the east, about three miles away, was a low ridge crowned with waving corn, a few thorn trees, and, in places, dark dots where horses or goats were tethered cropping the lush grass, marking the village we had last counted. Somewhere in the middle of the corn were the village Sheikh and his elders ruefully agreeing which animals

75

must be sold to pay the tax they thought they had so successfully evaded. Ahead, perhaps the same distance or a little more away, lay a similar ridge. A shout from behind, and I turned in the saddle to see the man carrying my bath which contained all my spare clothing fall below the water whilst his load bounced on the surface. Amidst the laughter of the others the man struggled to his feet and held the load above the water; relief carriers surged forward, it was lifted on to his head, and we all moved on again. I lifted my water-bottle and weighed the contents carefully. It was by now nearly two in the afternoon and we had been nine hours on trek, and apart from a cup of tea and a couple of biscuits as I had washed, shaved and dressed before dawn, I had yet to break my fast—as also had my motley crowd of followers. There were perhaps two mouthfuls of water left and I swilled one round my mouth slowly, before swallowing it. The other must be kept; something might go wrong and I might be glad of that water later in the day; if all went well, it would be the height of luxury to drink it as I rode up to my destination. Two mouthfuls and yet all around stretched water, millions of cubic yards of it; unsafe for at any rate the European to drink; teeming with disease: bilharzia, Guinea worms, dysenteries and other possibilities. The hot sun beat down on us. As this was October the sun temperatures would be somewhere in the 130's or more; I wore a large floppy *terai*, a bush-shirt, shorts and tennis-shoes; my legs felt delightfully cool as my horse dragged through the water.

Soon we were approaching the low ridge ahead of us and the water began to be broken by the stalks of various marsh grasses which grow round the ridges in shallower water. The going improved as we moved from mud on to harder sand marking where a path leading into the village commenced; the horses picked up their feet, pricked their ears and the foremost whinnied as a couple of hobbled mares started up from the tall grasses beside the path and plunged away. The relief carriers made a last change; the leader blew into his Pan-pipe and the rest broke into song; from the tall corn which crowned the ridge came a small deputation on foot to greet us, the village Sheikh—for this was the country of the Shuwa Arabs—the District Head's man (who had gone on ahead before dawn with my cook, a table and chair, and cooking utensils), and half a dozen of the village elders. We reached the edge of the sand, and I reined back to allow the District Head to go first followed by the Emir's representative; the welcoming deputation pressed forward. '*Allah ngubero,*' they said. 'May God greet you,' and they held out a hand to the District Head. We were tired and impatient, but courtesy demanded that we replied to their greetings, that we asked after their crops, after the latest news. 'All is well; all well,' they replied; though later, when we were rested, we should hear how there had been several highway robberies, cattle-thieving, a murder, how a *tum-tum* had been burnt to the ground, and so on. But now we were tired. 'All is well; come; come and rest,' and the villagers turned and led the way along a narrow path under the tall corn. We followed, and as my beautiful Njaro passed the corn, he leant out and snatched at the leaves, till, in order that he might not damage a stalk, I pulled off some of the smaller, more tender leaves and held them forward whilst he turned and took them. Behind us the carriers' song was interrupted by long warbling cries as they hurried forward, holding their loads at arm's length above their heads. These were professional carriers, men who would carry a sixty-pound load at a good four miles an hour under a burning sun, and with the pride to run in at the finish whistling, singing, calling, 'Behold Amadu's carriers; we are the strongest in Bornu. Here we are with *the* European. Out of my way old man. Maidens, we are here, we are the strong ones.' The horses began to tittup with excitement, the villagers started to run, the horses to canter, carriers to run; the corn thinned, hens scurried out of our way, a few women ululated in welcome, the corn ended and there, under a thorn tree, stood my table with the teapot on it, the small boy standing with a tray and a cooked meal all ready for me, whilst Karimu my cook called from behind, 'Welcome Master of the House, welcome.' I swung my leg over Njaro's neck, and he rubbed his head against me; Kamkura dropped from the other horse, handed the reins to a villager and ran to take Njaro. I drank that last hot mouthful of water, and then turned to the messengers, District Head and the others. 'Go you and eat; in an hour's time return and we will hear the news of the land. Headman, put the tent there and the loads so; go you and eat and drink and then return to the tent.' The entourage disappeared in various directions; a carrier limped forward to show me a bad cut on his foot; iodine and a bandage were wanted. The saddles and bridles came off Njaro and his stable-mate Shegin Miye, and the two horses dropped and rolled rubbing their backs in the sand in intense enjoyment. I sat down and poured some tea. 'There is milk,' said the small boy; 'greetings on your arrival. It was far today.' 'By God,' I replied, 'it was far. You have eaten? Is the food good in this village?' 'Good,' said the small boy, 'and they have killed a bullock so there is meat today.' Before me was my breakfast; fried chicken. 'Chicken again,' I said. 'By God, we are nearly at Maiduguri now,' and the small boy and the cook and the horse-boys laughed, for this was a time-honoured joke. I had once said that if all the chickens I had eaten were placed end to end they would stretch, from where we then were, for the eighty miles or so to Maiduguri, the provincial capital, or at any rate to Dalori, some ten miles short thereof; now on every other day, I made the same jest and all laughed, for who tires of a good witticism?

Half a chicken, killed only an hour ago, fried in groundnut-oil; queer bread made with dried yeast. Milk boiled to kill disease, but tasting of the acrid smoke of the wood fire over which it was boiled and with more than a suspicion of the urine with which the calabash had been washed out before the milk was taken from the cow. Then some Cooper's Oxford marmalade and Huntley and Palmer's biscuits, and Anchor butter—which I poured out as liquid on to the biscuits from a screw-topped jar. The many flies buzzed round and settled thickly on the food, or on the nets protecting it from their attentions; around me under other thorn trees watched the naked, pot-bellied children of the village. The circus had indeed come to town; for the first time in their lives here was a white man of whom they had heard but never seen; watch him eat; watch him use a knife and a strange iron instead of using his right hand to take his food as all well-mannered people did; sitting too on a chair instead of squatting cross-legged on the ground; eating alone instead of taking a handful in turn with others from the communal pot. From time to time sniggers and laughter came from over the top of a corn-stalk fence where the women of the village peeped at the white man, and teased some of the younger ones by asking them if they would marry him.

'More tea, Karimu,' I called. The small boy came forward and removed the dirty plates and I sat and drank cup after cup of tea,

replacing the pints of liquid sweated from me that day. The Headman of the carriers and my messengers reappeared and the
carriers struggled back in twos and threes, belching and praising
God for the food they had eaten, and we pitched the tent. My bed
was erected in it; the table was placed outside and a grass mat
brought and twisted round poles around a hole in the ground some
little distance away, my latrine seat erected and all was complete.
Home for another night was ready, and as the rainy season was
over, I would sleep in a tent instead of in a malodorous Arab *tum-
tum*. I looked at my watch, half-past four. 'Call the District Head
and the villagers and let us count their cattle; they will be re-
leasing them for their evening feed ere long.'

In a few minutes, into the open space came the District Head,
his dirty trek robes replaced by a glorious outer robe; bright
sandals on his feet; his staff of office in his right hand. With him
the Emir's representative, my messengers in sober white robes with
the Government golden crown on a black cloth pinned on to
their right chests, the village head and his elders. '*Allah ngubero*,'
greeted the District Head as he sank down on to the grass mats
which had been placed ready: 'Are you rested?' 'Rested,' I replied, 'and you?' 'By God, the way was far and the going bad
today,' said the District Head. 'And they say they have declared
all their cattle for the tax count.' I speak Hausa to my boys and
messengers; the District Head and the Emir's representative speak
some Hausa and understand more, but their language is Kanuri.
The villagers are Arabs who also speak Kanuri. So I think in
English and speak in Hausa; my messengers translate into Kanuri;
the villagers translate this mentally into Arabic and think of their
answers in that language and then reply. Progress is slow, and
intended by all to be, for this is the season of the cattle-tax—one-
and-sixpence per head—and unless a District Officer turns up, the
Shuwa will only declare about one-third of their herds. The
District Head will collect (privately and illegally) on perhaps another third, so my arrival is not viewed with enthusiasm by anyone. At any rate, counting is easy, as at this time of the year there
are so many biting flies about that cattle in these swamps must be
penned, both for most of the day and at night, and are only released
to graze for three or four hours, morning and evening. The day
and most of the night are passed in the *tum-tums*, huge thatched

huts built round four erect tree-trunks. Inside the area marked by the trunks is a raised floor of mats, walled with more mats, making a room in which sleep the woman of the house and her brood of children. There is no wall on the side facing the door; on one side of the doorway is a cooking space—a hearth with four lumps of baked clay on which to support pots; on the other side and round the back of the room, is a space in which are penned twenty, thirty or forty head of cattle. Each morning this space is cleaned out, clean sand brought in to replace that fouled by the animals, and by the time they return one could sit and eat one's food off the ground without any great offence. Miraculously, too, the *tum-tums* are almost free of flies, for these are kept out by maintaining a small fire of green wood in each doorway, in the smoke of which the returning cattle hang their heads and shake their feet to rid themselves of their tormentors.

'We have declared all our cattle,' say the villagers in reply to my questions, 'we have declared them all, and here are our receipts.' 'Tell them we will count the cattle just the same,' I say to the messengers; 'say that no doubt they are telling the truth but perhaps the District Head's scribe is not honest and perhaps he has not recorded the truth in his records,' so we rise and go to the nearest *tum-tum*. '*Salaam alaikum*,' I say at the doorway; tax agent I may be but at least one observes the niceties of civilized living. 'On you be God's peace.' '*Alaika assalaam*. And on you peace,' replies the housewife. '*Baggara fi?*' I ask, airing my small Arabic. 'Are there cattle?' '*Baggara mafi*,' she replies above their lowing, 'there are none'; for who would admit to wealth? '*Bismillah*,' I now say. 'In the name of God,' and I bend low to enter, followed by the village Sheikh, the District Head and my messengers. We count the heads; twenty-eight, and four calves. The owner of the *tum-tum* produces his receipts—one for ten and another for twenty-two animals. The former is dirty whilst the latter is suspiciously clean. We pass on, and in an hour or so have counted every head of cattle in the village. In every case there are two receipts produced—and in every case, one looks suspiciously new. I notice too that the old receipts are all in one numerical sequence, whilst the new-looking ones have a set of consecutive serial numbers far removed from the first. My suspicions are now confirmed; less than a third were counted originally; the rest were probably only counted last night—or even this morning—by the representative of the District Head who accompanied my advance party of cook and breakfast loads. But even so, I have won this battle of wits; it is my presence in the area which has had this result. I have won a great deal of face; they have lost—and they know it. But as the full tax has been paid—even if belatedly—there is nothing more to do but to plan tomorrow's trek, to listen to any complaints and to chat with them about anything they want to talk about.

The sun is getting low in the west as we return to my tent. We sit: myself in a chair, my entourage on mats around me, the village Sheikh and elders and as many as wish to come in front of us. 'All was well' when we entered the village; now we hear the truth. There have been highway robberies, a murder committed in another, near-by village, a *tum-tum* mysteriously burnt to the ground and the owner, family and cattle extricated with difficulty. On certain matters the District Head will take action; on others the Emir's representative will do so; on others I will write to my District Officer to say that I think such-and-such should be done. We reach the end of the complaints and the villagers leave; the Sheikh walks away with great dignity with his elders around him. We others sit enjoying the coolness after the heat of the day. 'Tomorrow,' I ask, 'how many hours to Gumsu?' The maps I have show the names of a number of towns and villages and gives some general idea of their position, one with another, but the scale is valueless and miles are an unknown quantity to my companions. I have noticed that in working out the distances of our daily trek, the results are Micawberish. If I anticipate three hours in the saddle and it turns out to be four, I arrive tired and peevish; if I plan for eight and it turns out to be only seven and a half, I arrive fresh and pleased with life. 'Gumsu,' says Yerima Boyi, 'about three or four, perhaps five if the way is bad.' 'Nay,' says the District Head, 'perhaps three at most.' 'Three!' exclaims the Emir's representative. 'Nearer four,' and so as usual we decide to leave at dawn and proceed via a largish village to the north, whilst the carriers can pursue a more direct route. As we reach this conclusion, the call to evening prayer is heard and I dismiss them until dawn.

Darkness falls; my chair has been placed outside my tent; on a box are a bottle of whisky and a bottle of boiled water wrapped in wet cloth to cool it a little by evaporation. As I sit down, my boys and some of the carriers start their prayers. A day has ended, the stars come out, my kerosene pressure lamp is brought and throws a little circle of light around me. Muttered scufflings come from the shadows where the youth of the village sit open-eyed watching this stranger in their midst. 'Boy!' I call. 'Bath!'—and into my bath are poured the contents of a couple of four-gallon kerosene-tins—the one of cold water, the other of hot. At this time of the year the water is clear and good, not as at some other periods when it is like potato soup. I take my bath with the flaps of the tent down and as I lie with as much of my body in the small amount of water as I can, I hear the gentle whinny of my horses and the stampings of feet as they eat, and shake off some fly or other. I dress and the flaps of the tent are hoisted again, and I return to my seat and my drink. The clear sky above with the tropical stars shining out; the far-off cry of a fox or a jackal; the noises of a village near at hand. I think of the long haul of the day, the endless heat, the end-less water and mud of this half-submerged world. I think of the tax that has been paid in full; the job has been done; I have gained face; I finish my drink. 'Boy, pass chop!' I cry, and, after dinner, to bed before nine for there is another day tomorrow and I shall be off in the saddle by five.

CHAPTER EIGHT

Jangali

I returned from leave in March 1938 and was again posted to Bornu Division, but after a couple of months the District Officer in charge of the Fika Division, with his headquarters at Potiskum 140 miles to the west, fell ill and had to be invalided and I was sent to hold the fort until a more senior officer arrived.

In the early 1930's the whole of North Africa had been infested with swarms of locusts; indeed the Egyptian army had been put on a war footing and sent into the desert to deal with this menace, and in Nigeria as many Government employees as possible, from all departments, had similarly been mobilized. In those days there was little one could do with a swarm of flying locusts beyond noting the direction of flight, the width of the swarm, the time they took to pass a given point, and whether they were copulating or ready to lay eggs. If egg-laying was imminent, then someone downwind could be warned and when the swarm landed, either the eggs could be dug up and destroyed or the area marked, so that when the hoppers emerged they could be dealt with. This information was sent by telegram to the headquarters of the campaign, whence warnings were sent to those downwind, and one, sent by a very senior officer, read: VERY LARGE SWARM FRONT ESTIMATED 10 MILES TAKING 30 MINUTES TO PASS GUMSU ON 11TH STOP DIRECTION FLIGHT SOUTH-WEST TO NORTH-EAST STOP COPULATING STOP RESIDENT ON TOUR. This was too much for the recipient; the reply—both original and reply were in the Maiduguri Provincial Office—read: STOP COPULATING AND GET BUSY KILLING LOCUSTS.

But with hoppers the story was different; when a swarm was found, everyone in the area was collected and a long trench, about a foot deep and the same in width, was dug across its line of movement. In the trench, at intervals of six feet or so, were dug deep holes, perhaps two feet deeper than the floor of the trench. The swarm was now surrounded by men, women and children armed with leafy branches; behind the trench were other men similarly armed, and others stripped of gown and with their trousers rolled above their knees. Village drummers started to beat out a rhythm, and the boughs came down in unison; ahead of them jumped the hoppers, into the trench and then along it till they fell into the pits. Into these jumped the men waiting for them to crush them into a heaving mass, and a sickly, sweet smell rose to scent the clouds of dust surrounding all involved. If the swarm was large, it consisted of millions of hoppers, and the pits had to be cleaned out time and again; the stinking piles grew higher and higher; the dust, the smells, the beating drums, the figures swirling through the dust, made an inferno-like picture.

There were lots of swarms of hoppers in the Potiskum area, and the Emir and I spent much time together dealing with them. By far the greater part of any swarm was destroyed in this way, and we were told that the few survivors did not matter as their herding or swarming instinct would have been destroyed and they would revert to being harmless, solitary grasshoppers. Locusts are eaten, and the previous year in Ashigashiya we had killed such vast numbers that everyone was satiated. I asked an old Pagan why he did not keep some of the paste of crushed hoppers in his corn-bins against a hungry day. Full of scorn, he replied: 'In life they destroyed our corn; their malignancy has not passed with death; if we were to place them in our bins, the corn would be destroyed.' To protect their corn, they kept in every bin a kind of python about four feet long which effectively dealt with mice and rats and other similar small deer; these pythons were on sale in every market.

When my relief arrived, I returned to Maiduguri and, after celebrating my birthday, left on 23 July on a trek which was to last until Christmas. From time to time I would meet my District Officer and perhaps another Touring Officer; in September I was to cross the border and join Dikwa Division again. My chief task was to check the cattle-count again as my success in Dikwa the previous year had been such that many of the herds were said to be hidden in Bornu. For the first week or so all went well. Whilst my carriers and boys made their way from where we had spent the night to some other village perhaps ten or twelve miles away, the District Head and I, with our respective followers on horseback, rode farther afield, covering perhaps fifteen, perhaps twenty or thirty miles as we moved round the District checking each cattle-camp. Everyone was out to see that he paid as little tax as possible, and whilst in the flooded areas largely populated by the Shuwa it was customary to declare one third of a herd, and by a little judicious bribery get away with no tax on at least one third, in this sand country of the west the cattle-owners were usually the nomad Fulani and they declared about one tenth only of their cattle, hoping to evade tax on the rest. They were up to every possible trick. They would divide a herd into perhaps ten sections, each of the same size, and by careful galloping through the bush, hope to be able to produce the necessary tax receipts as and if each section was discovered by an interfering European. One noted the serial numbers of receipts as they were inspected and where they had been issued, but when later in the week one met the same receipt fifty miles away, everyone would swear that the herd had moved and it was difficult to prove the opposite.

On arrival at one village my cook came to tell me that he had heard that one Fulani camp which we had visited ten days or so before had consisted of well over a thousand head of cattle and not the hundred or so we had found; the rest had been hidden away in bush until after we had passed—with the connivance of various officials. If this were true, I had lost face—badly; there was only one thing to do—to make a surprise visit when not expected. I trekked with two ponies so that whilst one made the relatively easy journey one day with the carriers and boys, the other covered a much longer distance; next day I changed ponies and the one that had travelled far had a relatively easy day; one was therefore reasonably fresh. I was about thirty to thirty-five miles from the cattle encampment, so that if I left that evening at about eight I could travel through the night and be there at dawn. I had a rest that afternoon, as well as one can in such a heat in a tent, then at seven called my messengers, the District Head and the Headman of my carriers. We would leave in an hour's time and I would take my horse-boy and four carriers with two loads—one my bed and the other a box with a little food and a lot of water.

So at eight we were away with instructions to the horse-boy and the carriers to stop at a village about ten miles short of the cattle-camp; we horsemen speedily outstripped those on foot and pressed rapidly on. The moon was out, it was almost as light as day, and from time to time we cantered. Trekking at night in this way was a constant delight, far different from the torture of the midday sun; by day the world lay dead and exhausted, by night it lived. At about 1 a.m. we loosened the girths on our saddles and walked, with the horses trailing behind, for a mile or so. Then, after tightening the girths, we remounted and made our way as before. At about 3 a.m. we passed through the silent village where later my carriers would arrive, and pushed on to the last stage of our journey, leaving behind us the dogs barking at the moon, disturbed by our passage. More cantering now, with the tired horses stumbling from time to time, and at about 5 a.m. we emerged from the bush into an area where we could see many fires and the forms of many cattle within a low fence of thorns. More barking dogs greeted us; then one or two shadowy forms emerged at the sound of the shouts of my followers—very hearty shouts to make quite certain that no one misunderstood who we were and sent a poisoned arrow our way. I told the District Head to tell the Fulani *Ardo*—the chief of these nomads—that no cattle were to be freed until we had counted them all and that we held him responsible for this being done. Confusion reigned, shouts came from some of the younger men, so my messengers told me, of 'Throw him out!' 'Loose the cattle!' and others of the same nature. But prudence prevailed; the time of prayer was at hand, and we dismounted, unsaddled our tired beasts and hobbled them.

A Fulani housewife brought me a great bowl of milk still warm from the cow, and in order not to offend and hoping that my typhoid inoculation was still potent, I drank and thanked her. Around me my entourage and the Fulani knelt in prayer; a final obeisance, and after telling his beads the *Ardo* came and greeted me. He was resigned to the fact that he had lost; God had ordained that this year he must pay in full—though it would break his heart to have to sell some bullocks to pay the tax. Next came the problem of counting the animals, but I and my staff were by now expert at the task. A gate was made in the fence and a small number of animals driven through to be counted, as they passed, by myself, the District Head and the Fulani *Ardo*, the latter using his string of beads to number the animals. With one herd outside, the rest were now more willing to be released, to run to join the others in threes and fours; the numbers mounted: five hundred had been counted, then six hundred, and so on till we topped the thousand mark. This was indeed a haul and I could afford to look away as the angry young men stampeded the last hundred or so through us so that we could not count them. We knew the total approximately; it now remained for the individual owners to be identified. As they collected I lay on the ground with my head pillowed on my saddle; the sun was well up now and it was beginning to get hot. For over two hours we had to sit and prepare the lists of cattle and their owners. A tall Fulani clad in the dirtiest of blue robes would sit in front of us and with the help of his beads tell off the number of his cattle by name. From time to time one of his family would remind him that such-and-such a cow had a calf or that some other calf was now grown up, had been named and listed. At last the total was complete—over a thousand head listed under the individual owners where but a hundred had been officially counted.

At ten I saddled up and with my followers turned towards home. At about 1 p.m., in the heat of the sun, we straggled into the village where lay my carriers; I erected my camp-bed, opened some tins of food, drank a lot of water and telling my horse-boy to call me at sunset, went to bed. At six we saddled up and set off on the twenty-five miles or so 'home', where we arrived at 1 a.m.

I next swung away to the west and south, crossing early one morning the one motor-road that traversed the Province, and making my way to the area about thirty miles south of Maiduguri. Here, from far away in the south, ran a great river-bed parallel with the ridge of the 'Little Camel-back' which it breached at Maiduguri itself to run east towards Lake Chad. For most of the year this river-bed lay empty and dry, but each year, more or less on the same day in August, a great wall of water came down the valley at night, and one woke in the morning to find a river as broad as the Thames at Putney where the previous evening one had been cantering a pony. It is said that, from time to time, the water arrives not by night but by day, and when it does men can see the noses of the great fishes sticking out of the wall of water as it passes them—fishes which weigh up to fifty pounds and which are caught during the next few months. By Christmas there is only a miserable little puddle left in the river-bed, and by January it is dry again.

But I had to cross it at its flood; and not only I but some thirty carriers, boys, messengers and others, all my loads and some dozen horses. From amongst my polyglot collection I found half a dozen swimmers; from a village on the bank, a half-dozen more. The harvest time was now upon us, so great bundles of corn-stalks, up to ten feet long and more like canes than the straw of English corn, were brought and bound with rope into bundles about three feet in diameter. Four of these were bound together and mats fastened on the top, and when this raft was completed we found it would carry half a dozen loads or about four men. The Thames at Putney is wide and this stream ran fast. I and my swimmers stripped and pushed the raft out into the stream with some loads and two of my boys on top. In due course we delivered them safely to the other side and so back with the raft for more.

Of the swimmers only I was also a horseman so in a short time I left the ferrying over of the loads and men to the others and swam over the horses. This was done by removing their saddles but leaving the bridles; I then mounted one bareback and with a couple of rope hobbles tied round my waist, I rode into the water leading the second. With a rider on its back, a horse swims deeply, with its head high out of the water, so that when we were about half-way over and I could feel him tiring I slipped off between the two and swam the rest of the way with a hand on the neck of each. In this way I crossed and recrossed whilst the carriers did the same with men and loads. When compared with the usual hot trek under a merciless sun, this swimming in gloriously clear water was a delight and I enjoyed every minute of my morning. Eventually all were over—and not before time, for by this time our raft had become very waterlogged and deep in the water. But at some time during the day I must have swallowed a germ, for three weeks or so later I lay ill another forty miles to the south with a swollen leg.

From time to time someone makes the classic remark 'Of course, things are very different in Africa now, the climate is so much better'; what has caused this dramatic change in the last few years is the progress of medical science which, whilst making the 'White

Man's Grave' safe for small European children, has by the same token started the appalling population explosion which gets daily nearer.

The histories of the early explorers and traders, and the large European cemeteries at each of the old trading and administrative centres, show that the title, the 'White Man's Grave', was not undeserved. The chief killers were the mosquito-borne diseases, malaria and yellow fever, and those carried in water or by flies, typhoid, bacillary dysentery and amœbic dysentery, together with blackwater fever, the final result of cumulative attacks of malaria and of the massive doses of quinine needed to kill each one. One was exposed to the risk of many other diseases; elephantiasis, also carried by a mosquito, smallpox, cerebro-spinal meningitis—of which outbreaks occurred every dry season—rabies, bilharzia and Guinea worms, though these, as with the physical dangers of snakes and scorpions, were avoidable with slight care.

By 1936 malaria was more a nuisance than a killer; one started with fever, took a massive dose of quinine and, in general, after a couple of days one was fit again and, if in bush, off on tour; in a station a doctor would keep one on light duties for a few days; blackwater was rare, but few recovered from an attack. The new drugs which have replaced quinine have killed blackwater and reduced the importance of malaria; in large towns, careful mosquito-control has still further reduced the dangers, but in bush a mosquito-net and one of the new insect repellents that the war produced are the best precautions. Yellow fever, the other terror of the past, has similarly been controlled since the discovery of an inoculation against it; without it the hundreds of thousands of troops and airmen who were stationed in or passed through West Africa during the war, would have suffered severe losses from this disease. Typhoid had ceased to be a problem, to those who insisted on their T.A.B. inoculations, many years before I first went to Africa, and bacillary dysentery has similarly stopped being a killer since the introduction of sulfa drugs; amœbic rarely killed but, as my wife was later to experience, was a general lowerer of health lasting for many years against which no drug is yet completely successful.

The crude death-rate amongst Europeans was low, but we were largely a male adult community who had all been A.1 plus when first appointed. For those who spent much time in bush, chiefly A.D.O.s and a few forestry and veterinary officers, there was always the danger of accident, not pleasant when it might take a doctor four days or even longer to receive the news and to reach one on horseback.

Mosquito-nets and quinine, a T.A.B. inoculation, and plenty of common sense, and one had minimized the risk of most of the above diseases; but we were dependent on our boys, and the way in which they carried out their work, to be kept free of the others. All our water was boiled and then kept in whisky- and gin-bottles; in bush we had these sewn into strips of woven cotton cloth so that, by being dipped in water and hung in a breeze, they cooled the contents by evaporation; in a station the bottles were, before the kerosene fridge was invented, placed in a large earthenware jar which was then filled with water; this percolated through the porous wall, was again evaporated, and the contents cooled. But in order to save work a steward boy would put so many bottles in the cooler that their corks were below the level of the water with the result that germs could enter. Covers made from old mosquito-netting kept the majority of the flies off our food but there was no defence against a lazy or dirty boy who came straight from an earth latrine to serve at table. Our health and even perhaps our lives were therefore in the hands of our boys and despite all the advances that have been made in medical science this still applies to those who go to bush; one can only hope that adequate instruction is given to the eager young volunteers of today.

In this particular instance, it was not malaria; I was ill on and off for a fortnight after whatever it was started, with recurring high temperatures and fever; my right calf swelled at one particular point and I tried to relieve the pain by cutting it with a razor blade; the result was a discharge the colour and consistency of shrimp sauce. Neither the fever nor the discharge was sufficiently bad to incapacitate me completely, and I struggled on, trekking and counting cattle. Then a fortnight or so after it started, I spent one morning swimming in a small river whilst my entourage was ferried over and that afternoon I started with a violent fever; next day my boys reported that I had been delirious in the night, so I sent off a messenger to the nearest doctor giving my symptoms and asking for help.

Next day we lashed a native bed on the poles of my tent and I started on my fifty-mile trek to home. That evening, after covering only about ten miles, I was awakened from a feverish sleep by the arrival of an African nurse, but I told him that we would leave everything until the next day when I hoped to cover another dozen miles. This we did and then, after some food, we started to dress the leg again. By now there was a black area an inch or so from where I had cut my leg, from which the skin was sloughing; the nurse eyed this with some concern, so I took a pair of tweezers from his hand, grasped some of this skin, and pulled; flesh and skin came away, more shrimp sauce poured out, and then in the middle of the hole we could see about a quarter of an inch of a black tube sticking out. This also yielded to a gentle pull, and we placed an inch-long tube in cotton-wool to show to the doctor in due course. We should have put it in gin or whisky; it was too dried for identification when it reached Maiduguri, but the probability is that when I first went ill, I had killed a Guinea worm, which is a thread-like organism perhaps two feet long, which had been slowly absorbed by my body over the period during which I was ill, leaving only one end to remain as evidence. I had my best sleep for weeks that afternoon and again that night; and next day, feeling well and tired of the motion of being carried, called for Njaro and finished the trek with one leg hanging limply from the saddle. The next dressing showed no discharge and the black area was regaining a more normal colour, so on the fourth day I crossed the river into Maiduguri and rode to the hospital to tell the doctor that I was recovered; a week later, bearing a small depression in my right calf which is still with me, I returned to bush.

Others were not so lucky; about the same time another A.D.O. died in Ilorin Province from yellow fever. A year or two after the war, when D.O. Gwandu, I met his successor on our common boundary, and after a couple of days bade him good-bye. A week later we got the news that he was dead.

The death-rate amongst African children was appalling, and those who reached manhood had in general survived an enormous number of attacks of fever and other diseases. The African is tough, and tough too where physical injury occurs. When I went to the hospital to be checked before returning to bush I saw a young girl aged about fourteen who had been brought in; she had had an infection of some kind in the hand, and this had progressed until her hand dropped off; she had been brought into hospital with the two bones of the forearm, white and dried like firewood, sticking out of the swollen upper arm and she had been like this for weeks. Next day she was operated on and in due course returned home. On another occasion I was told of a man in a bush village so affected by elephantiasis of the scrotum that he was unable to walk: he was reduced to mere skin and bones. With some difficulty we got him carried to the road, and then by lorry to Maiduguri; a month later I was greeted by a strong upright man who brought me a present of a couple of old chickens and who told me that not only had his wife returned to him, but he was marrying a new one, a young virgin of about thirteen years of age. Life was starting again at forty.

There is no place for hypochondriacs in bush, nor for those who worry and get depressed; the turn-over amongst European staff, as Heussler shows, was high and it was probably the retreat of those who could not stand loneliness to Europe or to the Secretariats that kept the suicide-rate to negligible proportions. One of the clerks in Maiduguri, a Mr Baiden, had been faced when at Potiskum with a District Officer who tried to commit suicide by shooting himself; this occurred in the middle of the rainy season. Mr Baiden therefore sent off a telegram which read: RESIDENT MAIDUGURI REGRET TO INFORM YOU THAT MR SO-AND-SO SHOT HIMSELF THIS MORNING STOP BAIDEN.

The road was closed, Potiskum was 140 miles away, there was nothing to be done but to arrange for an A.D.O. to leave posthaste to trek through in as few days as possible to take the dead man's place. Next day there arrived a second telegram: RESIDENT MAIDUGURI MR SO-AND-SO A LITTLE BETTER STOP WHEN WILL DOCTOR ARRIVE STOP BAIDEN. A mounted man was hastily sent along the road to the first District Head to tell him to have his best horse ready and to send another man ahead with orders to pass the word to each of the headquarters in turn to be ready, and the doctor left. After riding most of the way non-stop and with about eighty miles covered on one horse—which was far better than the proffered reliefs—the doctor staggered into Potiskum to find the would-be suicide sitting in a chair enjoying an evening drink. He had tried to blow out his brains but in some strange way the bullet had missed anything vital and had emerged leaving a clean wound which healed. Indeed, it was said that, after dressing the wound and making certain that his patient was well on the way to recovery, the doctor retired to bed for the next three days and was waited on by his solicitous host. In later years the tale received its inevitable embellishments: on hearing the shot, his boys rushed in to find him sitting on the bed with a little column of smoke emerging from the top of his head. 'Now look what you've made me do,' was his greeting. After the arrival of the doctor, Mr Baiden, so we were told, had to listen to the complaint:

'Why that chap comes to treat me, I do not know; all he has done is to put a dressing on my head and since then he has spent three days in bed. I'll be glad when he clears out.'

CHAPTER NINE

Rumblings of War

Dikwa Division, with its Moslem area and a relatively strong administration in the north, and its *mélange* of Pagans on the plains and mountains to the south, was almost an epitome in itself of what is to be found throughout Northern Nigeria. Like Dikwa, Northern Nigeria contains two types of people and two types of environment; on the plains of the north are the Moslems, whilst in the hills and mountains of the south and along the banks of the two great rivers, the Niger and Benue, are the Pagan areas. These had been raided for slaves from time immemorial but had never been permanently subjugated; the northern raiders were horsemen who had to dismount to enter the hills, or whose horses died when they came into the tsetse-ridden forests lying on the banks of the rivers. In some places in predominantly Pagan areas permanent slaving-camps came into existence which in some cases grew into towns of Moslems; these acted as bridgeheads for the Moslem religion but generally had little permanent success.

As in Dikwa, every area, whether Moslem or Pagan, contains many tribes and in some cases part of a tribe may be Pagan and part Moslem, and there is considerable tolerance between the two sections; generally, in the Moslem areas, the paramount religion largely supersedes tribal loyalties and the latter become to some extent similar to those which distinguish a Yorkshireman from a Lancastrian; there are no racial or colour bars in Islam, and once a man is prepared to repeat the Fatiha—'There is no God but God and Muhammad is the Prophet of God'—he is accepted as a member of the Faith; with the religion goes a system of law and a whole way of life, with proscribed foods and drinks, to act as a cement to the diverse peoples who embrace the Faith. In the Pagan areas there is no such cement; each tribe differs from its neighbour in language, dress, customs, religion, laws and every facet of life. In some of the Pagan areas there used to be powerful Priest Chiefs in whose hands rested life and death, for if the Chief were strong, the harvests were good, but if he fell ill, the whole tribe suffered. So every seven years the chief died and was ceremonially buried, and then replaced by a young, hale man who in turn, after his seven years in office, similarly disappeared. The best example was the remnant of the Jukon Empire of Kororafa, and our occupation of the area had lasted years before the seven-year period of office was extended.

In other Pagan areas the organization was that of the 'extended family', such as I have described in the Gwoza Hills; at some remote era, a mythical or semi-mythical father-figure founded the tribe and each of his sons became the founder in turn of each of the extended families or kindreds in the tribe. A kindred might number ten thousand people; within it, property was to a certain extent held in common; theft was therefore unknown; neither could anyone starve, as whilst food lasted it was available to all.

There could be no marriage between members of the kindred, for as they were descendants of the same father, this would be incest; nor could a man kill his kinsman for this was fratricide. Kindred could steal, kill and intermarry with another kindred although both were descendants of the sons of the founder of the clan or tribe, but on the occasion of some great danger to the whole tribe they would combine and tribal loyalty would be resuscitated, at least until the danger had passed.

The highly organized Pagan communities, such as the Jukons, were autocracies; the extended families were democracies or at least so the old men argued—though the younger ones would dispute the assertion—based on age and therefore on wisdom and knowledge.

In the Moslem areas the system again differed. There was a well-developed administrative machine, leading from the village head with his council of the chief men of the village, through the District Head—often a scion of the ruling house—to the Emir with his cabinet of half a dozen important men, one of whom would be the Chief Alkali or Judge of the area. To administer the Koranic Law, there was a system of Alkalis, ranging from a form of petty sessions with appeals to higher courts, then to the Court of the Chief Alkali and finally to the local 'House of Lords'—the Emir in Council.

Lugard when he became the first Governor on 1 January 1900

was faced with the necessity of ruling a vast area with the minimum of men and money; he found therefore, systems of indigenous rule which could be used as the basis for his administration, purged and cleansed of those aspects which offended against civilized customs. This was easiest in the Moslem areas; the separation of the executive and the judicial functions accorded with our own organization. The more extreme penalties of the Moslem code were forbidden—chopping off the hand of a thief for example—but others were accepted for, at any rate, the time being; such for example as the public beheading of murderers, which was not stopped until the late 1920's. A public beheading served both to show the common herd that justice had been done and to discourage others from the same path. The condemned man, his hands tied to his sides, was led through the market-place by two of the Emir's police—the *dogarai* as they were called; behind marched the *Sarkin Dogarai* swinging his razor-sharp sword from side to side. The men leading the condemned man called out in loud voices the facts of the case and why he had been condemned to death; the sword whistled round the unfortunate's head but still he was led on. A quiet whistle from the *Sarkin Dogarai*, his two men dropped to the ground, and the fatal blow was given. Eyewitnesses have told me of the headless body continuing to walk for many paces.

Whilst Lugard could accept the indigenous administrative framework on which to build, a more formal legal system had to be introduced which would integrate the indigenous systems with a British High Court culminating in appeal to the Privy Council. This was done by setting up two parallel systems, tied by cross-linkages at all levels, both leading to the same apex.

Lugard owed much to Sir George Taubman Goldie, the founder of the Chartered Niger Company, after whom Nigeria was nearly called Goldesia. Goldie destroyed almost all his papers but his introduction to Vandeleur's book *Campaigning on the Upper Nile and Niger* survives. In it he wrote:

It is certain that even an imperfect and tyrannical native African administration, if its extreme excesses were controlled by European supervision, would be, in the early stages, productive of far less discomfort to its subjects than the well-intentioned but ill-directed efforts of European magistrates, often young and headstrong, and not invariably gifted with sympathy and introspective powers. If the welfare of the native races is to be considered, if dangerous revolts are to be obviated, the general policy of ruling on African principles through native rulers must be followed for the present. Yet it is desirable that considerable districts in suitable localities should be administered on European principles by European officials, partly to serve as types to which the native Governments may gradually approximate, but principally as cities of refuge in which individuals of more advanced views may find a living.

The correctness of Goldie's views was shown a few years later during the Satiru revolt in Sokoto, of which more in due course; our principal failure in the rapid moves towards self-government from 1947 onwards lies in the fact that, whilst great thought was lavished by constitution-makers in Whitehall on the Central Governments of the various territories, little thought was given to the evolution or form of the Local Governments within the country.

In his first report for 1900–1, Lugard wrote:

The policy I am endeavouring to carry out as regards the natives of the Protectorate may, perhaps, be usefully summarized here. The Government utilizes and works through the native chiefs and avails itself of the intelligence and powers of governing of the Fulani caste in particular, but insists upon their observance of the fundamental laws of humanity and justice. Residents are appointed whose primary duty is to promote this policy by the establishment of native courts, in which bribery and extortion and inhuman punishments shall be gradually abolished. Provincial Courts are instituted to deal with the non-natives and to enforce those laws of the Protectorate, more especially, which deal with slave raiding and slave trading, the import of liquor and fire-arms and extortion from villagers by terrorism and personation . . .

Among the wholly uncivilized pagan tribes, who owe no allegiance to a paramount chief, it is often difficult to apply these principles of rule and the political officers have to undertake a more direct responsibility owing to the difficulty and the impossibility of establishing native courts, and to the lawless habits of the people.

Lugard the strong; Lugard the wise; laying the foundations with such great care; six years later, faced with unexpected reaction to our rule in half a dozen widely spaced places at one and the same time, with the possibility of the whole country going up in the flames of rebellion, he sent out rain-gauges to his Residents so that some basic data, without which no material progress would be possible, could be obtained.

Lugard is dead; now the denigrators try to destroy his image and to impute base motives. With the wisdom of hindsight they seize on errors and forget the massive accomplishments. Today there is instantaneous communication by wireless; large cars and aeroplanes cover in hours or even minutes distances that Lugard and his successors down to 1939 covered at the painful rate of thirty miles a day, day after day. It is easy to forget that decisions could not wait on the slow hooves of horses going to and from Government Headquarters, but had to be taken on the spot. Howard in Bauchi hanged two self-entitled *Mahdis* preaching holy war against the Infidel, and then sought, as was laid down, confirmation of the sentences.

Lugard is criticized by one of these latter-day writers, who believes, according to his book-jacket, that: 'Great Britain could have achieved her ends without the destruction of the Emirates.' What destruction? Do the Sultan of Sokoto or the Shehu of Bornu or the other Emirs of the North believe their Emirates to have been destroyed? When Lugard took over at Lokoja in 1900, the French were already on Lake Chad; they had occupied the territories north, west and east of Northern Nigeria and in so doing annexed large parts of the former Sokoto and Bornu Empires. Had Lugard not occupied Kano and the rest, there is little doubt that they would have become French, and then indeed the Emirates would have been destroyed. The justification for Lugard's actions lay in the help given to him and his officers after the Satiru Revolt in 1906 and in the loyalty of Nigeria during the serious revolt against the French in 1916.

Towards the end of 1938 I was again posted to Gwoza, but whereas in my previous tour the Pagan peoples of the plains had been peaceful and contented, after Munich the position changed, and both Hills and Plains murmured and gave trouble.

In 1937 the villages on both sides of the Anglo-French border, immediately north of the hills, had become the scene of the activities of a certain Bukar Amadiddi, an African Robin Hood to his own tribe for he looted only strangers and passed on much of his booty to his relatives, the Gamergu. He attracted in this way a considerable measure of passive support and a considerable following of lawless men. On one occasion when I was in Keraoua, astride the boundary, the alarm was raised that he had that very morning surrounded a village of Shuwa Arabs about three miles away, and had 'taxed' the inhabitants, taking two shillings a head from all householders, with smaller amounts from all other males. By the time the news reached me he was miles away on the other side of the border. Anyone who tried to resist was shot or speared or clubbed and the number of murders committed by the gang rose steadily.

A few weeks after the Keraoua incident I was proceeding on horse ahead of my carriers through the bush on the plains, accompanied by one of my mounted messengers, when we overtook and passed a small convoy of donkeys carrying loads of kola nuts; a mile or two farther along, I was greeted by a sedate man on a horse accompanied by a couple of followers on foot; we exchanged greetings and passed on. I reached my destination and an hour or two later there arrived the donkey-owners stripped of their animals and their loads. Following in my steps, they had reached a clearing in the trees to see the sedate-looking man sitting on a mat under the trees with his horse hobbled beside him; he called to them to approach and as they did so there appeared from behind the trees some twenty men armed with arrow to bow; they had been searched, stripped of their belongings and then told to run, whilst their donkeys had been driven away. An immediate pursuit brought no trace of the assailants beyond the clearly marked tracks through the bush as they fled to the border and beyond. I have often wondered where the gang was hidden when I passed by.

Matters reached such a pitch that soon after my return, in 1938, the French Officer at Maroua sent to ask for a joint consultation at Gwoza. Three French Officers arrived, and we agreed that the existence of the border gave our friend the sanctuary he wanted. 'Look,' I said. 'If I am chasing him can I cross the border after him? I certainly agree that you may do so as far as British territory is concerned. We'll forget all this nonsense about extradition.' For in theory the whole machinery of extradition with papers to be signed by the Governor had to be followed to hand over a petty thief—machinery which we consistently ignored as otherwise justice would have been a farce. The French agreed and we parted, but as if to mark the fact that he knew of our plans, the activities of Bukar Amadiddi redoubled and he became with his gang of ruffians more the ruler of the area than the rest of us, African and European, put together. The position was desperate and called for desperate remedies; amongst the proposals which we considered was one to the effect that I and two or three of my police, suitably disguised as kola-dealers, with my skin blackened and with rifles hidden on the loads on the donkeys, should trail our coat along the roads of the Division, in the hope that a hold-up similar to that related above might give us the chance to shoot it out, but this melodramatic plan was discarded as it would certainly be betrayed by the Gamergu villagers.

Some time later, again on tour, this time amongst the Shuwa of the plains and therefore without my police escort who were for use only in the hills, I was taken ill with fever and lay for a couple of days in a village called Wolojè. On the third morning I heard shouts outside and the Kanuri District Head with a great crowd largely composed of Kanuri and Shuwa following him rushed to my hut shouting 'Bukar Amadiddi is dead'. It appeared that unknown to me—but I should think well known to many of the Gamergu who were present—he too had been lying ill three or four miles away. A week or two previously, the French had told the Chief of Mora that Bukar had to be caught within a stated time or he, the Chief, would be deposed. The Chief in turn had called for one of his hunters, given him a modern rifle and fifty rounds of ammunition and promised him a large reward if he returned with Bukar, dead or alive. Hearing that Bukar lay ill with only two of his gang to keep him company, the hunter had approached the village and met a man going out to his farm. By cajolery and the promise of a reward he persuaded this man to go ahead of him back into the village and to drop a cloth as he passed the hut where Bukar lay. The man led the way, and the hunter, armed with his French rifle, saw two men washing in front of a hut prior to saying their prayers. The cloth was dropped and the hunter shot one of the two whilst the second fled into the hut. Screams from the surrounding houses marked the departure of the whole of the village: men, women and children. The hunter dropped behind a convenient tree and watched; from the door of the hut came a poisoned arrow and he shot into the darkness, to be rewarded with another scream. He then loosed off several shots into the hut; this was followed by the sound of a man bursting through the mat wall at the back. A fleeting glance as he fled, another shot, and this man too lay kicking in the sand. The hunter lay still and watched, listening for the slightest sound; of the men outside the hut one was dead and the other dying; from inside came from time to time a few groans. An hour passed; two; the wounded man at last lay very still; no sound came from inside the hut; a few heads appeared as the more venturesome of the villagers returned.

Afraid that he might now be shot in the back by some friend of Bukar's—and the village was obviously friendly to have sheltered him in this way—the hunter at last dashed across the open space into the hut expecting an arrow at every inch of his path. But nothing came and he found the third man lying alone, badly wounded and only just alive. This was Bukar; and now that there appeared to be little danger of reprisals at some future date, some of the men of the village were persuaded to help lash the two dead one either side of an ox, and to tie the wounded man on to a second. Then assisted by only one man the redoubtable hunter set out for Mora where he was received as a hero. The loads, when he arrived, had consisted of three dead men; the rewards were great, and I received a letter from the French to say that thanks to my great co-operation they had been able to rid the land of the man who had terrorized it for so long.

I was on my way to Bama to meet my District Officer and the then Resident, the late Mr P. G. Butcher, and I was uncertain what view they would take of the matter. My District Officer was perturbed. 'Heavens, man, you should never have given them permission to do that; you know what the French are,' and much more to the same effect. We approached the rest-house where the Resident was staying. 'Sir,' I said, 'I'm afraid I've a confession to make. I gave the French permission to cross the border after Bukar Amadiddi and they have done so and shot him and two others.' 'Are they dead?' asked Mr Butcher, 'and are they certain it is Bukar? Well then,' as I replied in the affirmative, 'this calls for a drink.'

The end of the story was on an open space in front of the District Office in Mora; three heads were placed on spears stuck in the ground and left until the natural process of decomposition and the attentions of the vultures reduced the relics to skulls. I felt sorry; I was the only European as far as we knew to have seen him alive; he had been an organizer of considerable ability and of some bravery. Life was more humdrum for his passing.

The Munich Crisis of 1938 was behind us; although Mr Chamberlain had talked of 'peace in our time', no one seemed to believe him. Certainly the French did not, as they started to move some of their colonial troops from centres such as Fort Lamy to North Africa and to France, replacing them by withdrawing most of the men from such outposts as Mora and Mokolo where my opposite numbers lived. In addition, I learnt that very gloomy talk went on in front of the household servants in the French stations, and as these were all prisoners from the local gaols, it was not long before the news got back to the hills that 'The white men are leaving'. Soon the news spread to our side of the boundary. In a short time, the French dared not show their faces in the hilltop Wulla villages and when tax was due in early 1939, I was told in effect, 'Come and get it'. Lokperè, the scene of the massacre recorded in a previous chapter, was the first to refuse, but it had to be left until I had dealt with all the others, for the madness was spreading. But by the usual mixture of cajolery and threats, patience and swift action, all was collected and by July Lokperè alone remained.

Tax was at the rate of two shillings per household and there would be perhaps two hundred compounds in Lokperè, or at least in that part of the village which lay on the Nigerian side of the boundary, so we were looking for twenty pounds. If we could lay our hands on about eight head of cattle to hold for ransom or to sell if not ransomed, we would be all right.

So inquiries were quietly made as to which households in Lokperè had cattle, and plans were laid for a dawn visit. The day came, and at midnight, with my sergeant of police and fourteen of his men, each carrying water-bottle, rifle and fifty rounds of ammunition, the gate in the leopard-proof fence was opened and we set out for a rendezvous a quarter of a mile away south of the native town. Here we were joined by the District Head and a score of his followers and guides and my two Government messengers. Five of us were mounted, the others on foot, and we wound our way through the farms and bush to where at the foot of the hills nestled the village of Hambagda where we had a small elementary school and a dispensary; it lay in the lands of the Hidkala tribe, bitter enemies of the Wulla, so we knew we should not be betrayed. A man was sent ahead to warn the chief elder in the village so that in the dark there might be no mistake of our intentions, for we did not want to lose any men from the poisoned arrows of friends.

My horse-boy and a couple of other men and all the horses were left behind in the compound of the school to await our return some time that afternoon, and the rest of us started the steep climb of about 2,000 feet to the hilltop above. This too lay in the lands of the Hidkala, so again a messenger was sent ahead to prevent any alarm being given. At last the hilltop was reached and by my watch it was turned half-past three; a short pause to let the stragglers arrive, then we formed up: ahead went three guides, then myself and my messengers, my police, and lastly the District Head and the rest of his party. Our way lay over the more or less flat hilltop, but as the whole of this area is terraced with stone walls, generally a couple of feet high, we were constantly climbing up or down two or three worn steps, and in the dark a fall was easy. After a time the last compounds of the Hidkala were left behind, and we wound along the terraces on one side of a valley running down to the east; from here we rounded a small hill and the terraces and houses of Lokperè lay below us, sloping down to where a small water-course marked the international boundary.

So far everything had gone well; my watch showed that there remained about half an hour to dawn; already the eastern sky looked lighter. 'Sir,' said my sergeant, 'the time for the morning prayer is at hand, may we pray?' Taking a rifle I slipped forward and sat on the hillside looking down on the sleeping and completely quiet village below me whilst the rest of the party, safely hidden behind the hill, said the early morning prayer; one by one the men rose to their feet and took their rifles; each man fed a clip of ammunition into his magazine and we were ready. A quiet word with the guides and we moved off; the plan was that I and my police would occupy an eminence in the middle of the village whilst the District Head and his men surrounded some half-dozen near-by compounds in which we were assured there were cattle. Half-way down the first dog barked; a man shouted; more shouts, and in a few seconds shouts and screams from all over the village marked where a precipitate retreat was taking place across the boundary. This we had expected, but we knew that in this first *sauve-qui-peut* the animals would be left behind. Dawn was now breaking and from my eminence I could see the dark shapes of women and children fleeing upwards to the hilltop beyond the French side of the village—women and children from not only my village but from the French one also. The men were collecting; war horns were being blown, and I could see that many of the younger men from the French side were armed with shield, spear, bow and poisoned arrows and in many cases crowned with the horse-tailed war helmet. Below me the District Head and his men were emerging from compound after compound either empty-handed or with a few goats. The sun climbed in the sky, the more adventurous of the younger men began to slip back across the stream, and our haul appeared to consist of about twenty goats, a few spears, a couple of shields and a few strings of pennies. Cows there were none; doubtless our spies had curried favour by warning our prey of our intentions, or more probably had told us the story to make life easier for themselves.

From one of the huts was brought a calabash full of groundnuts and a couple of eggs; I got a small pot of water and boiled the eggs; one was good, the other almost hatched. The one egg and a handful of groundnuts swilled down with water from my bottle formed my breakfast; the rest of our party had nuts only. I handed over a couple of shillings as payment for the food, to the District Head, to take as part of the tax of the village. Time for the next prayer arrived and sitting on my hillock I kept watch as the others prayed. It was now about ten and time to be setting out for home. My motley followers climbed the hillside half dragging, half carrying the goats and others prizes; giving them a good start, the police and I brought up the rear. It was on these terraces that the massacre of Malla Sanda's men had occurred a few years earlier, but now there was little danger as the hillmen had too great a respect for my escort.

We reached the saddle looking down on the village; already the men below us were back in the British village; already many of their women were coming down the hillside opposite. We sat and watched them to give the carriers time to get well on their way towards the Hidkala village. My messenger went ahead to watch their progress and then returned and shouted to us to follow, and at a quick jog trot, we set off in single file away from Lokperè. We were not followed and in a couple of hours time we all, men and goats, collected safely above Hambagda. But now the elements decided to take a part; black clouds gathered in the east and in a short time a torrential rain started. Our journey down the hillside was miserable in the extreme; cold, wet, hungry and with incessantly bleating goats; buffeted by the wind, cold and miserable, at last we reached the foot of the mountain. Now progress was quicker and, knowing that there was no danger to my charges, I mounted and with the other horsemen set off ahead for home. The rain pelted down, the path turned to a river, but at last I swung through the gate of the compound and one of my boys took the horse. 'Boy,' I cried, 'pass bath!'

The fortnightly mail had arrived and after reading the more personal letters I stripped and sat in my bath soaking out the cold and wet and drinking tea as I read the others. I had the righteous feeling of a man with a job well done; we hadn't got all the tax, but we'd made a start and taught Lokperè a lesson. From outside came the bleating of the goats as the rest of the party arrived and I saw the drenched police leave their rifles and bandoliers at the guard room. One letter was from India, from the man who in a couple of years' time was to be the godfather of my first son. He, in the I.C.S., had also been on tour—tax-collecting. 'In this part of the world,' he wrote, 'I trek with an elephant to carry my loads. A *zemindar* has refused to pay and I have therefore attached his elephant also until he does so, and I am now trekking on one with my boys and luggage on the other.' From outside came the bleating of my goats; would that it had been the trumpeting of an elephant.

To add to my troubles, Wala and Warrabè again started fighting and the two-year-old peace came to a violent end for, the young men said, the white men were leaving the land and it was they, not the elders, who would then rule. Forty years before these hills had been made part of the German Colony of the Kamerun by white men of whose very existence the hillmen were at that time ignorant. Now because of the quarrels amongst these same tribes of white men, a Wala man died suddenly and violently. The elders of both villages were disturbed at the turn of events and deputations came to see the District Head. Agreement to hold another peace ceremony to wipe out the sin of the spilt blood, and to hand over the five head of cattle to reimburse the family of the dead man, was soon reached and on the appointed day, with the District Head and his followers, my messengers and half a dozen police, I arrived soon after dawn on the common boundary of the two villages.

In a short time the elders of Wala appeared and greeted us by sinking on their knees and throwing a little dust over their shoulders as they repeated the Fulani words of welcome which they had learned in the past few years. *'Ussay, ussay, ussayko,'* they said, whilst we replied, *'Ussay, mboten*—greetings, all is well.' They sat in the shade of a near-by large tree and proceeded to smoke and hawk and spit. From the other side came about half of their elders to tell us, after similar greetings, that their fellows, having been upbraided and threatened by the young men, were refusing to appear. From the Wala elders under their tree came a shouted insult that the elders in Warrabè were no longer respected by the young men; Warrabè answered back, and some time was lost before quiet was restored. A Warrabè elder went to call his missing fellows and another stood and roared to the mountains towering above us, telling the missing elders to come, for the white man was angry.

The morning dragged on; from time to time an elder went; from time to time we had men shouting to us from vantage-points above us that they would not come; from time to time another reluctant elder emerged to join the rest—often no doubt prompted by the argument: 'The white man is still there; go and get it over and let us see him and his men depart and let us get back to our proper affairs.' The District Head went to a not far distant compound and argued with an elder who resided there; on outjutting points of rock above us stood the warriors of the two villages scissor-like against the sky; they were unarmed—a good sign—for despite the opposition to a ceremony, none ventured to appear in open hostility to the leaders of the village—not merely to those in this world, but to those in the spirit world, those who had gone before and those yet to be born. Midday came and I began to be anxious, when from Warrabè came a little procession of the missing elders and the Gidigil, the spiritual leader of the village, carrying a small puppy whose blood was to be used to wipe out that of Wala spilt by the young men of Warrabè.

The ceremony differed in no essential detail from that described earlier; it came to an end and the elders replaced the iron ornaments that they had doffed. From a near-by tree the glazed eyes of the dead puppy looked down on us, but the leaders of the white men knew no such certain way of keeping their warriors from each other's throats, and in a few short months the cries of the widows and mothers of Poland were added to those of the family in Wala whose son was perhaps the first to die because of the old hatreds between the white tribes.

The end of the story was not there, however, but a dozen miles to the north a few weeks later. Out on the plains where a river cut through the Dar-el-Jimeil ridge, was the small Kanuri village of Bulongo where there was a large market attended by the people of the plains and a few Pagan youths from the villages at the end of the mountain spur fifteen or so miles away. On this particular day a few men from Wala and from Warrabè, from Pulkè and Wija —two villages in no way related to the other two, which were cousins—attended the market. In the village of strangers they had naturally drawn together and had drunk of the beer brought to the market by the Gamergu women from the villages of that Pagan tribe which lay on the plains; as the sun sank in the west, the little group started for home. Some carried a spear, one or two a bow and a few freshly poisoned arrows in a quiver hung over the left shoulder; these weapons had been taken partly for defence along the paths of this lawless area, partly in case they met game on the journey; from their waists hung a few dirty rags or an old goat-skin, worn to hide their private parts when visiting a market of the clothed people of the plains.

Beer had been drunk and soon a warrior of Warrabè was threatening the Wala men; the recent peace ceremony had been no true ceremony for it had not been freely entered into but forced on them by the interfering white man; as all had heard at the market that day, the white men were returning to their own land and when they had gone, things would be different and Warrabè would demand the return of their cattle forced from them under duress. Tempers grew high and the men of Pulkè and Wija drew away from the others; those from Wala were conciliatory for between them and home stretched the compounds of Warrabè; but to no good. A drunken, raging, Warrabè youth drew an arrow from his quiver and at the same time tried to slip the slack bowstring round the notch which made it taut and ready for use. In some way, whether in his haste, or his anger, or because of the beer he had drunk, or perhaps because it got entangled in his unaccustomed loin-cloth, the arrow was dropped and pierced his foot. The men of Wala, Wija and Pulkè fled and twenty minutes later his companions lifted the still warm corpse and bore it home for burial.

The news spread rapidly; this was, as all could now see, no patched-up peace forced on the two villages by the white man, but one of great strength and potency; as all could see, the first man who had tried to break it had died, and, moreover, from a wound given by his own weapon as he drew it in anger against Wala. The young men pondered on these things and the elders rejoiced at this manifestation that indeed they were still the appointed leaders of those of the village on earth, still the appointed links between those now living and those in the shades.

Another headache in 1939 which caused everyone a great deal of trouble, stemmed from a famine which had occurred in 1929 or 1930. The Wulla, who were mostly in the mountains on the French side of the boundary, had been so badly hit that, in order both to obtain food for themselves and to save the lives of their children, they had sold hundreds of the latter to whoever would take them. The majority had gone to Shuwa Arabs on the plains of Dikwa and the purist would say that, on the latter's part, this was merely a return to the buying of slaves. But whilst they were no doubt taunted from time to time with their Pagan origin by the others in the village, the females were freely sought in marriage by Shuwa men as they reached marriageable age, and once they had borne their husband a child, they became in every respect free; as for the boys, they were not ill-treated or confined in any way; they mixed with the others, attended the markets with the rest of the village and could run away to their native home at any time. They had, however, been circumcised and become Moslem and the physical operation meant that they would not be accepted by their native village if they did return home. In the vast majority of cases, these Wulla children had exchanged a life of considerable hardship on the hills for one with much more food and safety on the plains, and were in many ways better off than their brothers and sisters.

Smaller numbers of these children had been bought into several of the Pagan villages on the Ashigashiya side of the spur. By 1939 the oldest of the girls were reaching marriageable age, but instead of their foster-parents being approached by potential sons-in-law with the appropriate bride-price, the girls were either persuaded to run away or were abducted, and in the latter case raped, sometimes by bands of youths who held them prisoner until they tired of them. Nothing like this had been known previously in the hills and some of the unfortunate girls passed forcibly from village to village, fair game for any band of youths who could get them away from where they then were without fighting. To add to the confusion and the resentment of the foster-parents, some Wulla had kept track of their children, and now that a bride-price might be obtained, they were trying to persuade their daughters to run away and return home. Endless cases of a most involved nature were brought before the Native Courts by aggrieved foster-parents seeking both the return of the money they had originally paid for the child, and some recompense for the corn and food lavished on the growing child. We cursed all famines and all Wulla, but the problem continued for several years.

Away on the plains to the west of Gwoza lay the villages of the Marghi, another Pagan tribe some of whose members were turning Moslem, strung along the banks of the River Yedseram which formed the boundary between Bornu Division in Nigeria and this part of Dikwa Division in the Mandated Territory. The bush between Gwoza and the Yedseram contained but few villages as a large herd of elephant roamed there. The chief village of the Marghi was Isgè, visited by Barth in 1851 and the scene of a sharp fight in 1898, before either the British or the Germans had arrived, between the French and the followers of the Arab Rabeh. There had never been any trouble with the Marghi in the Dikwa area since it was brought under British administration, but now the rumours from the French were being repeated amongst these people and a very worried District Head brought the village head of the area to see me.

A young Marghi from a section of the tribe many miles away had arrived at Isgè, and was telling the people that he had been to heaven and seen God; God had given him four small stones as witness that he had done so and told him to go to Isgè and warn the people. 'Tell them,' said God—or at least so said this messenger —'tell them that a time of great hardship is at hand; the Europeans are leaving the land; leopards will increase in numbers; it behoves the maidens in groups of four to sacrifice a hen; the youths in groups of four a goat; then let every man prepare his weapons and be ready for war. If the people of Isgè do as I tell them all will be well.'

But all was not well; armed men going to the weekly market and drinking vast quantities of strong beer fell to quarrelling and one was killed and many hurt. Such brawling was alien to the Marghi and rumour and discontent spread far and wide. 'I can do nothing,' said the village head; 'this man is sitting in the house of the head of the hamlet nearest to Gwoza; he is visited every day by large numbers of armed youths and they drink and eat and have no regard for me or the other elders. They say that they will kill you if you approach, and they are sending out to all parts of the Marghi country to tell them to sacrifice in like manner.'

This was a puzzler; if I did nothing the infection would spread; on the other hand if I was attacked in the thick bush of the plains I might lose many men. Whatever I did I would probably be blamed by those in the Secretariat who would have to minute on the matter, and, as this was Mandated Territory, to prepare the dispatch for the Secretary of State to submit to the League of Nations. Only five years had passed since the last A.D.O. had been killed in Plateau Province and amongst my police were two who had helped carry off his body under a hail of stones and poisoned arrows. Another dawn foray would be necessary; it was about twenty-five miles to Isgè, so to arrive at dawn we should have to leave soon after dark the night before. I would take fifteen police—though I was forbidden to take them away from the hill villages—and a dozen mounted men. We would march through the night; at dawn, on the edge of the Isgè farms, I would leave the District Head, my sergeant and eleven of his men, one messenger and all the mounted men except for five. Three of these would ride up to the house where the man was supposed to be and would seize him; I, Yerima Boyi, and another mounted man with three police on foot ready to take a stirrup leather each if we had to run, would get between that house and the rest of the hamlet. If the wanted man escaped and fled into the village we might catch him; if he created a hullabaloo and others rushed to his rescue we would try and hinder them; if the worst came to the worst we would all flee to the main body of my police who would have the shelter of the bush behind them and a clean field of fire to their front. If things went very badly, I should be lucky to get my footmen out of this bush alive, the more so as they would be fleeing after a night march of twenty-five miles.

But this time fortune was on our side—or the Marghi had forgotten how to fight. Our march was uneventful; as dawn broke we reached the edge of the farms; I repeated my orders to the District Head and to the sergeant of police, split the men into the two parties, and rode rapidly ahead. The three men who were to do the actual arresting galloped to one of the compounds that I passed and to my astonishment almost at once remounted and, with a handcuffed man tied with a rope to one of their saddles, called to me that they had got their prey. We others turned and less than five minutes after leaving the main body, we were back again with our prize. 'Are you certain that is the man?' I asked. 'Certain, certain,' came from the District Head and his followers. 'Then be off and don't let him escape; follow the track to Mutubè Hill and await me there. In a short time I will send off the police and then follow last.' The District Head mounted and his party started; off went the police and with my two messengers I sat on horseback watching the hamlet; but to our astonishment, apart from a few men running off in various directions nothing happened; no war crowd appeared; everything lay quiet and peaceful. After a quarter of an hour, we rode slowly after the others. And nothing happened the whole way home—we didn't even meet the elephants—but it was a tired and footsore party that got home in the late afternoon after a round march of about fifty miles.

In due course the captive was brought before the Court of the Emir of Dikwa and received a sentence of ten years. The madness passed; the village head brought in large numbers of bows, arrows and spears; we had a large bonfire.

All was well, no minutes were required, the League of Nations went undisturbed.

Life was not, however, all trials and tribulations. On Empire Day 1939 I received authority to spend two pounds on a celebration for the children in the small elementary school at Hambagda, alongside the even smaller dispensary where the devoted *Mallam* Zerma treated anything and everything with minuscule supplies of medicines and dressings.

The District Head, my messengers, Kamkura and a large and growing entourage rode out in the early afternoon of the great day; behind came the sergeant of police and three of his men. They carried their rifles as any celebration carried with it the possibility of some fight, but I had brought them not as an escort but as men skilled in the arts of running sports days.

It was the height of the dry season; the fields stretched bare and empty; the school-teachers and their charges had cleared a stretch of flat ground of stumps and twigs, and smoothed it over. Now, drawn up in classes they stood to greet us; under a large tree sat the elders of the Hidkala clan, whilst under other trees were spectators drawn by the news that the white man was going to do something or other of a non-unpleasant kind.

The police placed their kit in the school; a table was brought out on which I arranged the prizes for inspection. The District Head and my messengers explained to all and sundry that in a short time this unpredictable white man would proceed to give them away. The crowd grew; more and more pressed forward to eye the gaudily decorated enamel bowls from Japan, a few strings of German beads, a couple of lengths of white calico, heavy with dressing, and the same of gaudy prints from Hong Kong.

The usual programme of races for such occasions had been drawn up. The crowd swelled still more and the sound of laughter and cheering rose to the tops of the mountains above us as tiny, naked boys, often of most disparate sizes, struggled three-legged to the tape. The afternoon wore on; the winners stood round-eyed, with finger in mouth, as their prizes were shown to them and they were told that they would be able to take them home at the end of the afternoon.

I had retained three sets of prizes for adult races and after all had understood from watching the early events what I was up to, there were plenty of willing runners when I announced a race for elders only. We tried to handicap them by apparent infirmity and age, but as we placed older and more decrepit men closer and closer to the finish, furious shouts came from down the track as the haler pushed forward, and more and more halt and lame took up what they regarded as a suitable position a few yards from the finish. It would never do to have elders fighting amongst themselves so we dropped the whole idea.

For a race for maidens, we had a large entry of magnificently built and proportioned girls from about fourteen to eighteen years of age, naked as the day they were born except for a few beads worn on one or two thighs. With great difficulty we got them into line; there were several false starts before the sergeant of police dropped his flag; we spectators were able to admire without restraint the play of muscles under flashing brown flesh in a way no other audience is ever able to do. Yet even here I was reminded of the anguished cry from the poet: 'The poetry of motion is lost when women and cows run.' But there was little time for rumination for I and my two messengers stood on the winning tape to seize the first three over the line to ensure that the correct runners received the prizes. The horde of swinging wenches bore down on us; I seized one by the hand, and saw Yerima Boyi and Moman Biyu had done likewise; then each of us was surrounded by a jostling mass of sweating naked bodies as the less fleet of foot tried to pry our hands loose and transfer them to their own wet wrists. We were rescued by the Galadima and the grinning policemen.

For the young men I had planned something on the lines of a fell race at a Lakeland sports; one of the police climbed a thousand feet or so to where a prominent tree jutted out and another went a few hundred yards to his right and a couple of hundred feet higher; we lined a dozen contestants up and told them they were to run to the first man, hit his hand, then to the second and do similarly, and then back to us. I prayed that no one would fall dead from heart failure and they were off; the crowd below bellowed encouragement to their friends and sons and the climbers began to spread out; soon it appeared that the race lay between two or three of the stronger and some of those trailing far behind returned to the plains amidst the good-natured jeers and chaffing of their friends. Apart from the leaders three or four others hung doggedly on, spurred on perhaps by the thought that this strange white man would reward them for finishing. The first man rounded the first policeman and made his way to the second, rounded him and rapidly out-distanced his pursuers as he came down the hillside scarce seeming to touch the ground. Amidst the ululations of the maidens crowding round the tape, the winner romped home a hundred yards or more ahead of his nearest rival, and bore down on me to receive his prize.

The evening drew on, and we had the presentation of prizes to the schoolchildren by the Galadima; amidst the plaudits of the crowd we mounted and made our way home leaving behind us singing and dancing groups making their way up the darkening slopes, talking both tonight and for many days to come of the white man and his strange ways. It had been a great success but I received a measured rebuke for indecorum in an official letter when, in sending in an account of the day and accounting for the money I had received, I described the races for maidens and young men as 'going with a swing'.

To add to my many other difficulties in 1939, May brought with it an outbreak of smallpox from which hundreds died. I received vaccine by horse-messenger from Maiduguri, the eighty miles or so being covered in about three days. The tubes of vaccine were packed in ice in a thermos, and I tipped them out from warm water on receipt. The wife of one of my police died and we burnt the hut down to kill the infection; everyone in the compound was vaccinated and we tried to persuade the Pagans to be treated. At Hambagda *Mallam* Zerma was known and trusted and large numbers in that area were vaccinated. But elsewhere, the Galadima and I harangued and argued, and I would head a small queue to be vaccinated in sight of all. This went on day after day, and when my left arm was raw from shoulder to elbow, we started on the right.

Travelling over the pass behind Gwoza on which stood the

village of Guduf, Yerima Boyi and I were hailed by a man propped in the shade of a tree, who was little more than skin and bone. Yerima gave an exclamation of surprise and spoke to the man in the Mandara language; then turning to me, he said in Hausa, 'This is So-and-so whom we both know well; look at him, he was a black man; now after the smallpox he is a *jatau*—a red man.' It was true; from being jet black the man's skin had changed to the colour of milk chocolate.

My three years' probationary period was drawing to a close; I was to go on leave during the first week in September. Margaret started the arrangements for our wedding.

But this was not to be. The war clouds grew and I was told that whilst I was to hand over on 1 September, I was to be embodied from the Reserve into the Nigeria Regiment.

In the late afternoon of the last day of August, I rode out of Gwoza for the last time accompanied by the Galadima, the two messengers and a large number of horsemen. A mile along the track that led to Bama we came to the first of the flooded patches; I turned and said good-bye and accompanied only by Kamkura rode forward.

Two days later I was guarding Maiduguri aerodrome from Heaven knows what. My army service was, however, not of long duration. From Maiduguri I was posted to Zaria to join the 5th Battalion; here Njaro and I finished second in the six-furlong race for European riders in the Outbreak of War Meeting. Six years later, when we had won the same event at the Victory Meeting, *The Field* published our photos and inquired if this was a record.

From Zaria we were sent to the Cameroons to safeguard internal security amongst the German-owned and -manned banana plantations and I was thus able to visit parts of Nigeria I would normally never have seen. But Italy, contrary to all expectations, did not enter the war; we reservists, black and white, were therefore 'disembodied' and sent home. At Lagos I was put into hospital for the only time in my life, but eventually reached Liverpool on 24 January and was married on the 26th.

As I still spoke some Swahili from my East African days in addition to my Hausa, I was assured by the Colonial Office that I would soon be recalled to be sent to East Africa to meet the Nigerians, in anticipation of the entry of Italy into the war. But nothing happened and finally, in June, leaving Margaret to face the black-out and bombing and to bear our first child, I returned to Nigeria for my third tour.

I was sent first to Zaria; then, after a month spent in trekking the country to the south of that place, to Benue Province. This was a very different matter from Bornu; no horses, no desert, no mountains; a great river, open grass plains, canoes, tsetse flies and endemic sleeping sickness. Njaro was left with a friend in Zaria.

PART TWO

Benue

CHAPTER TEN

The Opening-up of the Interior

In Bornu, as we have seen, contact with Europeans consisted until the death of Rabeh at the hands of the French column based on Fort Lamy of a few visits by explorers crossing the Sahara from the north; from 1832 onwards, however, the country bordering the Niger and Benue rivers was brought into almost continuous contact with European traders, traders who in time became administrators and who were finally replaced by the British Government on 1 January 1900.

Africa was the unknown continent until comparatively recent times, protected from intercourse with the rest of the world by a great desert in the north and by jungle and disease elsewhere, with no great bays or navigable rivers leading deep into the heart of the continent. The Carthaginians are believed to have circumnavigated the continent over 2,000 years ago, and certain of their youths are said to have crossed the great desert and returned in due course to their Mediterranean homes. The Romans pushed far south into the desert but never crossed it. The French claim that at the end of the fourteenth century certain Breton fishermen voyaged far down the west coast of Africa, but there are no proofs. It was the Portuguese under the inspiration of Prince Henry the Navigator who ventured southwards along the coasts of Africa, to the Cape and so to the eventual exploration of the coast of the whole continent at the end of the fifteenth century. For the next 300 years, whilst there were many points of contact by European nations at places on the coastline, and many settlements were made—Goree near the modern Dakar, Elmina near the modern Takoradi and Fort Jesus at Mombasa are examples—little was known about the interior.

At the end of the eighteenth century the penetration of the interior of West Africa by members of European nations commenced. Mungo Park, a Scot, made his way alone from Goree to the headwaters of the Niger in 1795. He returned safely and in

1805 set out a second time with a large party consisting of himself, Messrs. Anderson and Scott, four carpenters and two seamen from England, and Lieutenant Martyn and thirty-five soldiers from the garrison at Goree. Of the latter, the Directors of the African Institution—the body behind the expedition—when they came to prepare an account of the death of Park, wrote:

The detachment of the Royal African Corps which was to escort the expedition, consisted of a lieutenant and thirty-five privates. It was not to be expected that troops of a very superior quality could be furnished from a regiment which had been serving for any considerable time at a tropical station such as Goree. But there is too much reason to believe that the men selected on the present occasion notwithstanding the favourable opinion of them expressed by Park, and although they were the best that the Garrison could supply, were below the ordinary standard even of troops of this description; and that they were extremely deficient both in constitutional strength and vigour and in those habits of sobriety, steadiness and good discipline which such a service peculiarly required.

The party was doomed from the start; Park reached the Niger with only Anderson, Martyn, six soldiers and one carpenter. The rest had died—or been left to die—at places along the route. Yet the difficulties that the expedition had to overcome were not very great; they did not have to fight their way; the climate is the same as that of today; the sole difference is the knowledge of disease—that it is the mosquito and not 'bad air' which brings on the dreaded malaria and blackwater fever.

Park and his companions prepared to start their voyage down the mighty Niger. Where did it lead? Opinion in Europe was divided; some held that it was a tributary of the Nile, others that it led to a great inland lake from which there was no exit, others again that it was a tributary of the Congo. But death still further reduced the little party and when, in two canoes fastened together and christened 'H.M.S. *Joliba*', they left Sansanding there appear to have been left only Park, Martyn and three others.

After various adventures, these intrepid men reached the town of Yauri, the first of the Nigerian Emirates which pay homage to Sokoto; from here they sent back Amadi Fatouma, their guide down the river, with their last letters and journals. In one of these

Martyn wrote: 'Whitbread's beer is nothing to what we get at this place; as I feel my head this morning, having been drinking all night with a Moor, and ended by giving him an excellent threshing.'

No further news came from them and in January 1810 their first guide, who had been with them from the Senegal to the Niger, a man called Isaaco, was sent back to find out what had happened. Twenty months later, after contacting Amadi, he returned with the sad news that, after leaving Yauri, the little party had been attacked and eventually, to escape capture, the survivors had jumped into the river and been drowned. The scene of Mungo Park's death is usually assumed to be the rapids at Boussa, but having been the District Officer in charge of the Yauri area, and having in my turn travelled down the mighty Niger from the French border to the Boussa rapids, I doubt the accuracy of this identification, and in a paper published some years ago I tried to reconcile the differing accounts of what happened.

A sad and little-known sequel to the story of Mungo Park concerns his second son Thomas, who, with his mother, refused to believe in his father's death and clung to the hope that he still lived, a prisoner somewhere in the Western Sudan. In 1827 he made his way to Accra and set out to seek his father. In a final letter to his mother he wrote that he expected to be away for up to three years; nothing more was ever heard of him.

Then in the 1820's the expedition from Tripoli consisting of Dr. Oudney, Commander Clapperton, R.N. and Major Denham crossed the Great Desert and arrived in Bornu. The first named died in Bornu, but the others—Clapperton after penetrating as far west as Sokoto—returned safely to Europe. Denham became Governor of Sierra Leone—where he died—but Clapperton returned to the coast near the present Lagos, and with his manservant, Richard Lander, marched inland to Sokoto, crossing the Niger at Boussa. At Sokoto Clapperton died, and after great dangers Lander returned to the coast and eventually to England. He too had now been bitten by the bug of African exploration, and in turn returned with his brother to Boussa, embarked below the rapids, and in due course emerged on the coast near Fernando Po, showing that the mighty Niger ran into the sea through hundreds of small mouths none of which had previously been taken to be

the debouchment of a great river. The secret of the Niger was un-
ravelled.

In 1850 the German, Dr Barth, working for the British Government, followed the route of the earlier expedition and arrived in
Bornu from Tripoli. In the next four years he ventured as far
west as Timbuktu, and as far south as Yola on the River Benue.
Miraculously he returned to Europe—to die a few years later in
the Levant—but he left behind a monumental work on his travels
written with typical Teutonic thoroughness. But Barth is guilty
at times of considerable exaggeration and is not always accurate
in his statements: he describes the Marghi of Bornu as consisting
of jet black and brown people, when the latter are in fact merely
adorned with red ochre, and he accuses Denham of geographical
errors when, as I was able to show to the Royal Geographical
Society, Denham was right.

Meanwhile, following Lander's descent of the Niger, attempts
were made to establish trading-posts on its banks. In 1832 the
Liverpool trader Macgregor Laird placed two steamers on the
Niger which ascended both it and its great tributary, the Benue,
for about a hundred miles above their confluence. Of the forty-
nine Europeans who went out, nine survived. A Government expedition to establish a post at Lokoja in 1841 was equally
disastrous, and gave Charles Dickens the material for Mrs Jelleyby
and her scheme for the settlement of two hundred healthy families
cultivating coffee and educating the natives of 'Borrioboola-Gha
on the left bank of the Niger'.

Lagos was occupied in 1851 and in the succeeding years Macgregor Laird made many attempts to set up trading-posts along
the Niger and the Benue, but a hostile climate and hostile inhabitants, some of whom were being raided for slaves whilst the
others were their raiders, defeated his earlier efforts. Success came
at last and with it many other traders, with the not unnatural
result that competition became ruinous. There then came on the
scene Mr G. D. Goldie-Taubman, a remarkable man later
known as Sir George Goldie. In 1879 he formed the United
African Company and proceeded to buy up the various concerns
on the two rivers, English and French, to form in 1882 the
National African Company; four years later he obtained a Royal
Charter for his company, which now became the Royal Niger

Company and ruled Northern Nigeria until the abrogation of the charter.

Meanwhile, Leopold of the Belgians had called the Brussels Conference of 1876 which led to a short-lived international surveillance of Africa in the shape of the International African Association. The Berlin conference a few years later ended the scramble for Africa by drawing up the rules by which the Continent was divided—rules that paid no attention to such matters as geography or peoples or economics, for the maps were white and Europe was less concerned with these matters than in preventing war about the colours which would replace the white.

Goldie's National African Company inaugurated a new period of expansion and on the Benue river the first effect was the foundation of a trading-station at Ibi, just over the boundary of what is now Benue Province. Following the custom in the trading-posts of the Palm Oil Rivers, this first station consisted of the hulk of a wooden sailing-ship, the *Emily Watters*, and from this point other trading-stations were opened up the main river to beyond Yola and along the various tributaries of the Benue. These stations again were generally hulks, as these allowed the experimental occupation of a site, which could be abandoned if the venture proved a failure and the hulk taken elsewhere. The hulks also gave a considerable measure of security, particularly in the rainy season when they floated. Often they were steamers specially built to ground, which, if not employed in this way, would have had to retreat with the falling waters at the end of the rains, to lie at anchor in the delta somewhere. With the formation of the Chartered Company, the trading operations were now protected by the presence of a disciplined force under British officers called the Royal Niger Constabulary, instead of being solely dependent on the audacity of individual agents.

In the *Gazetteer* for Muri Province, issued in 1922 (Muri Province has long since disappeared, being divided between Benue and Adamawa), was a note by Mr W. P. Hewby, C.M.G. on the activities of the Company, of which he had been an employee. He wrote:

The administrative policy of the Company, with a comparatively small staff of energetic young men, largely engrossed in commercial development, was modest and simple. Their aim was to maintain friendly relations with the important Mohammedan chiefs, whilst keeping trade-routes open by any means feasible; and to put a stop to, or at any rate check, slave-raiding amongst the Pagans on the south bank of the Benue below the Katsina river by north-bank Mohammedans, chiefly Nassarawa.

In 1894 a party of four Arabs sent by Egypt to make contact with Rabeh, the recent conqueror of Bornu, arrived on the river, but the Emir of Yola refused to allow them to pass that way to Bornu; they reached Dikwa in due course by a roundabout route but I have never learnt what finally became of them. Two years later, Rabeh tried to make contact with Ibi and sent a caravan of ivory to exchange for gunpowder.

During these years a number of French and German travellers passed through the area, the most notorious being Lieutenant Mizon of the French Navy. His first journey was in 1890 when, with one white companion, he voyaged up the Niger to the confluence and then up the Benue, eventually abandoning his boat and reaching the French Congo overland; his life was saved on one occasion by an agent of the Company and his journey was only made possible by the unstinted assistance he received whilst in their territory.

In the wet season of 1892 he returned with two steamers, one fitted out for trade, the other with a large number of French officers and arms, and both vessels were declared 'in transit' through the area of the Company's operations. With the fall of the river both grounded, and Mizon made friends with one of the Fulani rulers, the Emir of Muri. He distributed arms of precision and used letter-paper headed 'The French Protectorate of Muri'; he landed two field-pieces and men to man them to join the Emir in an attack on the Pagan town of Kwona which submitted after his bombardment although it had resisted Muri's attempts at conquest for many years. In 1893 Mizon went on up the flood tide to Yola followed by Mr Wallace, the Company's Agent, in the steamer *Nupe*, well armed and with a contingent of the Constabulary on board. There are no accounts of what transpired, but Mizon was left in no doubt of what the Company thought of his activities. Leaving his trading vessel at Yola he returned downstream in the other, and when the Company seized and confiscated the latter he sent for the one at Yola and withdrew, leaving at Yola half a dozen Senegalese and Arabs to whom the French Press referred in the next few years as 'the French post at Yola'. It was the activities of such men as Mizon and the counter-activities of resolute men such as Wallace which brought England and France to the verge of war, and which led ultimately to the abrogation of the Charter of the Royal Niger Company.

The agents of the Company and the members of the early administration were men whose deeds deserve recording. We are satiated with the deeds of the Americans who 'opened up the West' but we tell our children and the world little of the men who opened up, under far more difficult conditions, the continent of Africa: of Captain Moloney who occupied a hostile town in the Benue area, building a small redoubt in the middle, for, he wrote, 'I was unable to hold a 4,000-yard perimeter with fifty men'; he was later crippled for life in the Brass raid on Akassa in 1895 and murdered at Keffi in 1902. Captain Parker of the South Wales Borderers faced poisoned arrows with his steward boy attending to the wounded with a razor and a bottle of carbolic acid. Parker was wounded on three separate occasions and killed by a spear thrust when attempting to give a leg-up to his tallest man onto the top of the wall of the fortified town of Suntai.

The area of the Tiv tribe, or the Munshi as they were generally called, had always been regarded with doubt by the Company's staff, though trading-posts were opened at fishing villages of the Jukun along the river bank, including Katsina Ala which lies up the tributary of the Benue of that name. In the dry season of 1885–6 the Munshi attacked the various trading-posts and killed four of the five Europeans in charge; as a result, the Company abandoned its trade in their country.

The whole area, being one in which slave-raiding took place, had attracted adventurers from all over the Hausa country; in about 1870 for example a raid from Sokoto brought a certain Dankoro, a man of considerable notoriety. He raided Wukari and became of great influence amongst the Munshi, many of whom joined his war camp; he eventually died from the kick of a horse in 1899.

Nineteen-fourteen brought to the area its share of war scares, including an attack by a German column. In 1916, near Donga in

Benue Province, a Pagan calling himself the 'Invulnerable One' attracted a large number of followers and the early pattern appears to have been similar to that I have described as occurring amongst the Marghi of Bornu in 1939. This man attacked Donga town, was captured by the then Resident with his escort of twenty police, tried for murder and hanged; it was commented at the time that, but for his arrest, the rising would have spread and assumed serious proportions.

CHAPTER ELEVEN

The Tiv

The organization into provinces of the country near the great rivers had not been easy; an area like Bornu consisted, except for the Gwoza Hills, of the Kanuri and their related peoples and others who had for long acknowledged their suzerainty; along the rivers, however, were inchoate jumbles of once mighty states, petty emirates founded by masterless men or the leaders of war parties, from where slave-raids had been carried out, and Pagan tribes from whom the slaves had been taken and whose relationship with the others formed a complete spectrum from war to active collaboration. In these areas it was not a question of pro-British administrative units being grouped together to form provinces of convenient size, but rather of the facts of geography determining which areas could be best reached and therefore be administered from some selected centre. After several different groupings, the building of a railway bridge at Makurdi where the River Benue was at its narrowest—though still 900 yards wide—determined the site for the headquarters of a new Province spread on either side of the railway.

This new Province was named Benue and was formed in the late twenties; it contained five Divisions, of which the biggest, to which I was posted, was the Tiv Division, largely conterminous with that virile and populous tribe. The Province was a hotch-potch of completely unrelated peoples, speaking at least six totally different languages, and whilst Bornu was said to be the Holy Kingdom to which only the Administrative élite were posted, Benue was still regarded as a punishment posting.

Makurdi, the Provincial Headquarters, was built on a low hill overlooking the river. In the desert parts of the north, coolness and darkness, if not synonymous, are inseparable, and in Fort Rabeh in Dikwa and the great mud houses of Kano, we would close all doors and windows and draw the curtains by 8 a.m. to keep the coolness of the night within the walls of the house as long as possible. But where the humidity is high, you want a current of air, so the houses of Lagos and the south have tall french windows to open to let the welcome breeze freshen the heavy water-laden atmosphere. Makurdi's houses were of the southern type, and although the temperature never reached the 124 degrees of Dikwa, the high humidity made it seem lifeless and airless. I visited it as infrequently as possible, but I had to spend three weeks there in charge of the Provincial Office when the then incumbent went for some local leave; this visit was noteworthy for the fact that in the files I rediscovered the origin of one of the delightful jests which were famous in the country, and of which I have been said to be the author.

Heussler comments in his book that the majority of those recruited to the Service in the inter-war years were classical scholars, and notes with surprise the Latin and Greek tags and quotations which appeared in official papers of all kinds. I was a mere scientist and Greek was Greek to me—as it had been to one of my predecessors in Makurdi. Apparently what had happened was that he received one day a file from his Resident containing a minute in Greek. In those days—and this may still be the case— with every tin of the delectable Lyle's Golden Syrup there was a small booklet which presumably extolled the virtues of that product in a dozen different languages, each in a different alphabet— Arabic, Chinese, Japanese, Urdu and so on. The A.D.O. must have gone home to breakfast and with his syrup had come inspiration; on his return he too had minuted, and there for me to read were the two minutes:

A.D.O. OFFICE—My only comment after reading the papers on this lamentable affair is the immortal words of Aristotle:

$$\mathrm{\mathring{α}νθρωΠος\ φ\mathring{υ}σει\ Πολιτικ\grave{ο}ν\ ξ\^{ω}ον}$$

K. POOP, Resident.

RESIDENT—Or on the other hand, as Confucius so truly remarked on a similar occasion:

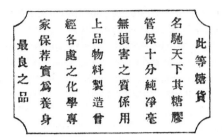

A.D.O.O.

The country occupied by the Tiv was probably at some earlier period well timbered, but these assiduous but wasteful farmers have destroyed whatever tree cover may formerly have existed and now live on a rolling, smooth grass plain, cut by the great River Benue and its smaller—though still respectably large—tributary, the Katsina Ala, with one or two small granite hills breaking the monotony of the surface, of which the largest is Mkar in the centre of the Tiv country. Yams are the chief crop of the Tiv, like potatoes in that they require to be grown in ridges or individual heaps, and the yam heaps of the Tiv may be up to eight feet high; the labour of construction is formidable. Guinea corn is also grown and used for brewing beer, and other crops are maize and cassava.

The problems that face the improvement of farming in countries such as Nigeria are well illustrated with the maize grown by the Tiv. This was a small-headed variety of low yield, but a useful crop as it ripened earlier than all the others and thus fed the growers at the beginning of the rainy season—generally a period of hunger in Africa. At the foot of the Mkar hill, which rose to about 800 feet above the plains, the Dutch Reformed Church of South Africa had established a mission in the 1900's when, as a result of a conference in, I think, Jerusalem, an attempt was made by the Christian Churches to establish across Africa a line of mission stations along the southern edge of the Moslem penetration, to act as a sort of *cordon sanitaire* behind which Christianity could become the dominant religion. The Boer missionaries at Mkar were of farming stock and they introduced from South Africa varieties of hybrid maize, sweet and large-headed, which gave large yields. The variety ripened late, which did not matter to the missionaries with their plentiful supply of foods of all kinds, but to the astonishment of the Tiv, in an ever-widening arc round Mkar as converts took home a few heads of the new maize, their own maize ripened later and later as the years went by. The reason was cross-pollination between the introduced stock and the native variety, so that the date of ripening became progressively later as more and more of the heavy-yielding Boer variety was grown. But the chief merit of the Tiv maize lay in the fact that it ripened in what was otherwise a period of hunger, and late-ripening varieties, no matter how prolific in yield, were of little value to the Tiv. The result was that all the maize grown in a large arc round Mkar had to be uprooted and destroyed, the import of new varieties forbidden, and the area restocked with seed of the unpolluted, early-ripening, low-yielding maize native to the area. The way of the crop-improver is both a long one and one beset by many difficulties.

Contact between different types of plants can therefore lead to unforeseen difficulties, but as with the maize remedial action can be taken by destroying the seed of the new variety and returning to the pure native variety. But it is very different when in place of plants we have men; when in place of varieties of plants we have differing kinds of social organization; then contact between peoples of two cultures may bring in its wake a great deal of hardship and suffering to those of the culture which eventually disintegrates or which becomes submerged by the other. This has been seen time and again in recent times, and we assume too easily that it only occurs when the dominant culture is that of Europe; it can also occur—and the hardship can be equally great—when two African cultures clash.

When the dominant culture is that of Europe and the rulers of a land are Europeans, the various forces which are pulling in different directions within the dying culture may at one time combine with one another against the ruling power, and at others split, so that some work with the ruling power against their own tribesmen; the forces change from time to time in their grouping, in an ever-changing kaleidoscope. For example the younger members of the more primitive culture may be attracted to the superior one with the result that there is a schism between them and the older generation who cling to the known and well-tried tenets of their ancient faith and traditions. No doubt such a schism appeared in these islands at the time of the Roman conquest, particularly around the Roman camps and cities, away from the great forests in which the natives dwelt; certainly it has played a very important part in the disintegration of the Kikuyu under British rule when the forbidding of female circumcision—which appeared to the Administration as a barbarous rite and to the missions as a sign of Paganism to which no convert must submit—was to the elders a blow aimed at the very existence of the Kikuyu as a tribe. The problems of the Kikuyu and of Kenya have no part in a story of Northern Nigeria, but the problems of the Tiv tribe, numbering perhaps 750,000 people, have; these problems are no longer the concern of the British; it is to be profoundly hoped that they will not cause trouble to the Government of independent Nigeria.

It is necessary to understand some of the trouble and stresses of the past sixty years which affected the Tiv in order to appreciate some of the problems that the present rulers have to face. As the years pass and the old men die, stresses of this nature become weaker and weaker, but the tribe which has been so affected may be left floundering without faith or sheet anchor. In the past the cry of the old men was, 'The white man has spoiled the land'; what will they say today? It is only too easy for young, unscrupulous politicians to promise salvation; in the past the kaleidoscopic changes were all within the tribe, for or against the European rulers; today in a Federal State they may be replaced by demands for changes in regional boundaries; the unhappy Tiv, torn between many influences, may be the rock on which the Nigerian Federation will founder, and the cause lies in the circumstances in which their fathers first came in contact with the people of the plains outside the great forests of the Congo basin.

The first members of the Tiv tribe, the north-western extremity of the Bantu race of East and South Africa, arrived in Northern Nigeria some 150 years ago from the dense forests of the Congo basin out on to the relatively open plains around the Benue to the south of Wukari, the capital of the ancient Empire of Kororafa. The Tiv are another tribe with a very rudimentary social organization based on the extended family or kindred. All believe that they are the descendants of the original founder of the tribe who had two sons; these in turn had sons each of whom became head of a clan; their sons in turn headed the separate kindreds. On entry into the country where they now live, the Tiv came into contact with the alien modes of life not only of the Jukun of Wukari, but also Moslem Hausa such as the adventurer Dankoro, and other tribes such as the Chamba with a well-developed system of chieftainship. Before the tribe could be affected to the extent of completely accepting the system of any one of these other peoples, the European arrived, who not only had yet another kind of organization but did not accept all he found in the organizations of the others—to the further bewilderment of the Tiv.

Moreover, they were moving into a completely different physical environment from that which they had previously known, with horses and cattle for example, and corn and other kinds of foodstuffs which were unknown in the great forests of the Congo basin. In this latter area cannibalism existed until recently; not a ceremonial, fear-creating eating of human flesh but the prosaic eating of dead bodies because of the protein shortage in the available diet. To what extent the Tiv ever practised cannibalism is not known, but some of their neighbours in the Sonkwalla Hills to the south are said to have done so as recently as the 1940's; when anyone died, the body was taken to a certain spot on the boundary, a signal given to the neighbouring village, and in due course the word went round the latter, 'The butcher has called, go and get it'; the course of nature meant that eventually the debt would be paid back in kind but on occasion, it is said, when four, five or more banquets were unrequited, the first village would send over to urge that something should be done to liquidate the debt, possibly by hitting old Bill over the head—he obviously had not many days to see before he would appear naturally on the butcher's slab, and it would make matters easier all round if he were assisted on his way. It may be that the Tiv had long since abandoned the custom but had some tribal memory of the fact and some ceremonial in which pretended cannibalism played its part.

The Divine King of Wukari must have made a tremendous impression on them; he was not allowed to touch the ground with his bare feet for that would have brought disaster to the crops;

he held office only as long as he was young and healthy and so was ceremonially killed at the end of seven years in order to ensure that the divine essence of kingship should not be damaged by residence in a weak and failing vessel. The concept is difficult for us to understand; it was probably never understood by the Tiv. The Divine King, of necessity, had to be surrounded by a vast train of helpers who, in course of time, had received high-sounding titles and were surrounded by much pomp and ceremony. The wise men of the Jukun, generally older men, office holders and participants in the ceremonial of the court, in whose hands the real power lay as it was they who decided when the Divine King must die, remained in the background so that the common herd were unaware of their real standing. The whole organization must have appeared both awe-inspiring and attractive to the elders of the Tiv clans, and there is little wonder that they hastened to buy titles from Wukari as a first step towards knowledge of this new mystery, so that they could apply it to their own clansmen.

In earlier times the Tiv had only one system of marriage, that of exchange; before a man could marry he must produce a woman of his own clan, whether of his own generation or older or younger, to take the place in the other clan of the woman he married. This led to great stability of marriage; the women were secure from ill-treatment as there was a hostage in the other camp. It also played into the hands of the old men, for, as fathers of their families, it was they who said for whose benefit such and such a woman might be used in exchange, and to many of the younger men it appeared that they used too many of the pledges to obtain many wives for themselves. There were of course restrictions on such exchanges but they are too complex to be entered into here.

From contact with other tribes, the Tiv learnt that exchange marriage was practised only by themselves; others paid a bride-price or obtained a wife partly by payment, partly by working in the farms of the prospective father-in-law. It should be stressed that, whilst in these latter days, commercialism has entered into this field as it has into all others, the payment of bride-price is not the act of buying a wife in the way that in the past one bought a slave or today a horse. The Tiv bought slave wives from stranger communities with whom they came in contact but these 'bought' women were in quite a different category again from the free woman for whom a proper bride-price had been paid.

The Tiv are a litigious race and from all these methods of marriage endless cases were brought before the courts established by the white men; those which gave the greatest trouble were those based on exchange; the ramifications of an involved case were endless and might result in large numbers of women being forcefully removed from various households and returned to others (leaving their children behind) in order to straighten matters out. To the European this was repugnant in the extreme. Moreover, the younger men working for the European on railways and roads and thus easily obtaining money became whole-heartedly in favour of marriage by payment of bride-price; similarly the women, for not only did they advise their father or guardian not to accept payment from those whom they did not favour and only from the man they wanted, but once married they could obtain fair treatment from the husband by the threat, 'And if I run home to Father, he'll be in no hurry to repay you the bride-price.' Many of the adult men also looked on the system with favour; bride-price was the system of the surrounding peoples; many of the Tiv wanted it and it only.

In 1927 therefore, in answer to what appeared to be the general wish, the European Administration called the elders together and told them that they wanted them to drop exchange marriage, and the leaders of the clans were given a period of time in which to consult with their people. This gave rise to an example of the condition to which we have referred above; the old men, the rulers of the tribe, were against marriage by payment; the younger ones and most of the women were for it; the tribe was split with the elders anti-administration, and the younger of both sexes ready to support it against their elders.

At about the same time, the European Administration, looking at the considerable degree of over-population in the Tiv country and the vast empty wastes of bush around Kaduna whither the capital had been moved within the past ten years, conceived the idea that, were parties of Tiv taken to Kaduna to see for themselves, they would agree to move, for after all, were not the tribe recent immigrants into Nigeria? Such a move would relieve the pressure on the Tiv farms and would help feed the inhabitants of

the new capital. Had a concentrated effort been made to persuade
a large kindred to move *en masse*, success might have followed, but
to expect odd men and their households to move with men from
other, unrelated clans was unrealistic in the extreme. The result,
as anyone would have expected, at any rate a year or two later
when much attention had been given to the Tiv and much
knowledge obtained of their organization, was a complete failure.

Having failed to persuade, the Administration next decided to
exile one of the clan leaders who had been found guilty of many
wrongs, including the amassing of a vast number of wives, with
his personal household to Kaduna, hoping that this would lead
to those so moved eventually realizing the advantages of Kaduna
and agreeing to stay voluntarily. Once a Tiv village existed it was
hoped that others would join it of their own accord. To the Tiv
elders these completely unrelated actions were all part of a plan;
the European was against marriage by exchange and those who
stood in his way were exiled to a place where no men would go
willingly; better to agree than to suffer, so exchange marriage was
ended.

In the eighty years or so between the arrival of the Tiv in
Nigeria and the arrival of the white man, they had been brought,
as shown above, under the influence of different kinds of chieftainship, a concept foreign to their own clan organization. The
Wukari system, which to the Tiv appeared to be the setting up of
a figurehead with the real wielders of power in the background,
had many attractions for the older men—and of course for the
young one who was made into the figurehead chief, for the Tiv
had no conception of the necessity of ensuring the physical
strength of the Divine King by killing him at the end of seven
years. Simple and incredulous, the Tiv were also exploited by
other stranger communities on their boundaries; for payments of
various sums, these kind strangers sold them protective amulets
of different kinds and later they sold 'titles'.

Whilst therefore the elders kept much power and knowledge
in their hands, the years from 1820 until about 1920 saw many
kinds of 'chiefs' being created in the Tiv clans without destroying
the real power of the elders. These artificial chiefs, rather than
the true elders, were the ones brought to the attention of the
British and were first recognized as the rulers of the Tiv; they

it was who were responsible for many of the abuses of exchange marriage; it was one of these men who was exiled to Kaduna. But in societies such as the Tiv it is not 'vidth and visdom' that go together but age and wisdom, so that a man who might in the prime of life have been one of those put forward as a figurehead chief or who had bought a drum from Wukari, became, as the years passed, one of the elders and a power in the land in his own right, independent of his former puppet position or his purchased grandeur. A Tiv could understand this, a European never; so that not only was the tribe split over the marriage question but it became 'agin the Government' over the matter of chiefs. As the years passed, to many of the younger men, this ambiguity of power with the old men and younger figureheads recognized by the Administration contrasted unfavourably with the apparently powerful Emirs of the Hausa, and they began to demand such a paramount chief for themselves. The schism between older and younger generations became more and more complete and conditions more and more confused. The time had come for the elders to try and reassert their power and prestige, not only in the matter of 'exchange marriage' but in all aspects of their position as leaders of the clans.

As with that of so many other forest tribes, Tiv life is ridden by a multiplicity of charms, devils, benign spirits and the rest, with intermediaries between man and supernatural in the way of certain old wise men, who might be ignorantly called by the European 'witch-doctors'. To a certain extent all men of mature years have powers in this direction; all mature men possess what is known as 'tsav' except for a few men whom all know to be fools, who are 'empty-chested'.

So whilst the Tiv were torn asunder on the questions of marriage and chieftainship, all—men and women, elders and youths—believed in the power of the supernatural and all respected—and feared—those who possessed tsav—the 'Mba-tsav' as the Tiv called them. What then was more natural than that some of the elders should use the supernatural powers for which they were respected to try and bring the younger generations to heel in matters of temporal rule?

To attempt to explain more would only still further confuse the reader; to simplify: within a year of the abolition of exchange marriage it appeared to the European Administration that the Tiv were permeated by a powerful secret society called Mbatsav which apparently had a whole series of beastly ceremonies based on cannibalism—and it will now be seen why I referred above to the possibility that the Tiv did have some memory of such practices in the past. A mass hysteria seized the tribe and a reign of terror apparently held sway. It was said that the paraphernalia of the dread society included certain decorated human skulls—and such skulls were produced; human leg-bones made into a kind of 'bull roarer'—and such bones were produced; there were special ropes and hooks for dragging bodies from graves—and hooks were handed in; mats on which the bodies were cut up—and mats were produced, stained deep brown with gore; human skins were believed to be important—but none were found—and to the astonishment of the Administration the dark brown stains on the mats when analysed were always vegetable dyes, not blood, not even goat blood. The question arises: were they manufactured to meet the needs of the Administration threatening penalties if such trophies were not surrendered or were they part of ceremonial equipment to frighten the uninitiated, similar to that found amongst other primitive peoples?

The hunt was on and the mass hysteria increased; accusations of cannibalism were frequently made. On one occasion, one of the Administrative Officers trying to find out what was really happening heard a howling mob approaching his rest-house; on going out to see what was occurring he saw that at the head of the party was a man so tied up that he was scarcely alive. Two policemen rushed out, the man was freed and the most vociferous of his captors were asked the reason for the whole affair. It appeared from what they said that the captive had been caught eating human flesh; it was alleged that he had opened the grave of a newly dead man, had extracted the body with the hook, had cut it up on the mat, all in the 'traditional' manner—for so it appeared at this time. A grain of doubt existed in the District Officer's mind. 'Does anyone know this grave?' he asked, and when all there said they did, 'Lead me to it,' and with the accused tied securely by the arms and with two of the crowd carrying shovels, the procession set out for the scene of the alleged grave-robbery.

On the outskirts of a village they found a mound of newly

turned soil, which, however, gave no appearance of having been disturbed since it had first been filled in on the body beneath. Two helpers were set to work with the shovels; the hole was again excavated, and in due course the watchers saw unmistakable evidence that a corpse was indeed in the grave. Mastering his revulsion, the District Officer looked into the hole as the grave clothes were removed and there was a dead—a very dead—body, but one which showed clearly that it had neither been tampered with nor cut up. As this evidence sank into the minds of those surrounding the grave, a great roar went up and the crowd rushed at the accused. With great difficulty the European and his two police saved the unfortunate man's life; other help arrived and the people were quietened. 'Why on earth,' asked the District Officer, 'do you still want to kill him? You can see that the body has never been touched and that therefore he is innocent.'

'Innocent,' shouted the nearest in the crowd, 'why, he is even worse than we thought. Not only has he killed this man by witch-craft, not only did he take the body from the grave, not only did he cut it up, not only did he eat some of the parts of the body, but then, even though he was tied up by you and despite the fact that we were all watching him, he is so strong a wizard that he has replaced everything in the grave to make it look as if nothing had been touched. We thought he was wicked before, now we are certain of his great evil. Even to a European that must now be clear. Kill him'—and the crowd came on again.

The man's life was saved, but many others were accused of sorcery and it was said that as well as the bodies of those who died naturally being taken from the grave, numbers of otherwise healthy people were killed by witchcraft in order to maintain adequate supplies of the organs necessary to perform unspeakable ceremonies. Then almost as suddenly as it started, the whole madness passed and the Tiv became sensible again.

The Administration moved in specially selected officers to investigate all aspects of the life of the Tiv; their language is difficult but all the Administrative Officers who were posted there were ordered to learn it. (We count in tens; some people count in fives; the Tiv count one, two, three, four, five, two-threes, five-and-two, two-fours, five-and-four, ten—which gives some idea of the various influences which have affected them in their recent development.) A full investigation brought to light the true organization of the tribe, the clans and the kindreds which form them were recognized, and Native Authorities were set up, based not on an alien idea of chieftainship but on the council of elders of the clan. This work of reorganization was only completed in about 1937; three years later other officers claimed that there was a yet older indigenous organization which might be preferable to that recently set up; four years or so later again the Tiv surprised everyone by suddenly demanding that they should have a paramount chief, similar to an Emir, and an ex-sergeant-major of the Nigeria Regiment who by this time was the Chief of the Tiv Police was the unanimous selection.

The wheel had gone full circle; the last true Tiv organization—that discovered in the 1940's—might have been of value in the 1900's; that brought to light in the 1930's could also have been of inestimable value at that time. By 1945 the old men, the ones who in their youth had been impressed by the Jukun court and its ceremonial, were almost all dead. It was they who had been the supporters of what were known as the 'drum chiefs' of the early British Administration; when they had reached old age, the European had turned to their generation on which to build his resuscitation of the past, the new Native Authorities, the Councils of Elders; but they were too old, too affected by the events of the past thirty years, and too few to put back the clock. The men who had been young during the years of the mass hysteria were, in 1945, the sedate men of the tribe; large numbers of the Tiv had served in the army in the war; for the first time there was a generation of sedate men who had little faith in the resuscitated organization and a younger generation who wanted a supreme chief; the schism was no longer present, and a paramount chief emerged.

Fifteen years later the ballot-box was introduced and in the eyes of many of the younger generation of today, the paramount chief is an anachronism. What now lies ahead of the Tiv? Are they to become mere ballot-fodder of unscrupulous politicians? Only the future can tell, but in the Tiv lies one of the main possibilities of a rift in the Northern Region; if attempts are made to exploit that rift by parties hostile to the Fulani and Kanuri rulers of the Region the consequences may be grave not only for

Northern Nigeria but for the whole Federation and so for Africa.

What was the truth of the events in the late 1920's and early 1930's? Did the old men, in their attempts to reintroduce tribal discipline, really try to reintroduce cannibalism? Or was the whole paraphernalia of hooks, mats, skulls, and the rest merely an elaborate means of frightening the women and the younger men and maintaining the authority of the old men? If there are still some of the *Po'or* skulls and *Imborivungu* pipes available it would be interesting to have them dated by radioactive carbon or other modern and reasonably exact methods, to see if they are of the period of 1930, or very much older. The possibility exists that they are the skulls and bones of tribal elders of very long ago, carried on their long travels from some nodal point away in Central or East Africa through the Congo basin to the present home of the Tiv, carried to maintain a link between those of the tribe now on earth and those, the majority, who have passed to the Shades.

Although I have told the recent history of this tribe at some length, I have of necessity had to be superficial in dealing with their problems and have only been able to indicate the nature of the involved skein of religion, administration and marriage which is the social environment of a tribe like the Tiv. Many Europeans are surprised when they learn of the diversity of the peoples in the African countries; the problems of the Tiv are as involved and incomprehensible to some of the present leaders of Nigeria as they are to the European. Should a mass hysteria again afflict the Tiv, who knows what may happen?

On the other side of Africa, in the southern Sudan, are the Zande. When I visited them in 1951, I was astounded at their close physical resemblance to the Tiv; even their face-marks were not unlike and as both are Bantu, I could recognize some similarity in a few words I was able to compare. Both tribes may, at some not too far distant epoch, have sprung from the same nodal point in the northern part of the Congo basin, the Zande to move north-eastwards, the Tiv north-west. In the Sudan it is the Zande who have bitterly resisted the rule of the alien Moslem Arabs of the North; it is they who have taken a major part in the present armed rebellion which has reduced the southern Sudan to a battlefield. Meanwhile, in July 1964, political rioting in Gboko, the main town of the Tiv, has resulted in at least nine deaths. The omens are not good; patience and much sympathy are necessary in dealing with the Tiv, and an understanding of why they drift rudderless from one system of administration to another, unable to find an answer which will satisfy all members of the tribe.

Stocky, cheerful, hard-working, the Tiv retain the friendship of all who served with them. Exasperating on occasion, said to be the best and the worst recruits who joined the Nigeria Regiment, they produced a very high percentage of the company and battalion sergeant-majors in the years before the war; yet on one occasion during the war, they were alleged to have refused to continue until they had been issued with yams instead of rice. Perhaps here is the secret of their contentment.

CHAPTER TWELVE

Eighteen Months in Tivland

The headquarters of the Tiv Division were some miles away from Makurdi, at a new town called Gboko, and here I became the Assistant District Officer in charge of the Native Treasury and other chores which kept me in an office chair. But each month I managed to get in about ten days' trekking, generally on foot or on a bicycle, for the tsetse meant that there were no horses in the area; on one occasion I trekked down the Katsina Ala river, and spent most of one day in the water swimming between the two canoes carrying my boys and loads. There were no crocodiles to be afraid of, but one had to be careful wading in shallow water for there lurked what was known as the water scorpion, but is, I believe, a form of sting-ray. There were hippos and also manatees, both protected but both greatly in demand for food amongst the Tiv.

The Tiv were not as untouched by contact with the outside world as were the Gwoza Hills Pagans, but their patriarchal system and their clans and kindreds were not dissimilar. Payment of tax called for no direct action, and during the tax season caravans of elders would converge on Gboko carrying heavy loads of strings of pennies in respect of their respective kindreds. I did not like the idea of these elderly gentlemen arriving late at night with nowhere to place their burden for safety after the Treasury had closed, so I installed in my house four heavy cash tanks used for the transport of money, and late arrivals made their way to my bedroom to place their tax in my charge and to take the keys of the tanks away with them. The counting and custody of huge sums of pennies was an enormous labour, and as this was an area in which pennies were in over-supply, we received during the season orders from the Government Treasurer to send hundreds of pounds' worth to other places. It was an incredible fact that there were quite large numbers of both forged pennies and half-pennies in circulation, an interesting pointer to the low cost of labour in the area. In the late afternoon of Monday, 11 November

1940, I received a lorry with two messages, the first to dispatch by return several hundred pounds' worth of pennies, and the other to say that my first son had been born.

Whilst stationed at Gboko, I found some old papers, which had been lost for many years. I was alone in the station which consisted of four houses for the District Officer and three A.D.O.s strung out along a low ridge; away to the east, across a small stream, was another ridge on which had been built a capital town for the Tiv (on the model of Canberra, as it were), consisting of the Divisional Office and the offices of the Native Administration, the prison, police lines and the small but growing town of Gboko. At about five-thirty in the afternoon my boys called me as a big bush fire had been started in the valley between the two ridges and was rushing towards us through the dry grass. In a short time it swirled through the grass near my house, but did no damage to the house itself and I then went to see that the other three were also safe. This was the case; but I could see that the flames were now close to the Divisional Office; I ran down the hill and up the other side and arrived as the first sparks fell onto the thatched roof. The two men on guard had raised the alarm and already others were running from the police lines; I shouted to them to turn out twenty prisoners and then ran to help men climb onto the roof to beat out the flames which were beginning to appear. But the roof consisted of thatch fastened to mats over a frame of bamboos which rested on asbestos sheets, and the space between the thatch and the asbestos allowed the flames to spread rapidly; in a few minutes most of the roof was in flames and I concentrated on getting what I could out of the place; we rushed in and out; typewriters, files, paper, clock were saved; then I got the strongroom open and we carried out the money; one bag of halfpennies burst; as the last load came out the roof collapsed and a cloud of sparks went roaring up and the heat forced us many yards away.

A quarter of a mile away were the Native Administration offices. Many willing hands cleared one part of these, the N.A. strongroom was opened, in went the Government money and into the corner of the N.A. offices went tables and chairs and files. I had to hurry for the next day was to see the arrival of the Chief Commissioner—later the title was Governor—for Northern Nigeria, on an inspection; lamps were brought and by nine I had order out of chaos and had found these old files which had not been seen for years. (In a similar fire in another station some years before, it is said that as quick as the files were brought out through the front, the District Officer threw them in again from the back.)

So to bed, to be wakened at about midnight by an anxious District Officer and his companion, another A.D.O. They had returned from the Provincial Headquarters at Makurdi by car, having dined with our next-day guest, and on passing the Divisional Offices had seen nothing but a pile of glowing embers, whilst the crest of the ridge where were our houses was lined with fire, where bushes, trees and clumps of grass still smouldered.

'My God, the Tiv have revolted,' said one to the other. 'They've burnt the office down and there go our houses. Poor old Sam, I wonder where he is,' and they had come to seek my remains in the embers of my own house. Reassured at seeing the house standing, they were more reassured still when they saw me asleep in my bed on the veranda. A relieved party sat round my last few drops of whisky.

Next day all went well, and the Chief Commissioner was impressed with the sense of having the Divisional and Native Administration Offices in one and the same building, so that the District Officer could approximate to the position of clerk to a local authority in England; on his return to Kaduna he urged that the possibility of similar arrangements elsewhere should be pursued. When we came to check, the only things lost were the pendulum of the clock and twopence-halfpenny from the burst bag. Having been responsible for the money I had to replace the lost funds, but I received no thanks or congratulations for saving all the rest of the Government property.

Whilst serving in this Division I had to play my part in two human tragedies. On Empire Day 1941 we were called in to Makurdi, the Provincial Headquarters; war or no war, our Resident decided that this children's day should be observed in proper form. So in the morning there was a parade attended by all the Administrative Officers in full dress—white uniform and helmet, sword and all: doubtless a very brave sight. The parade over, the Resident sent for me and said I should have to leave at once for Katsina Ala, a one time Divisional headquarters where there was now a secondary school with a European Headmaster, and one member of the trading community, who had newly arrived there complete with a young wife and a baby born six weeks before in Lagos. This child must have been one of the first European children born in Nigeria—apart from those of missionaries—as until yellow fever had been tamed by the inoculation discovered at the outbreak of war by the Americans, no children were allowed. Word had come that the wife was ill with a temperature of 99 degrees; the doctor in Makurdi had two sick Europeans on his hands as well as a large native hospital but was uneasy about the girl; I was to go at once the fifty miles or so to Katsina Ala and send back if I thought the doctor was needed. I set off as soon as I had changed, called in at Gboko for some more kit and for my clinical thermometer, and reached the village of Utur on the west bank of the big unbridged river opposite Katsina Ala before dark. I crossed by canoe taking with me the driver of the lorry so that when I had decided what to do he could return to Makurdi with a message.

It was well after dark before we had covered the mile or two from the ferry to the rest-house, and I went at once to the house of the young trader. I introduced myself and he took me up the steps of his bungalow—which was on stilts—to his sitting-room. In a cot in the corner lay the first European child I had seen in Nigeria, fast asleep under a mosquito-net. From this room opened the bedroom, and when he went in to his wife carrying the pressure-lamp, I heard him tell her of my arrival, and a very weak voice ask where I came from, and if he had any food to give me. I had asked him about his wife's temperature and was horrified to find that he had been taking this by holding a cheap room-thermometer in her armpit: this had showed 99 degrees for several days; my clinical showed 103 degrees—and she had been this or more for the whole of this time. Leaving them and saying I would be back in the morning I sent off the driver at once with a letter to the doctor saying that I had not seen the woman, but that it appeared her temperature might well have been over 103 degrees for several days. I urged an immediate visit and promised to have the ferry ready for him on the far bank from nine o'clock onwards.

Next morning I found a very worried young man; his wife was delirious and appeared to have an even higher temperature;

leaving him I made my way down to the ferry and in a short time was delighted to see the doctor and the Education Officer arrive at the other bank. They crossed—and the latter went off to bed as he had started with fever on the road down. With the doctor I returned to the sick woman; in a few minutes he came out with a very grave face and called me to one side; she was dying and he suspected typhoid. A lorry was sent back and late that afternoon we got a microscope and he took blood counts at intervals. As dusk fell another member of the trading community arrived and taking advantage of his arrival, the doctor called me again to one side.

'I can do nothing here,' he said. 'I'm afraid she will not last out the evening; she is sinking fast. Get him out; say he needs a breath of air; take him up the hill to see how the Education Officer is, but don't let him come back here.'

Leaving the newly arrived trader at his Company's rest-house, I set off on foot with the young husband up the slight hill to where the secondary school was; arriving here we sat for some time with the Education Officer—he had an attack of fever but was not very ill—and then we set out in the dark for home. Outside the rest-houses we were met by the last arrival who insisted on us going in for a drink with him; I was resentful, but he managed to tell me out of the corner of his mouth: 'She is not yet dead; the doctor says for God's sake keep him out.'

What the young husband was thinking I do not know; but for me it was a ghastly evening, making jokes and conversation knowing that we were waiting for the doctor to arrive to say that all was over. At last we saw the light of the doctor's torch and he came slowly into the circle of our lamp. It was all over and a stunned young husband faced the fact that he was now a widower with a six-weeks-old child.

After the first frantic grief, we had to discuss the arrangements for the night. He must go back to the house to look after the baby; he must indeed sleep on the bed where his wife had just died. 'Please remove her before I go into the house,' he begged us. Leaving him with the other trader, the doctor and I went out into the dark; first we got a stretcher from the small dispensary—where incidentally they had several clinical thermometers which the unfortunate husband could have borrowed had he not had a fear of infection from them—and then proceeded to the house. Together we lifted the poor girl on to the stretcher and carried her still warm body downstairs. We placed stretcher and corpse in the dispensary whilst we got the husband back into the house and busied over the child. Next we got a message over the river for the lorry-driver to take to Makurdi to say the girl was dead, asking for a coffin and prayer-book, and to ask the missionaries at Mkar if they could send someone the next day to take the child. Then we consulted the Dispensary Attendant; he was a Hausa not a Tiv; I have told of the Mbatsav and their possible horrible ceremonies with dead bodies; if there were any truth in the stories, the body of a white person would be beyond price. The Dispensary Attendant agreed with me that the dispensary was not the place for a body—it might be taken during the night; we returned to the trading-station; the large stores in which produce was placed were empty; we put the body in one but hastily came back when the night watchman said, as he locked the doors, 'Look at the rats, they have smelt the corpse.'

Were the circumstances not so appallingly tragic, we might have been participants in some farce, dragging from place to place a stretcher on which lay the body of a young girl not two hours dead. There was only one solution; what with rats and potential Mbatsav, the stretcher and body could only be safe in one place, in our rest-house, and the only space there was at the foot of our beds.

Next morning, I marked out the grave in the little graveyard where there were already three others, and set men to work. When I returned to the rest-house, the doctor said 'I must conduct a post-mortem and you will have to help,'—so, for the first and only time in my life, I helped at the autopsy. From the inside of the stomach cavity was cut out a length of the lower intestine, which when slit open revealed large red patches each the size of a five-shilling piece.

'Typhoid, I was right,' said the doctor. We covered the body with a mosquito-net to keep the flies away from infection which they could carry to our food, and had breakfast.

Others now started to arrive: first the senior member of the firm to which the bereaved husband belonged; he sat enjoying the breakfast we gave him until, in answer to his question, we told him that the mosquito-net behind him covered the corpse; he left to sit under a tree in the compound, unable to eat more. Then the Sanitary Superintendent with the coffin; we placed the body in it. Next came two members of the mission: one a lady to take the baby, the other instead of the prayer-book for which I had asked from which to conduct the burial service, to do it himself. They brought wreaths; we made others and I lined the bottom of the grave with the red petals of bouganvillæa.

When all was ready the doctor and I went to see the young widower to ask him if he wished to see his wife's face again; he lay on the bed with his arms clasped under his head. He was very quiet; we told him what we had done and how everything was ready and he thanked us; the lady missionary had already left with the baby and was in one of the traders' rest-houses; he lay without moving and then said, 'I shall not come with you; I cannot look at her again; leave me.' The doctor looked at me and I at him. 'Ka ji Hausa?' he asked the young widower. 'Do you understand Hausa?'—but the latter looked at him without understanding. Turning to me the doctor said in Hausa, 'Go and ask his boy if he has a revolver and if he knows where it is.' A startled boy confirmed what we feared: it was in the bedroom in an unlocked chest near the bed. I told the doctor in Hausa, and added, 'Watch him, and I'll get it.' I crossed the room, and said, as I removed the revolver, 'Forgive me for doing this, but we can take no chances and in a few years' time you will thank me.' I slipped the revolver in my pocket and when we were outside removed the six rounds which were in it.

The Education Officer was too ill to attend, so the two traders, the doctor and myself, the Sanitary Superintendent and the missionary were the only mourners. The coffin was lowered into the grave and the doctor and I stayed with the Sanitary Superintendent to fill it in. I handed the empty revolver to the senior member of the widower's firm, and told him to keep it for a few months. The grave filled, the Sanitary Superintendent left and the doctor and I sat on the low wall looking at the new heap of soil.

'What a bloody business,' he said. 'Had she come in to Makurdi when she first went ill she might now be alive. But fancy letting a young girl like that come to a place like this without her typhoid inoculations. How foolish can people be?'

148

A town-house in Kano

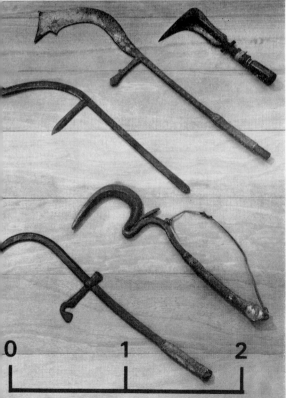

These handbills, in the author's possession, are among the most murderous of African weapons of war. The two at the bottom are from the Gwoza area

D.O. on tour—Young Africa poses a question

Education in the North. A Kano *Mallam* with his class

The Emir of Kano in council

The author's is the only cheerful face at a tax announcement gathering

▷

Court Jester, Nigerian style

Dogarai in armour

The Emir of Kano

The Emir of Gwandu

D.O.'s tea-party—a familiar scene in an exotic setting

Bush D.O. and household

We sat and talked: of other similar funerals; of the famous one in a tin-mining area where the deceased, a veteran of the First World War had been too large for the coffins in the store of the Public Works Department, and how one had had to be made out of a packing-case. Of the look on the officiating clergyman's face when as the body was lowered into the grave, the medals of the deceased and the Union Jack were whisked off the coffin to reveal its obvious origin with THIS SIDE UP and STOW AWAY FROM BOILERS stencilled on its sides.

The baby was taken away that afternoon; we sat and talked and drank until late with the widower; next morning he left for Makurdi with the other two traders; the doctor also; I went up to the school to see the Education Officer to ask him to watch that the grave was not tampered with—I suggested that he keep the wreaths on the grave as long as a stick lasted, as the Tiv would be certain to think that they were strong witchcraft of some kind.

A few weeks later as I sat alone in the station at Gboko, a lorry drew up at my house at about eight in the evening and out of it came a Yoruba man of about my own age, followed by a woman of the same race. 'I am Doctor So-and-so,' he said, 'and this is my wife. I have been sent to take over the hospital at Wukari but when I got to the Katsina Ala river, I was told that I could not be ferried over until daylight; there was no furniture in the rest-house, so I came back here.'

In addition to the four houses of the Administrative Staff there were a couple of rest-houses in Gboko. All six buildings were basically similar—cement floors, brick walls, thatched roof and steel-framed windows. None contained a stick of furniture and we Administrative Officers lived with our trek loads of camp-bed, camp-tables and so on. One or two went to the trouble of getting curtains; generally we did not bother; a few native mats on the floor and home was complete—it was far preferable to a tent. My visitor had thought that here in Gboko he would find a furnished rest-house with beds, linen, tables and so on, and was very down in the mouth when I told him that the accommodation in Gboko differed in no way from that at the ferry. I gave them a drink whilst the boys got some dinner ready, and over dinner I advised them to return in their lorry to the river, so as to be able to cross first thing next day. But my guest would not agree.

149

Before they departed next day, I gave them breakfast and learnt a lot about my guest. He was a Yoruba—one of the great nation which comprises most of the population of the Western Region and of Lagos the capital. He had started life as a clerk, then gone to England to study and qualify. His knowledge of Nigeria was confined to Lagos and one or two of the larger Yoruba towns; it was far less than my own, and he was far less fitted to face a trip into bush than any newly arrived cadet in the Administrative Service straight from England. He had no idea of the conditions under which he would live; I told him that at Wukari was one European D.O. famous for the fact that he walked round and round his veranda for an hour or two every day; there were the native Jukun, some Hausa traders, Ibo fishermen, and a very small community of five or six Government clerks and employees of the trading firms with their wives, one or two of whom might be Yoruba. I told them all this as gently as possible so that on arrival they would know what to expect. His wife looked at me from large eyes with obvious dismay; she had not been to England and had never in her life left Yoruba land. They were one of the most pathetic pairs of Innocents Abroad that I have ever met.

Four months later the wife was buried at Makurdi. She had been pregnant when they fed with me and at Wukari they found that the sole person with any similarity of outlook and civilization was the District Officer, and he, as I indicated above, was a bachelor set in his rather *outré* ways. The poor girl had fretted and fretted and at last was taken to Makurdi where she died. No disease had killed her, she had simply been killed by the loneliness of a bush station. The unfortunate English girl, buried at Katsina Ala, had been better able to face this than had the Yoruba.

After eighteen months' service in Tiv, I felt like leave; in peacetime our tours were of that period followed, for health reasons, by a leave in the United Kingdom of eighteen weeks; but because of the war this was now impossible, and we were urged to take three weeks' local leave at the end of eighteen months, as no one could say when we would get home on leave. At the end of 1941, therefore, I decided I wanted to leave my chair and to stretch my legs by a trek through the montainous country on the borders of Nigeria and the Cameroons.

150

As I stood at Katsina Ala on a clear day in the rains, from the south round to the east was a quadrant of magnificent mountains, the highest of which, over the border of what is now the Eastern Region, in the Sonkwalla hills, was almost 6,000 feet above sea-level. In the south-east was the hill called Swem, across in the Mandated Territory of the Cameroons, the holy hill of the Tiv, by which they swore, to which the spirits of the Mbatsav were supposed to fly on iron horses each night to hold ghostly conclave, and which was regarded as the umbilicus of the tribe, the nodal point after their wanderings across the Congo forests from which they had sprung. It is a commentary on the ridiculous way international affairs are run, that the 1900 boundary between British Nigeria and German Cameroons, drawn on a map in complete ignorance of the ethnology and native organization on the ground, and which by chance cut off the Tiv from this point of pilgrimage by about ten or twenty miles, has been perpetuated, so that the holy hill of the Tiv is now across an international border in another country. This was not the state of affairs in 1941 as the then Cameroons Province was administered by Nigeria.

It was not the best time of the year to go on a trek of this nature as the long grass had not yet been burnt; however, I left on 8 December on a lorry which was carrying payments to the various road gangs, for the small town of Obudu where, in peace-time, an A.D.O. of the Southern Nigerian service had his head-quarters; his house was empty but I had permission to spend the night there. I had brought no reading matter and I found a well-stocked library from which I borrowed a book called *Tsushima*, which, as I had nothing else with me, I read several times during the next sixteen days.

The following day, with the carriers I had brought from Gboko, I trekked some twelve miles to a place at the foot of the mountains, and the next day again, leaving my loads behind me, I set off up the hillside with some twenty-five local people to beat down the grass on the mountain-top, which they did in a very rapid manner; they were each armed with a heavy staff with a length of rope attached to either end; the rope was held in their hands while the staff was half thrown, half pressed by one foot on the grass, and the weight transferred on to that leg. With men doing this alternately on either side of the path, it was surprising how rapidly the grass was cleared from the track. This was not necessary at first, as the path ran steeply up through the high forest in deep shade. Emerging from the forest, my path-clearers got to work as we passed on to the grassy downland above; the path wound ever upwards, but crossing from time to time deep little valleys down which ran crystal-clear streams of pure water—for here we were far above human habitation. The mountains contain both gorilla and chimpanzee, and a number of leopard, but although I had brought a rifle, we saw nothing. Seeing that progress was better than expected, I sent back for all my loads, intending to sleep on the hilltop; but with the many languages in use, or possibly because my carriers had no intention of sleeping anywhere other than in a warm hut, only my lunch-box appeared, so at about 3 p.m. we cleared a space alongside a small stream where a rest-house had once been built, and I had my first food of the day.

Still expecting the other loads to arrive at any time I, my three boys, two of the Tiv carriers and half a dozen of the local people spent the night round large fires at about 4,800 feet, whilst the rest returned home. Next morning, these half-dozen cleared the way to the top of the mountain and we returned to where we had spent the night as the rest of my loads arrived. At the beginning of the rainy season the view from this top must be stupendous, but in December there was a heat-haze everywhere. I now paid off my locals from the foot of the hills—members of the tribe who were said at that time to eat human bodies as almost their sole form of protein—and after all, a human body cannot be very different from the two kinds of huge apes which they also ate—and with my Tiv carriers and three guides, made my way down the east side of the mountains.

During the next few days I wound up and down through most delightful country which had rarely been entered by Europeans as it was right away from the usual routes followed by A.D.O.s on tour; in time, and given communications, if the tree cover has not been destroyed, this area might become a holiday centre for Nigeria. We crossed the Cameroon border and entered the Mamfe division and on the 15th reached a village which was an anthropologist's paradise, for people here appeared to be doing all the things that one finds in the books. Beer was being brewed, a woman was making pots, children had cross-bows, and they played making string figures. My carriers were most truculent and I feared an outbreak of fighting, particularly when the beer-drinking started, so next morning I left at dawn and moved on. We now started to run across the grain of the country; at every mile or so we dropped precipitously down about 500 feet to cross some fast-flowing stream, often spanned by hammock bridges.

At last we came to the Moan river, on the farther side of which we knew there to be Tiv villages, and possibly as it was on the border between them and the other tribes to the south, the hammock bridge was in ruins. We had therefore to wade through chest-deep, swiftly flowing water; to get the loads over, four of us who could swim held hands to form a chain in the middle of the stream with others holding the hands of the end men; then each carrier in turn crossed with his load, pressed by the power of the current against our bodies. Up the other side, instead of the forest through which we had been travelling since we left the grassy tops of the Sonkwalla mountains, we entered an area where every tree had been destroyed by the Tiv. We were nearing the foot of Swem, and every house in the Tiv village we now entered was surrounded by *akombos*, which are pots and succulent plants forming, as it were, small shrines for the various spirits guarding the village. Every Tiv village has these, but nowhere had I seen such an abundance of them. When I asked for a guide to the foot of the mountain, I was met with complete ignorance—no one had ever heard of Swem, in any case the country in that direction was thick bush, there was an easy route back to Tiv land, and so on.

'Swem?' they said; 'never heard of it.'

'Oh, *Swem*—ah yes, our fathers have told us of it.'

'Near, oh no, many days away and we do not know the way.'

'Within sight in the rains? Really?'

and eventually:

'A guide; oh all right, anything to get rid of you, but we warn you, the last man who went to Swem died.'

During the night my carriers were got at and hair-raising tales were poured into their eager ears. To make matters worse, back in Gboko a meeting of the Central Council of the Tiv was being held, and my entourage knew that whilst the human forms of all the elders of the Tiv would meet by day with the European District Officer, at night their spirits would fly to discuss those parts of the agenda that really mattered on Swem. If in passing they saw below the forms of my apparently inquisitive and inter-fering carriers, they would no doubt show their displeasure at such an intrusion in the time-honoured way—sudden and terrible pains in the belly and all the limbs, followed in a short time by death.

I spent a long time persuading and ridiculing them; surely they, men who had seen the great world of Makurdi with its rail-ways and steamers on the river, were not going to be made laughing-stocks by bush-men who had never ventured from their village. What would the maidens of Gboko say when I spread the news of their cowardice, and so on. At last they agreed to go on, and with a guide we went some six miles to the first villages of the Iyon people—relatives of the Tiv. Here our guide left us, with a whole series of farewell messages to those at home from my carriers, in case their worst fears were realized.

The Iyon had many characteristics of the Tiv and also some of those of the neighbouring tribes to the south; the houses of their chief men had huge mounds near them surmounted with four horse-hooves and with young silk-cotton trees growing from stakes. These marked where horses, bought in the north, had been slowly beaten to death over several days, a horrible business but part of the religious beliefs of these people.

A few miles beyond the Iyon village we met a party of men working at clearing new farmland, and we were addressed in Hausa; these were members of a village of the Bamenda people, who had been here five years, seeking new lands, away from their overcrowded villages. The complete change of dress, ornament and house-building was remarkable; their houses were two-storied and they were cultivating rice and coconuts which they had brought with them. Their presence had been resented by the Tiv, for some of the Bamenda who could speak Hausa came and spoke to me without reserve. Apparently the senior elder of the nearest Tiv clan had sent to say that they must leave as the smoke of their fires hindered the Mbatsav on their flights to Swem; when they refused, a messenger came appealing to them, on the 'old boy' basis, to keep their women at home and not to allow them to wander far from the village for there are certain things no woman, no matter of which tribe, should ever see.

It occurred to me that this request might be due to genuine

journeys on foot, not by spectral steed, to the foot of the mountain by Tiv elders, but my informants either could not or would
not tell me more. But there was the mountain, and by three in
the afternoon nearly all of my Tiv were hidden in a house from
which they did not stir till the sun was well up next day.

At dawn the next day, with my cook, a Bamenda man, and two
Tiv, one of whom was a Christian, we tried to climb the hill; but
now I had no team to press down the grass; there were no paths,
and we tried to make our way up a stream-bed. Our guide was
another Duke of Plaza-Toro, for he was in the rear, encouraging
our climb with tales of what would happen if we were caught on
the mountainside in the dark, with spectral visitors not only of the
Tiv, but from the Obudu, Utangè, Ndiri and Iyon tribes, to all
of whom Swem was holy. At about one in the afternoon our stream
died out; we were in tall grass, and about 1,000 feet, as far as I
could judge, from the summit; we were tired and in rags. We
turned back and reached the village as dark fell. Judging from
what I had seen on the Sonkwalla mountain, it would be best to
try and climb this hill from the east, not the west, and after the
grass had been burnt. We were in no shape to try again, so to the
delight of my carriers, next day we turned northwards and reached
the northward-flowing Tunga valley, a place as beautiful as many
of the best parts of East Africa and easily the most lovely I had
seen in Nigeria. From the 22nd until the 26th I wandered through
country well known to District Officers from Wukari, and on the
26th reached Takum where there was a relatively large European
mission station.

Invited to dinner, I was for some time completely stunned with
the news they gave me; I had left on the day of the attack on
Pearl Harbor and for seventeen days had been unaware of the
fact. During this time I had read several times the book I had
brought from Obudu, telling the story of the end of an earlier
fleet at the hands of the Japanese, in 1904 at the great battle of
Tsushima. Why of all the books in Obudu something had made
me borrow that one, we could not say; 'perhaps,' said my host,
'you have *tsav*, and can pick up the vibrations of happenings
elsewhere.'

Had I but thought to have borrowed one of the model iron
horses!

Kano

CHAPTER THIRTEEN

The Walled City

With the entry of Japan into the war, the whole tempo of life in Nigeria changed and the rationing of foodstuffs, petrol and motor spares required more and more staff. My organization, in a matter of a few hours, of a new office after the old had been burnt down had impressed the Chief Commissioner; a man was wanted to get these controls going in Kano, the great trading centre of the north; I appeared to have organizing ability, so on my return from Swem I was transferred to Kano in January 1942. I was sorry to leave the Tiv for I had grown to like and respect them, but I was glad to get back to the arid north and recover from a friend my horse Njaro, left behind when I left Zaria for the Cameroons in November 1939. His stable-mate, Shegin Miye, had passed from my ownership, for when I left Zaria I had sold him. His name meant 'the bastard of Miye' for it was at that town that I had bought him; although a wonderful ride, he was a savage beast; to mount or dismount was not easy, for Shegi had his ears back, and either lashed out with his hind feet or came round biting. Once one was mounted, he strode out at a most comfortable walk approaching six miles an hour, and was easily the best pony I ever had for long trekking. On one occasion he got his horse-boy's arm and carried him for about twenty yards shaking him like a cat with a sparrow but without breaking the bone; on another occasion, when both I and Kamkura had fever, Njaro threw the horse-boy who was riding him on exercise and disappeared; when dark fell, Shegi went nearly mad at the non-appearance of his bed-mate and managed to break two of the posts supporting the roof of the hut which was their stable, and we had to leave our beds of fever to rescue him from the mass of thatch which fell over him. His new owner had him gelded, but this had no effect, and Shegi ended his days at Enugu where, when any newly arrived subaltern from England boasted of his riding and hunting, he was invited to ride Shegin Miye. His owner was said to have regained many times over the amount he had paid me by taking bets as to how long it would take each new arrival to mount and, once on, how long he would stay on. He was a grand horse but useless for polo.

A traveller from Bornu moving westwards and keeping to the north of the Pagan belt, first crosses the lands which were the marches of the old Bornu Empire, and then comes to the country of the Hausas. Hausa is a language, not a tribe, and there are many Hausa-speaking tribes of whom the Kebbawa in the far west of Nigeria are the most important. Why tribe became subordinated to language is not known, but in about A.D. 1000 several great city states of the Hausa-speaking peoples came into existence of which the greatest was, and still is, Kano. Its fame became known in Europe in the Middle Ages but its resemblance to Ghano or Ghana, a state of the Middle Niger area, led to confusion as to its true position. We do not know as yet who were the founders of this great city.

In Kano itself, one tradition is that the earliest inhabitants were a race of blacksmiths called the Abagayawa of whom there are still descendants within the city today, pursuing their ancestors' craft. The tradition in Bornu on the other hand is that the founders of Kano were the giant Sau of whom I have written earlier, and another of the Kano traditions is that the founder was a giant called Dalla, who worshipped a snake in the sacred grove surrounding a stream at the foot of the hill bearing his name. Those who have visited the great market in the middle of Kano and seen the evil-smelling drain down the centre will have some difficulty in believing that this open sewer was once a limpid stream on whose banks grew a sacred grove in which the ancient rites of snake-worship were carried on. Yet such appears to have been the case.

Kano today spreads far beyond its great walls, which are about twelve miles in circumference. Within the space encompassed by the walls there are two low hills, that nearer the market being called Dalla, at whose feet ran the sacred stream, the Jakara. Standing on either this or the other, called Goron Dutse, one can see away to the north and west several other similar hills, and it is presumably the presence of the Jakara stream which led to the first settlement, as apart from the stream there appears to be nothing to distinguish the site of Kano from a dozen others.

Neolithic remains have been found throughout this northern part of Nigeria, so the possibility exists that Kano is another Jericho built on a very ancient foundation; perhaps one day some Nigerian archaeologist will be able to unravel the early history of this fascinating town and relate it to the history of the Sau towns in Bornu which also await excavation.

Despite the many oral traditions, we have no certain idea of the date of the foundation of the town. In an earlier chapter I wrote that the arrival of the first Kanuri in Bornu, about the tenth century A.D., led to the emigration to the south and west of the Jukons, who had arrived some hundreds of years earlier. Some of the people moving from Bornu at this time, settled in Kano, where they found an earlier settlement but we do not know exactly who these emigrants were, whether earlier inhabitants of Bornu or members of the Jukon racial wave. It is said that they introduced the horse into Nigeria but this appears to be unlikely at that very late date. This wave of immigrants appears to have found a people not only in Kano but also in Daura to the north, who had some form of snake-worship, for, in true fairy-tale tradition, one of the handsome strangers from the east killed the great snake of Daura and married the lovely princess of the town who had been held in thrall by it. The happy pair had seven sons who, tradition says, each founded one of the great city states of the Hausa, and the first ruler whose name appears in one of the written histories of Kano is Bagoda, grandson of the serpent-killer, who succeeded to the throne of Kano in A.D. 999.

Kano and the other Hausa city states lay on the marches of three Empires, that of Bornu to the east, Kororafa to the south and Kebbawa to the west. Kano probably attained its greatest power at the time of Mohammed Rumfa in 1463–99, in whose reign arrived the first Mohammedan missionaries, though it is probable that for many years earlier there had been Moslems in the country. Ibn Battuta, the great North African traveller who was born in 1304 and died in about 1369, who travelled widely in Asia and Africa, never penetrated to the Hausa country though he was very close to it at Gao on the Niger. During his travels around Timbuktu he was in a Moslem state with Pagans, possibly cannibals to the south, and this pattern probably existed across Hausaland and Bornu at the same date.

161

Following the death of Mohammed Rumfa, Kano was conquered by the Kebbawa of the west and remained subject to them for about a hundred years, to be followed for a like period by the Jukons from Kororafa. In about 1730 they in turn were driven out and Kano became tributary to Bornu. The people of Kano were traders not empire-builders, and their trade continued no matter who ruled.

From the beginning of the thirteenth century there had been arriving from the west members of the nomadic Fulani tribe with their great herds of cattle. These nomads settled happily amongst the hard-working Hausa-speaking farmers and many of them adopted the settled life of the latter. These settled Fulani became largely Moslem whilst their nomad brothers mostly remained Pagan, but the two sections retained their tribal loyalties. By the beginning of the nineteenth century there were five Fulani clans present in considerable numbers in the vicinity of Kano, and to their ears in 1804 came the news of the revolt of their brothers under Shehu Uthman dan Fodio against the Hausa rulers of Gobir to the north-west. Three years later, the Kano Fulani chose a certain Dan Zabua, chief of the Daneji clan, to visit Sokoto and find out just what was happening; in due course he returned with a flag to which to rally the Faithful and a commission to revolt against the Hausa ruler of Kano—who as far as can be ascertained had a better claim to the title of Faithful than the majority of the Fulani herdsmen. Be that as it may, fighting broke out, but the Fulani clans acted independently of one another at first, with the not unnatural result that they got the worst of the exchanges. Combining together at last, at Dan Yahaya some twenty-five miles north of Kano, their forces were attacked by Alwali, the Hausa ruler of Kano, with an army of 10,000 mounted men, with men and horses protected against the arrows of their assailants by chain-mail and quilted cotton armour. The battle lasted three days and was decided less by any religious fervour on either side than by the archery of the Fulani, who broke the power of the Kano cavalry with their steady hail of arrows. This Nigerian battle of Hastings ended with the flight of Alwali—a flight in deadly earnest and not just a stratagem to get the Fulani ranks to break; he was killed shortly afterwards to the south of the town.

162

The Fulani sent the news of their success to Sokoto and asked that one of their number be appointed Emir; but, probably to prevent the rivalry of the five clans breaking out in open warfare, instead of one of their leaders, an inferior named Suleimanu was appointed to rule, and he died ten years later after a reign devoid of incident. In 1825 Bornu invaded, but was driven back, whilst in 1844 the still independent Hausa rulers to the north and west tried to drive out the Fulani upstarts who had seized so many of their ancient kingdoms, but without success.

Clapperton and Barth both visited this great trading centre of the Sudan, and Barth's description of the great market near to the foot of Dalla Hill is, except in one respect, little dissimilar from what can be seen today. He wrote on his first visit in February 1851:

Here a row of shops filled with articles of native and foreign produce, with buyers and sellers in every variety of figure, complexion and dress, yet all intent upon their little gain, endeavouring to cheat each other; there a large shed, like a hurdle, full of half-naked, half-starved slaves torn from their native homes, from their wives or husbands, from their children or parents, arranged in rows like cattle and staring desperately upon the buyers, anxiously watching into whose hands it should be their destiny to fall. In another part were to be seen all the necessaries of life, the wealthy buying the most palatable things for his table, the poor stopping and looking greedily upon a handful of grain; here a rich governor dressed in silk and gaudy clothes, mounted upon a spirited and richly caparisoned horse, and followed by a host of idle insolent slaves.

The last great change in the Government of Kano came with the arrival of the white man. Lugard was appointed Governor at Lokoja as we have seen. Nineteen hundred was largely a year of marking time as, just when everything was ready to advance northwards, the Ashanti War—in the present Ghana—drew off as many men of the West African Frontier Force as could be spared, with the result that Lugard's men had to confine their activity to the country south of the two rivers. Even here progress was not without setbacks; one of the best of Lugard's civilians, Carnegie, was shot with a poisoned arrow in the thigh, and died in convulsions begging for someone to take his revolver and end his agony. His small escort fought like demons to bring out his body, a fight that lasted for over two hours and cost three of them severe wounds.

In 1901, the return of the troops from Ashanti allowed the forward progress of government to be restarted. A small force marched on Kontagora, consisting of two companies of the West African Frontier Force with two Maxims and two quick-firing 75-mm. guns. Approaching Kontagora, they were attacked by a force of about 400 horse and 5,000 foot. These were still the days of the small British square, but for two or three minutes matters were touch and go, as the troops, many of whom were having their first baptism of fire and who could see that they were hopelessly outnumbered, forgot all the training they had received. Things looked black, and order was only restored by the British officers running up and down the line hitting up the rifles as unaimed and ragged fire broke out. Control was regained just in time; volleys rang out and the untrained opponents fled.

In 1902, a column marched on Bauchi and Bornu and occupied this vast tract of country, whilst in the same year, in Keffi, a Moslem outpost on the borders of the Tiv country and a great centre of slave-raiding, the new Resident, Captain Moloney, went alone into the town to try and persuade the right-hand man of the ailing Emir that resistance was useless. As with others of the Administrative Service, Moloney paid for his efforts to prevent bloodshed with his life; his killer fled to Kano. Here he was welcomed as a hero. 'If such a small place as Keffi can do so much, what cannot Kano do?' was the comment. In May 1902 Lugard received an Arabic letter from the Sultan of Sokoto which read:

From us to you. I do not consent that anyone from you should ever dwell with us. I will never agree with you. I will have nothing ever to do with you. Between us and you there are no dealings except as between Mussulmans and Unbelievers, War, as God Almighty has enjoined on us. There is no power or strength save in God on high.

This with salutations.

War could not be avoided, so in 1903 Lugard ordered the march on Kano of a force of 722 rank and file and some 38 Europeans. Lugard in his report for the year comments on the fact that many of the troops bore the distinguishing names of Kano,

Katsina or Sokoto, yet they were as eager as the rest of his small force. As it was feared that the men available would not suffice, some 300 reserves were ordered up from Lagos, but they were not required. Opposition was slight until Kano was reached, where the force was faced by walls thirty to fifty feet high, and about forty feet thick at the base, with a double ditch, and flanking towers at intervals. After a fruitless attempt to enter at one gate, a small breach was made at the next and a storming-party entered the city. Inside, resistance collapsed and in a short time the British party was master of this great city—the trading centre of the western Sudan. Lugard's description of the gaol is worth repeating.

A small doorway 2 feet 6 inches by 1 foot 6 inches gave access. The interior is divided by a thick mud wall with a similar hole through it, into two compartments each 17 feet by 7 feet and 11 feet high. This wall was pierced with holes at its base through which the legs of those sentenced to death were thrust up to the thigh, and they were left to be trodden on by the mass of other prisoners till they died of thirst and starvation. The place is entirely airtight and unventilated except for one small doorway, or rather hole, in the wall through which you creep. The total space inside is 2,618 cubic feet and at the time we took Kano 135 human beings were confined here each night.

In the next few months, Sokoto and Katsina were similarly captured and with them the effective occupation of Northern Nigeria was completed. At each place Lugard installed a member of the ruling house as Emir and in a letter of appointment promised amongst other matters that there would be no interference with the Moslem religion—a promise that evoked murmurs of delight from the crowd when it was read out at the installation, and a promise that was kept, even though Church interests in this country and in the United States violently opposed it. At Sokoto the then Sultan fled and another was installed in his place.

The ex-Sultan fled to the east and as he passed through the country between Kano and Zaria he was joined by many thousands. In Kano I found a number of old files which I saved from destruction and which were sent for safe custody to the Secretariat at Kaduna as these are the life-blood of history. Amongst them was one of 1903 containing a letter from F. Cargill, Resident of Kano, to the Resident of Sokoto Province:

Sir,

I enclose herewith a circular telegram which I have no code to decipher. I think it means that a force from Zungeru is going to attack the ex-Sultan of Sokoto who is now in force at Burmi.

Capt. Sword harried Attahiru as far as Messau, fighting six engagements with various parties of his followers. The people of the Chera district joined Attahiru *en masse*. After leaving Messau Capt. Sword was joined by the O.C. Bauchi and the combined force of 130 men, two Maxims and five white men continued the pursuit as far as Burmi. At Burmi there is a holy *Mallam* or *Mahdi*, who successfully intercepted our force. After a five-hours fight during which he twice got into the town, Capt. Sword was compelled to retire at night with sixty casualties including four killed and Sgt. Hayes severely and Capt. Plummer slightly wounded. The enemy lost 300 killed (verified) and the *Mallam* himself was wounded. Capt. Sword retired unmolested to Bauchi . . .

It was a pretty severe engagement in which almost half of the attacking force was killed or wounded. To complete this history, though it has nothing to do with Kano, on 27 July, Burmi was attacked with complete success. Major Marsh was killed and three other officers wounded; four soldiers and six carriers also died, and there were some seventy wounded. About 800 dead bodies lay round the town, and examination showed that they included the ex-Sultan, Moloney's murderer from Keffi and many more of the recalcitrant leaders of the country. The rest surrendered, and were either exiled or allowed to return home. As throughout its long history, the traders of Kano accepted their latest rulers with the same equanimity as they had accepted Bornu, Kororafa, Gobir and the Fulani and the opening of the Lagos–Kano railway set the final seal on Kano's economic importance. The years from 1903 to 1939 saw the annual growth of this great trading centre.

Amongst the old files that I found in Kano was one of some interest in view of the allegations of homosexuality which are levelled at Roger Casement. This file—which my Resident and I destroyed—recorded the trial for sodomy of one of the first European traders to arrive in Kano in the early days of this century. The evidence, recorded in sickening detail, was conclusive; there was no defence but the accused tried to excuse his actions by alleging that such activities were common amongst Government Officers, and were condoned as he well knew from his many years spent in the Oil Rivers before coming to Kano. The Court was unimpressed and he was sentenced to a term of imprisonment; he then asked for the facts of the case to be placed before the acting Governor, Temple, and he elaborated on his allegations. Temple was unmoved by the plea and was indeed highly indignant at the accusations against the members of the Government Service in the neighbouring Territory. Pending his removal to some prison in the south where a European could serve his sentence, the prisoner was confined in the small European hospital—consisting of a couple of rooms only—and the morning after he had been told that Temple refused to intervene, he was found dead alongside a broken poison cupboard. It appears incredible that this possibility had not been foreseen; someone, perhaps the Medical Orderly, had had compassion on his shame.

Was there some truth in the allegations? Was sodomy a common failing amongst Europeans in the Oil Rivers Protectorate at the end of the last century? Roger Casement served there until 1895; perhaps those who have been refused access to his diaries may find the clues they seek in papers in the old Foreign Office Archives referring to those who served 'on the West Coast in the earlies'.

After the fall of France in 1940, Governor Eboué, the West Indian Governor of Chad, had declared for de Gaulle, an example followed by the other colonies that formed French Equatorial Africa. But French West Africa and the territories along the Mediterranean did not follow suit, although a number of both European and African members of the military forces and Civil Administration of Niger Colony deserted and fled to Nigeria, many of them helped by the redoubtable Father Charles, a French missionary of great repute who had spent nearly thirty years first in Kano, then in the Zinder-Agades area. With the closing of the Mediterranean to our shipping, the airfields from the port of Takoradi on the Gold Coast, which led through Nigeria, Chad and the Sudan to Egypt became the only route by which thousands of planes could reach the battlefields of the Middle East. After the attack on Russia this route was followed by a number of high-ranking Russian and Polish officers making their way via Persia and Egypt to Great Britain. My arrival in Kano coincided with

167

that of the first members of the U.S.A.A.F. to prepare the way for the great American bombers winging from the States, via Ascension and West Africa to Egypt, India and China. This air route had therefore become, by January 1942, of considerable strategic importance and a German attack on the northern fields could not be ruled out; a second line of fields was therefore started in the south of the country, at Makurdi and Yola on the Benue, and we heard rumours of another line still farther south through the Congo, for on these life-lines depended the strength of the R.A.F. in the Middle East.

The aerodrome at Kano had a considerable R.A.F. contingent; the U.S.A.A.F. were starting to pour in—and to show that Pearl Harbor could not happen twice, they arrived armed to the teeth and moved round Kano with loaded revolvers at hip. Near the town was a Free French detachment in light tanks; not far off a brigade of Belgian Congo troops (large numbers of whom deserted when a year later they were moved home) and two brigades of Nigerian troops. There was a supply mission for the Free French force which had started to move north from Fort Lamy across the desert towards Mourzuk in the Fezzan, part of the Italian Colony of Libya, a force which linked up eventually with the Eighth Army moving west from Egypt. This force, when it started from Fort Lamy, was already over 500 miles from its railhead at Kano, and every mile north took it farther away and made its supply more difficult, so that the members of the mission in Kano looked to me to help them with tyres, lorry spares and the loan of lorries themselves.

At the end of January it appeared that our worst fears were about to be realized, for a plane appeared over Fort Lamy, circled once or twice, and then destroyed the main petrol dumps and other stores lying on the open plain. The chief result was that we had hastily to introduce the whole paraphernalia of blackouts and air-raid precautions; an impossible task with a town like Kano. On one of the first A.R.P. exercises, an ambulance carrying 'casualties' to the African Hospital in the city, stuck in the gateway through the ancient thirty-foot-thick walls, so a new, wide motor passage was made through the wall alongside the old gate. Four days after that exercise, large numbers of the inhabitants of the town left their houses and went to the villages around, returning the next day; some were questioned, as it appeared possible that they had received news from some source or other of an impending raid. One grey-beard replied, 'Lord, when the canoes-of-the-sky first started to come weekly from the land of the Europeans, we were told they took four days on the journey; when therefore you warned me that some had left to bomb us we waited until they were close before we left the town. Have we not done right?'

More serious than the raid on Fort Lamy was the fact that the printing-presses for the currency of French Equatorial were in Paris, in German hands. They were now turned on at full pressure and in the markets of Niger, north of Nigeria, notes were sold at a great discount for Nigerian money; the purchasers then made their way through Nigeria to Chad or the Cameroons, and bought cattle which they brought back to Nigeria; the trade in currency had to be stopped or Eboué might find himself faced with a hostile African peasantry with its faith in both its currency and its Government destroyed. Great efforts were therefore made to stop this trade and some spectacular hauls resulted, but others were less spectacular: one day a man arrived at my office, sent by the District Head of Dambarta to the Emir and by the Emir to me. It appeared that this man had been caught at Kassala in the Sudan by the Italians, on his return journey from Mecca in late 1940. He and other pilgrims from Nigeria had had to hand over their West African currency and in return had been given the notes which the returned pilgrim now handed to me. I opened the bundle and found that I held not French Equatorial francs but magnificent pre-1914 high-value mark notes, with the figure of Germania.

Later in the war, one of the Kano traders told me that he had accepted from an American airman some English banknotes; would I confirm that they were five- and ten-pound notes. Again fine pieces of paper appeared—five- and ten-yuan notes of the National Farmers Bank of China—worth about threehalfpence each as far as we could make out.

The success of the 'James Bond' stories underlines the fact that at heart large numbers of us are still small boys; but when these dreamers-of-cloak-and-dagger-and-blood-and-thunder-adventures are placed in positions of authority with money actually to spend on such matters, the results can be laughable rather than thrilling. Before and after the First World War such efforts in Nigeria were directed towards the discovery of *Mahdis*, 'Messengers of the Prophet', organizing Holy Wars against the Government of the Unbelievers: one or two very successful careers were founded in this way. By 1930, the obvious absence of any *Mahdi* led to the bottom falling out of that market, and in its place some desultory efforts were directed towards discovering what the French were up to in Zinder and Agades and Fort Lamy and the other centres not far from the borders of Nigeria. It was of course quite simple to visit any of these centres openly and indeed to ask one's French host what troops there were in the place; this was too easy, so a sum of about twenty pounds was made available each year to the Resident of each of the frontier Provinces to use on the employment of male agents to obtain this information. One such Resident, faced with the offer of information by an Arab woman who claimed to be straight from the still warm bed of the French C.O. in Fort Lamy, sent a code telegram asking to what head and item her services should be charged. The reply, in an open telegram, read: HEAD 34 ITEM 65. A glance at the estimates showed this to be *Upkeep of amenities in out-stations*.

From June 1940 until November 1942, Nigeria actually had on its western and northern boundaries a hostile government; the cloak-and-dagger experts really came into their own and whilst it is untrue that they wore the flash *Secret Service* on their shoulders (it was in the Gold Coast that this occurred) everyone knew what they were up to; not that this discouraged them from making supposedly secret journeys or entering their houses after dark when no one could observe their movements; perhaps more Edgar Wallace than Fleming. One, to the astonishment of all, donned Hausa dress and made his way through the streets of Kano to sit, in the character of a beggar, unobserved against the wall of the house of one of the leading men, who was believed to be in the pay of the French. Thus disguised he hoped to be able to see who entered and left the house, but as he made his painful way through the streets—for he was unused to wearing sandals made from old motor-tyres—he was greeted on all sides by the surprised but still polite Hausa peasantry, with the usual salutation *'Sanu Bature,'* 'Greetings, O European'; he ended this charade in some indignation, when the suspect, who had a sense of humour, approached him and dropped two-tenths of a penny at his feet with a call to God to lighten the afflictions of the sufferer—employing the Hausa phrase used in polite circles in respect of those who are mentally unbalanced.

In addition to the large profits that currency smuggling made possible, even larger ones could now be obtained from the sale of information; the house in Kano used as the Headquarters of this new espionage service became known to everyone as 'The House of Secrets': its occupants paid well for information received; it was not long before word went forth that these new Europeans paid by the size of the lie; to swear that one had seen ten tanks at such and such a place brought in a much greater payment than if one said one only. Moreover, after being paid, it was desirable to lend verisimilitude to the next lie, by actually visiting Niger, and there too it appeared that good money could be earned by selling the French bogus information about matters Nigerian. So certain wise men spent several months in 1942 trekking up and down between Zinder and Kano, to be closeted secretly in turn with the Europeans in these two strange establishments.

In 1943 I went over the boundary with a Forestry Officer who for a time had been with the British establishment and we lunched with a Corsican officer not far from Zinder. Our host had been in the area in the French Intelligence in 1942 and the two compared their memories of what each had found out about the other; neither appeared to bear much resemblance to what had in fact been the truth. One very large tank, for example, which had occasioned much perturbation in Kano was actually, we learnt, a road-roller encased in plywood.

With the concentration of troops in the Kano area, foodstuffs had become both scarce and dear and the Kano Native Administration had to introduce a system of requisitioning in the south of the Emirate in order to release the supplies of corn so obtained, together with maize and cassava flour from Southern Nigeria, on the market of Kano. This became another of my jobs, and I went out to organize supplies in the districts, and with the Madaki, the District Head of Kano City, organized the sale of our daily quota in the great market where Barth had seen the slaves waiting to be sold. To control the crowds, we built a long narrow passageway of stout timbers, leading to several points where a measure of corn was poured out on payment of the exact sum; the crowds would gather well before dawn to get as close as they could to the passageway. I would arrive at about six as would the Madaki, and we would then order everyone in sight to sit down. Those already in the passageway were supplied, and we would point to groups of twenty or so at a time to scuttle across the space cleared by the supply of the first-comers, to take their places. So long as we maintained an open space between the head of the passageway and the waiting crowds, we could control the hungry mob: if we did not, a fighting horde burst over us.

As I was a European, my heart had been wrung by the sight of old women, the halt, lame, blind and leprous caught up in these crowds and trampled underfoot when they got out of control, and at first I would call them out and get them served. Within a day or two every handicapped person within miles of the city had been cajoled and bribed to come to act as corn-obtainer for some family. We never had enough corn for everyone, but at least our supplies helped. As a result I obtained a new nickname (every European was known by his nickname) and became known as Baturen Hatsi, the 'European with the corn', and as long as I stayed in Kano I was so known.

The great market of Kano and the palace of the Emir are little changed from Barth's day, and it fell to my lot to take many distinguished visitors round the former. I knew many of the regular traders by name and as they knew that I generally brought them a customer I was a welcome visitor to their stalls. On those of the vendors of clothes, amongst the most interesting specimens were the camel-wool blankets brought to Kano by the Tuareg of the desert. These blankets consisted of strips of woven material sewn together, each strip being about nine inches wide, and embroidered with intricate designs in black and red in the form of diamonds and crosses, said to be the last memorial of the time when this desert-living tribe was Christian. Many were the distinguished visitors who left carrying one of these.

Others were interested in the silver coins of which large numbers are always available. Some of these were French and Italian coins of the period from about 1850 to 1914, but one coin that never failed to excite comment was the Maria Theresa dollar bearing the date 1780. During the middle part of the war, when Kano was an important staging-point for American planes *en route* to India and Burma, their crews were keen to find some suitable memento of their overnight stay. Before long the word had passed along the line of communications that if diligent search were made in the market at Kano, genuine antique coins could be found; in a short time too, the word circulated round Kano that these strange Americans would pay not the usual two or three shillings for a dollar but up to a pound or even two or more, if, and this was the important point, they were allowed themselves to find one hidden in a pile of French and Italian coins. Not for the Hausa traders to ponder over the strange behaviour of this latest tribe of the white man. As all could see, they were immediately suspicious if they saw a pile composed solely of dollars and would not buy one, but were filled with delight if they were allowed to pursue their strange game of search to victory. So the Maria Theresa dollars disappeared from the fronts of the stalls, and were hidden behind. Two or three Americans would arrive, and after much search would find their booty; they would pay perhaps two pounds and, as they left, another coin would be produced and hidden in the same pile in time for the next party.

The Maria Theresa dollar has been used as currency in parts of the lands bordering the Red Sea and particularly in Abyssinia since 1780, and it has also been common in Bornu and Hausaland. For some reason or other, at a very early stage of their use, it was found that the one date only was acceptable—any other being rejected. The mint was, until the First World War, in Vienna, and in 1916, following their usual custom, the Abyssinian Government dispatched to Vienna a ton or two of silver bars and old worn coins for the Austrians to mint into shining new dollars. But the road was no longer open; the silver was sent on to England and the Abyssinians were told that we could carry out the order. In due course the new coins arrived back in Addis Ababa—to be indignantly rejected, as they all bore the date 1916. Explanations had to be given, and the whole consignment was reminted, but it is said that one of the rarest collectors' pieces is an Austrian Maria Theresa dollar made in England for use in Abyssinia bearing the date 1916.

In Bornu it is believed, despite the fact that traders get them from the banks still individually wrapped in tissue paper and boxed in twenties as they come from the mint, that they all fell in one miraculous shower at Mecca. They are no longer used as currency in Nigeria but either for ornament or as a source of silver for melting down to make rings and necklaces. The fact that there was no demand for them as currency was apparently unknown to the War Office as at an early stage in the war, several million were sent to Nigeria. They spent the war in a strongroom and were then sold off to one of the banks.

Prior to the arrival of the Americans, no one had ever descended on the great market of Kano without either spending some time in the country or arriving accompanied by someone who had lived long in Nigeria. But the members of the American Army Air Force came direct from the States to the strange medieval atmosphere of Kano; they were on their way to war and were careless with their money. One old grey-beard friend of mine was a dealer in leather goods, saddles and bridles with their gaudy trappings, swords and daggers in leather scabbards and small wallets made out of the cut-off ends of half-tanned goat- or lizard-skins, crudely cut and thonged round the edges. These were sold to those who had lived some time in the country for a shilling or so; to others the first asking price was twice that amount and the final price depended on the patience of the purchaser and the time available for bargaining. One day early in 1942 a small group of strange white men wandered slowly through the market, stopping and admiring from time to time the goods on offer. They stopped at the stall of my friend to admire his colourful goods, particularly the swords with their great tassels of red and green wool. They were interested and spoke amongst themselves and then regretfully replaced the goods they had handled; one squatted and picked up one of the wallets and turned it over in his hands.

'Sule biyar,' said my old friend, seeing that they had no guide with them who knew better, and extended the five fingers of his right hand. The stranger turned the wallet slowly over in his hands and held it up to show it to one of his companions; then he drew a roll of currency notes from his pocket and threw a Nigerian ten-shilling note to the seller and walked away admiring his purchase.

'*Wallahi*,' the old man wailed to me, 'by God I was a fool; now I am the laughing-stock of my companions in the leather workers' guild. I asked five shillings and he gave me ten without question; would that I had asked a pound.' I was unsympathetic, but his grief evaporated when I told him that this was but the first advance party of many thousands. Word soon went round, and when future groups of American servicemen made their way slowly round the great market, a score of dirty hands thrust wallets in their faces: 'Ver' cheap, fifteen shillings,' was now the cry. The months passed, the faces of the traders became wreathed not only in smiles but in unaccustomed rolls of fat as they prospered on this unexpected harvest.

And not only they, but many others as well; wealth beyond the dreams of avarice was apparently at the disposal of these Americans; they rarely queried the price first asked, and those stationed at Kano adorned their rooms with bridles and bits, swords and daggers, ostrich eggs, and indeed anything that the great market offered. They paid to be photographed on the animals of the area, and soon at the gates of the American base a keen Yoruba photographer had set up in partnership with a Hausa donkey-owner; their clientele were photographed on camels, on donkeys, on horses almost invisible behind the masses of trappings with which they were bedecked; in some cases the cost of their mounts was recovered by the enterprising pair in one morning.

But Christmas of 1942 saw the finest *coup*, which earned the equivalent of the Salesman's Oscar of Kano for old Alhaji Ibrahim dan Aluwa who by this time had become a supplier of poultry to the Americans. The tale came to my ears by roundabout ways, and I heard the end before the beginning and from many mouths. Had Alhaji Ibrahim ever told the full story it would have been in the following form.

For some months he had supplied the Americans with meat and eggs, not only for their own use in Kano but to ship out by plane, particularly to a place which they called 'Accra G.C.' As Christmas approached he told the American victualling officer with whom he dealt that if he wanted any turkeys he must take action quickly for the English ate them all each year. The American gave no immediate answer but a few days later asked if Ibrahim could supply four hundred live birds for the following Wednesday. 'By God,' said Ibrahim, 'you have but to command and it will be done.'

'And look here,' said the American, 'I shall only pay you the price that the English judge has laid down for a live turkey. I find that I've been giving you twice and three times what I should have done.'

Alhaji's son looked at his father with some disquiet when the latter told him of the order. 'Master of our House, how shall we obtain four hundred live turkeys? I doubt if there are as many in Kano and Katsina combined. We can never buy them all, and if we try the price will rise.'

'Wait my son,' replied his father happily; 'God will provide.'

The following Wednesday his son drove him to the American base in the old car which they had now acquired, and after greeting his friend the old man sat down on the floor of his office.

'Turkeys—have you brought them four hundred birds I wanted?'

'*Zaki,*' said the old man, using the Hausa word of salutation but carrying on the rest of the conversation in the English he had quickly learnt, 'Lion; they are outside; I got the best in the market and they only are fit for you; pay me what you will, for I know you are just.'

'Threepence a pound live weight is what the Local Authority has laid down; I'll pay you that and not a penny more.'

'Threepence, but I paid sixpence in order to get them, then I had to pay the man who killed them and dressed them . . .'

'Killed them and dressed them, but I told you I wanted them live,' said the American. 'We Americans don't eat turkeys at Christmas like the English; I was wanting the birds to keep, to eat one by one.'

'*Wallahi,*' wailed Ibrahim. 'Surely my Lord is in error; dressed you said to me. I swear by everything we hold holy that my Lord you are in error; dressed you said.'

'There's no ice-box here big enough to hold four hundred turkeys. They have at Accra G.C.; there's a plane due through today. I'll send them a signal to ask if they can take them.'

Ibrahim rose with dignity and went outside to wait.

'My father, have they refused to take them?' asked his son anxiously.

'Nay, it is just as I said would happen; here they cannot keep them, but they will be glad to take them to that other base of theirs. Wait, my son.' And the old man squatted in the shade and told his beads.

In half an hour, shortly after a great plane had landed, he was summoned again to the office.

'Let me see those birds,' said the American, and the first box of beautifully dressed carcasses was placed before him, covered with a spotless white cloth.

'*Wallahi*,' said the old man, 'I have slept not since yesterday preparing these birds; they are ready for eating, my Lord.'

'They're a bit small, more like an old hen than a turkey,' said the American. 'Ten shillings each; the plane leaves in twenty minutes.'

'*Wallahi*, I cannot,' wailed the old man. 'Take them away,' he said to his son urging him from the room with his right hand whilst with his left he kept a close grip on the box. 'Lord, they cost me a pound each.'

'I asked for live birds, you brought dressed ones; you've robbed me a thousand times in the past; I'll give you two hundred and fifty pounds for the lot. Take it or leave it,' and the American took a big pile of notes from the safe behind him and waved them in front of Ibrahim.

The old man rocked backwards and forwards in his grief, wailing that in his attempts to help the war effort of the Allies, he had ruined not only himself—which did not matter, as he had but few years left—but also his son, and his son's son.

His grief was so great that the American's heart was touched. 'Two hundred and seventy-five pounds,' he said, and counted the notes on to the table. '*Zaki, Toron Giwa*,' said the old man, 'Lion, Bull Elephant, make it but three hundred pounds and I will die content. All right,' as the American gave no sign of yielding, 'two hundred and seventy-five pounds, and I am ruined.'

The boxes were whisked away into the waiting plane, and the American returned the rest of the notes to the safe.

'*Zaki*, you are a hard bargainer,' said the old man, 'and you have taken advantage of my error in killing the birds. Had I sold them to the British I would have received five hundred pounds. Master, add a little, even if but five pounds more.'

The American was adamant, and shaking his head and wailing a little from time to time, the old man made his way to where his son waited in the old car. Still clutching his notes and calling on the heavens and the onlookers to see how he had ruined himself in the cause of righteousness, he disappeared down the dusty road.

'Father,' said the son once they were out of sight of the aerodrome and the old man was purring with delight over his notes. 'Remember that it will be necessary to pay the Master of the Market twenty pounds to keep his mouth shut; and the Market Judge will require a like present; what too of the police? That is fifty pounds of your total, my father.'

'True my son; then I gave the man who caught the birds twenty pounds, and the two old women who plucked their feathers another ten pounds each, and the Cook of the Resident another ten pounds for dressing them. That is a hundred pounds of our profit gone.'

'Father, I think you should give the cook another twenty pounds lest he tell his Master.'

'True; I had hoped for three hundred pounds from this day's work, but we should thank God for this harvest; it has more than paid for the car.'

As I said, I only learnt this story from the end, for I might never have heard it had I not commented to the Market Master on the sudden diminution one day in the numbers of vultures in the market drains, picking away at carrion and human excrement; only his obvious embarrassment led to my pursuing the point.

CHAPTER FOURTEEN

The Hausa

I spent from January 1942 until May 1946 in Kano, taking leave twice during that time; the first of these coincided with the invasion of North Africa and the decision of French West Africa to follow the Allied cause. As this removed any threat to the airfields, the Congo troops—less their many deserters—went home, the French joined Le Clerc's column and the units of the Nigeria Regiment moved to the Western Provinces for training in jungle warfare before leaving for Burma. I became the District Officer Finance in the Kano Division, a post which, in addition to looking after the finances of what is the largest local administration in Nigeria, included being responsible for a survey and printing-works, and for the Kano prisons—the large Central prison, the Goron Dutse convict prison, a criminal lunatic asylum, a women's prison and a reformatory for boys, with a total population of over 1,600.

More and more posts were being created in the Secretariats in connection with some aspect or other of the war effort, no officers were being recruited, and the Nigeria Regiment hung on to every man it could get hold of. As a result touring officers pretty well disappeared. Kano Province had two divisions: Kano, consisting of the great Kano Emirate and the tiny independent emirate of Kazaure, and Northern, with the two emirates of Gumel and Hadeija, neither of which was very large. In peacetime the administrative staff for some two-and-a-half million people had numbered eleven or more. For about three months in 1944 we numbered five, and in addition to being in charge of Finance, I became touring officer Kazaure and District Officer, Northern Division. One weekend a month, I would leave for Kazaure about 3 p.m. on the Friday afternoon; it was only two hours away by road and I would devote the next morning to its office affairs and Treasury. On the Saturday evening I would trek away and spend Sunday and the Monday morning touring the area on horseback, returning to Kano in time for a late breakfast at about midday. A fortnight later I would go by train to Hadeija, have a day there, then to Gumel, the same there, and then back by train to Kano.

Kazaure was not an ancient emirate such as were Daura to the north and Kano to the south; it had been founded by a certain Dan Tunku, one of the Kano war chiefs at the time of the *Jihad*, who had set himself up as an independent chief in the area where Daura, Kano, Katsina and Gumel met; he made himself such a thorn in the sides of his neighbours that they had sent to Sokoto for someone to come and solve their problem by taking from each as small a portion as possible of their territory with which to placate this unruly man. This had been done, and a new town had been built at the foot of the small hills of Kazaure, to which had flocked the discontented and the injured from each of its larger neighbours. Their descendants had retained their spirit of independence and at the slightest injury or affront, men would 'go home' to the village in one of the neighbouring emirates from which their grandfather or great-grandfather had fled a hundred or more years before.

On one of my weekend visits to Kazaure, sitting outside the rest-house in the cool of the evening, I looked across the shallow valley to the walls of the town; outside these was the cemetery, and the rays of the setting sun illuminated a large number of new graves. The rest-house keeper was in the kitchen talking to my cook and I called for him; yes, there had been a number of deaths recently, many more than usual; no, it was not smallpox, but the disease which strikes every dry season—in other words, cerebro-spinal meningitis. I got into my ancient fifteen-year-old Ford kitcar and returned to the town; the Emir and his Waziri were called, and confirmed that there had been over twenty deaths and that several people were still lying ill and not expected to live. I was taken to the home of one, and by the light of a torch could make out a very sick man; for the next hour criers went round the town and we established that some fifteen men, women and children lay very ill. Down at the produce market outside the walls were some lorries ready to leave for Kano; on one of these I sent off a messenger reporting an outbreak of C.S.M. and asking for help.

The school was closed for some holiday, so next morning, with the dispensary attendant supervising their removal, we cleared the classrooms and brought into them the sick; two of these appeared to have little chance of survival as they were already arched backwards and were breathing with difficulty. About midday an African nurse arrived from Kano complete with a microscope and supplies of M and B; he took one look at the very sick and immediately gave them injections; from the others he took spinal fluid by means of a lumbar puncture, and examined each specimen under his microscope; in all cases he diagnosed cerebrospinal and the inoculations started at once. By nightfall we had another three or four new cases, but the first two he had treated were relaxed and sleeping. Leaving instructions for the thorough fumigation and disinfection of the school, I returned to Kano; in the event not one of those treated died, and when next I visited Kazaure there were no new graves to be seen as I sat taking my evening whisky. I reproached the Emir and the Town Head for not having taken action before I came. 'It was the will of God that they should die,' said the Emir. 'But all those who were ill when I went round the town are alive,' I protested. 'It was the will of God that *they* should live,' replied the Emir. 'So it was; God is great; praise be to God,' mumbled the others present.

With the end of the war in North Africa and the opening up of a line of communication along the southern shore of the Mediterranean, the usefulness of Kano Airport to the British war effort ceased (whilst it was still of importance for the supply of Forts and Super-Forts to India and China), so the number of convoys of fighters dwindled and eventually ended. However, before it did so, one day late in August 1943 saw the worst loss of planes suffered in a single day. A convoy consisted of six or eight Hurricanes or Spitfires escorted by a twin-engined bomber in which was a navigator, whose responsibility it was to get the convoy from airfield to airfield across Africa. The pilots of the fighters were a very mixed lot; many were men who had flown in the First World War, others young lads straight from flying school; they were of all nationalities: Poles, Norwegians, Frenchmen, Dutchmen, Yugoslavs, in addition to men from every white Dominion in the Empire.

On this particular day, a tremendous rainstorm swept in from the east at about 11 a.m. whilst three convoys were airborne north of the Niger making for Kano, and in a matter of minutes all radio contact was lost. At 11.30 the Officer Commanding rang up to say that he feared some planes would have been forced down; he was getting a rescue party ready, would I go in charge. I had had a couple of days' fever, so I went home, fed, and got my mosquito-net, quinine and blankets, and was ready to leave by noon. Meanwhile the R.A.F. were fitting up a four-wheel-drive lorry with a two-way radio, but it was after 4 p.m. before this was ready, with a set borrowed from the U.S.A.A.F. It reached me equipped with four coffins, the same number of stretchers, food and water, a driver, wireless-operator, medical orderly and a spare man—this despite the fact that the R.A.F. had two doctors on their staff at that time and the crashed men might be in need of medical care.

By this time, all the planes of two convoys had arrived after first touching down in ones and twos at airfields spread over 400 miles of ground, and of the third, the bomber and two of its charges had arrived safely. It appeared that this last convoy had been close to Kano when the rain squall hit it, and had flown north until it emerged out of the murk; by this time the navigator was lost, but over the Kazaure hills two of the fighter pilots, who knew the country, recognized their position, and, as petrol was getting low, turned back, flying at tree-top height along the motor-road to Kano. The others flew on until they saw an aerodrome below them with the word ZINDER for all to see; the navigator was now able to pinpoint his position and turned the convoy back for Kano, forgetting that the fighters were near the limit of their petrol. One pilot left the convoy and made his way back to Zinder, gliding in to the runway as his engine stopped.

Now there were five, and whilst four followed the bomber, the fifth saw the main Zinder–Daura–Kazaure–Kano road below him and decided to follow that. When his petrol ran out, he landed in a groundnut field alongside the road at Kazaure, got out, stopped a passing lorry and two hours later was in Kano. Alerted by the news of a crashed plane, the Emir of Kazaure and his Waziri rushed to the place by car; there was no sign of life and fearing that the pilot must be dead inside they set off down the road to

Kano to tell us. One by one the other four had crashed as their petrol ran out; the question was, where?—for the navigator had not pinpointed where each left the bomber, and by now nearly five hours had passed since they crashed.

By 5 p.m. I was at a point on the main road where a second dry-season track from Babura joined it. It appeared probable that the missing planes lay in the triangle of land between the two roads, and I had to decide which would bring me nearer to them. Various planes were flying overhead, and we now received a radio message to say that one plane had been spotted on the ground near the Babura road; then the radio broke down and I got no more messages. As dusk fell I was stopped by a messenger on the road to say that a plane lay a mile or so to the east , and when I got there on foot I found the local village head with most of his men around the plane. They had brought a roof and mats and erected a shelter; they had a roast chicken and groundnuts, water and milk, but the pilot had refused, despite all their signs, to leave his plane; he had not known, he told me, 'if the natives were friendly'. What more they could have done to show their feelings, I did not ask.

Darkness came, and we set off again; at about ten a man, attracted by the roar of our engine, dashed on to the road to say that a second plane lay nearby and the pilot was in the house of the village head of that area. In the entrance hall of the village head's house was my quarry; he too had been provided with a bed, a mosquito-net, a roast chicken and some tea; he had a bang on his forehead and was slightly concussed. We regained the lorry, and the medical orderly collapsed with fever. We put him on a stretcher with all the blankets we had on top of him, gave him a massive dose of quinine, and went slowly north. At midnight a horse messenger held up his hand to stop us and handed me a letter addressed to the O.C.R.A.F. Kano which I opened. 'Sir,' I read, 'I have the honour to report that I have crash-landed near a place called Babura.' Three in the bag, and three coffins no longer required. We could stop for the night—indeed we were near the banks of an unbridged river which stopped our further northward progress.

We therefore camped, and as my companions got the lorry ready to sleep in and brewed some tea, I wrote a couple of letters for the horseman to take straight back. I told the District Head to provide his guest with a horse and to bring him to me next day; I told the R.A.F. Officer to mount, not to drink anything but boiled water, and that he would reach me at noon. And so to bed. None of the others would sleep out; they told me next day that they had been afraid of lions and hyenas; so I took a stretcher, fixed up my net and, as the sick man needed my blankets, wrapped myself in my mackintosh and got onto it; it promptly split from end to end; so did a second, so I spent the night huddled below my net on the remains of the two stretchers.

Next morning the sick man was much better and we brewed tea and used tins of potatoes—to my horror—as a tripod round the fire to support a frying-pan in which tinned bacon was cooking. Overhead appeared a plane, which inspected us as we waved and then flew off. We stood up to be counted so the pilot must have seen I had two of the missing men; soon another plane arrived which dropped a packet on a small parachute. This contained a map marked with the position of each of the four planes; one was not far from Zinder and far beyond my possible aid. With it was a letter saying that, as they assumed my radio had packed up, there was enclosed a code with which I could show the pilot circling overhead how many pilots I had, whether I wanted a doctor, and whether I was stuck in my lorry, based on placing men in various positions round the lorry. This we did and for good measure gave a final signal of everyone in line with both thumbs extended heavenwards. A few minutes before twelve I crossed the flooded area by canoe to see the last of the trio approaching on horseback. On the way back my last pilot told us that at Babura the District Head had been accompanied by an English-speaking clerk from the sole canteen in the place, who addressed him, 'Welcome to Babura, sir'; he too had had the bed, net and roast chicken treatment, but in addition he had been asked if he would like a virgin with whom to while away the time until help arrived. The natives *were* friendly.

We set off for home with a plane coming over every half-hour to watch our progress and a little after five we reached the main road to find the O.C. and one of his doctors waiting for us. There was to be a big party in the mess, the last of the missing men having been flown in by the French an hour before, and I was the guest of honour. I was dog-tired and still off-colour from the effects of my fever, and I had not been impressed with the rescue efforts which had been mounted. I had however to attend, and before the coffins went back to store I was placed in one and carried in triumph round the mess. The navigator was court-martialled, but all the planes were recovered, repaired and sent on their way.

In an earlier chapter I have given Lugard's description of the prison in Kano that he saw in 1904. Forty years later we had erred, if anything, in the opposite direction, and when the near-famine in the area still further reduced food supplies in 1943, large numbers of men deserted their families, and committed some petty theft in order to obtain three or six months safety in my care. Every prisoner was seen on the Friday morning, when the Chief Alkali and I, and sometimes the Emir himself, toured the prison. I had the power to review every sentence that had been passed, but instead of exercising this power, which I always regarded as the ultimate sanction to be used on very rare occasions, I would tell the sentenced man of his rights of appeal. To deal with the large number of petty thieves I arranged with the Chief Alkali, a wise old man, that he would take these cases as if a formal appeal had been entered, and where it appeared that a family had been deserted the man would be lectured as to his responsibilities before having his sentence quashed and being returned home. In this way we kept numbers below 1,500.

The most distressing part of any large prison in Nigeria was the section where criminal lunatics were confined. It needed a strong stomach to visit this before breakfast on a Friday morning, as conditions were little different from those portrayed by Hogarth. Often naked, with matted hair and horrible vacant eyes, lying about in their own filth, there was little that anyone could do for them. To have to look after these people was both degrading and brutalizing to their warders and I was glad whenever death removed one of these unfortunates.

In Kano, amongst the score or so detained there, was one who had been a member of the Treasury Staff, and had apparently been a depressive maniac; the first signs of violence had occurred one morning when not only had he hit the sedate and rather frail

Treasurer over the head with a very large and heavy cash book, but he had then proceeded to tear up large quantities of files and other records. Violent, of that there was no doubt; mad, I sometimes wondered. On those days when he was lucid, it was a sad business to speak to him and give him the latest news of the Treasury. I arranged for him to be given sheets of paper and pencils but when violent he destroyed them all.

He reminded me of a certain Colonial Governor who also went mad; it is said that the first time this became apparent was when he left his train wearing only a bath towel to inspect a guard of honour of the local regiment drawn up awaiting his inspection. It is also said that he ended his days writting endless minutes to all and sundry, showing that there is no hard and fast boundary between sanity and madness but a slow imperceptible progression from one to the other. Some of his later minutes were no doubt as sensible as others written many years before; some of the latter as foolish, had anyone dared question him, as some of his last.

Hausa is a rich language and will never die as it is ever ready to absorb new words, as I first learnt in the Women's Prison when a warder referred to an inmate as a *'dambelo'*. In the First World War, Nigerian troops went overseas to the East African campaign and on the ships that carried them, they learnt the words 'down below' for the vast holds in which bunks had been knocked up for them. In due course they returned and a *dambelo* became a large barge on the Benue; next it was applied to the large store in which produce was kept on land before being transferred to the barge; lastly to a cheap prostitute who takes any number of men each night.

I once returned from an evening polo game to find one of the Kano warders awaiting me, with a message that certain prisoners refused to go to their cells until they had seen me. Still dressed in sweat-soaked polo gear, I drove the mile or so to the town and into the main reception hall of the prison. Squatting on one side were a dozen prisoners armed with brushes, shovels and head-pans in which to carry away rubbish. 'What's the meaning of this?' I asked. 'What are these men doing here, and why won't they go to their cells?' 'Master of the House,' said one of the prisoners, 'we have a complaint to bring to your ears and yours alone. You alone

186

will see justice done to us; you, Lion, Protector of the Poor, we have suffered; may I tell you our tale of hardship and ill-treatment?' I looked a bit astonished at this; from the warders surrounding the room came various little grunts of agreement with the speaker. This could only be serious; I sat down and told the speaker to continue.

'Master,' he said, 'we here with one other, that son of Eblis himself, Haruna Dambarta, were sent to the market this morning in charge of two warders, Mohammed Kano and Hussain Kazaure. We were sweeping the market as is our wont, when that deceiver Haruna Dambarta flung down his brush and fled. At once Mohammed Kano and Hussain Kazaure ran after him and we continued with our work. We swept the market as is our custom until the time of the afternoon prayer and no one had come to look after us. So we sat down and waited; still no one came, so as evening approached we returned to the prison. All day we have been out Master, all day we have sat in the heat of the sun waiting for someone to come for us. Then we have had to return unescorted to the prison. We have refused to go to our cells until we have brought this our complaint to you, our Father, protector of the weak. If this occurs again, we shall have no recourse save complaint to the Governor himself.' A murmur of agreement came not only from his fellows, but from the warders; in some way I was responsible; humbly I promised that such an untoward happening would be unknown in the future. Mollified at last, they agreed to go to their cells.

In due course one of the warders returned having chased the escapee for about fifteen miles; two days after this, the remaining warder returned triumphantly with his prisoner. But the matter did not end there; at the request of his fellow prisoners, Haruna Dambarta was assigned to jobs inside the prison and not allowed to accompany working parties outside; he had let the side down and was unfit to wear, if not the prison tie, at any rate the prison shirt in public.

I may perhaps end with an unsolicited testimonial not to me, but to the way that the Kano Prison appeared to one of the first local prison visitors who were appointed towards the end of 1943.

DAN BANA

FROM ALHAJI ALI NA ABBA,
VISITOR, KANO PRISONS,
C/O P.O. BOX NO. 99 KANO,
30 JUNE 1944.

THE RESIDENT, KANO.

Sir,

With reference to the District Officer Finance Kano's memorandum No. 5382/14 of the 15th January 1944, I have the honour to inform you that I have today completed my six months' tenure of office as a Visitor to Kano Central Prisons.

Throughout the whole period I exercised greatest care to detect any anomaly, but can assure you that there was no hitch whatever. The few repairs I suggested were speedily effected, and the place carries with it marks of cleanliness and tidiness. The latrines, gutters, bedrooms and the yard are all neatly kept and airy.

My respect goes to the D.O. Finance, Mr White, who has a blazing interest over his job. He is conscientious and painstaking, and possesses an indefatigable spirit. In short, no promotion would be too much for this omnivorous worker, and we should be thankful to see him elevated, as your honour knows that 'encouragement is a needed incentive to efficiency'. I could see that his present work is too far below his capabilities, and I am quite sure that if greater responsibilities were imposed on this industrious D.O., the Government would gain by it. By his side are the Madakin Kano and the Serikin Aiki who are as clever and duty-bent as this gallant Mr White. Their supervisory activities leave no room for criticism. Suffice it to say that the Prison House is a Paradise in miniature, and the Prisoners are cheerful and satisfied.

It may interest you to read the attached Testimonial (to be returned) which is a token of my good services to the Nigerian Railway Administration during the Managership of Mr Bland C.M.G.

To God's gracious Keeping I commend you,
I remain, Your Obedient Servant,
ALI NA ABBA.

The ruler of this great town and of the important emirate of which it is the centre, from 1926 until 1954, was Alhaji Abdullahi Bayero, a slow-spoken old gentleman who astonished us from time to time with his flashes of wit. An early member of the Nigerian Administration, later Sir Richmond Palmer, was the expert on the early history of all the lands west of the Red Sea. To those not so well versed as himself, some of the conclusions he drew from the similarities of names of places 1,000 or more miles apart, appeared at times to be a little far-fetched.

In 1944 or so, the Resident was giving a dinner-party for some visiting notable, a Governor or Resident Cabinet Minister, and amongst the guests were the Emir and two or three of his Councillors and myself. The Notable Visitor regaled us with his views on the course of the war, and I translated from time to time to the Emir. Fighting on the Russian front was at this stage of the war around Gomel, and in translating I carefully told the Emir 'Gomel is a place in Russia; he does not mean Gumel in the Northern Division.' The Emir looked at me with his very reflective eyes: 'I wonder if Mr Palmer has heard this news,' he remarked, 'and if he is trying to show now that the Russians are relatives of the Hausa?'

One of the most interesting evenings I spent with the Emir was in 1946, when, with the end of the war, our wives were at last able to join us. I had taken my wife and a New Zealand engineer and his wife some twenty-five miles to Wudil, where a great steel road-bridge crossed the dried-up bed of a river. On the far side was a plantation of trees which made a pleasant spot for a picnic. We enjoyed the coolness of a late afternoon and then, shortly after dark, started our return home. On the Kano side of the bridge was a country house of the Emir to which he could retire when he wanted a day or two free from the cares of state, and as I approached this I was stopped by a Kano Native Administration policeman. 'Mr Waayit,' he said in Hausa, 'the Emir is here and would be pleased if you would stay and have some tea with him.' The two New Zealanders were delighted, and in a short time we were sitting with the Emir drinking a little sweet tea by the light of a kerosene pressure lamp. I acted as interpreter between the Emir and the rest of the party and we told him how we too found Wudil a pleasant change from Kano. After some time, the Emir's interest in my companions ended and he started a long conversation with me, less a conversation than a thinking aloud on his part to a sympathetic listener, on some of the problems that beset him. He did not seek my advice, but my sympathy, as he told of his worries about his family, and how he wondered who would succeed him.

The Emir had several brothers and several sons; of the latter, the eldest, bearing the title of Chiroma, was in charge of the Central Offices of the Native Administration. Over the past two or three years there had been a number of near scandals involving the Chiroma; his house had been searched by the Nigerian Police looking for stolen property; there had been a theft of some £3,500 from the Treasury and the man responsible, the Cashier, had made a series of allegations against the Chiroma and members of the Central Office staff who were known to be his creatures. I had been a witness at the trial and I reassured the Emir that the Cashier had stolen this money for his own purposes and the Chiroma was guiltless. The Emir was unconvinced; one of the exhibits at the trial had been a piece of paper bearing the Emir's seal which was always in the custody of the Chiroma. On this point I had given evidence, and I was certain that I was correct, that the piece of paper had been cut from an old form on which the stamp had been placed quite legitimately. The Emir was only half reassured, but he turned to other half-hidden scandals of which he knew I was aware. How the Treasurer had found that at the Friday Mosque he had been seated next to the most notorious pickpocket in Kano and how he had sat throughout the prayers holding the keys of the strongroom, and how, to make quite certain, he, the Treasurer, had slept that night across the strongroom door. There was much more to the same effect and the Emir ended with a long sigh that he feared that after he was dead, either his son would never become the next Emir of Kano or would not stay long in that position. I respected his confidences but when in due course an annual return on the possible succession to the Emirship had to be sent to Kaduna, I told the Resident a small part of what the Emir had confided to me, with the result that when I typed the return, in place of the Chiroma who had been so shown for many years, we put the Emir's younger brother, the Galadima of Kano, District Head of Dawaki ta Kudu, as the most suitable successor.

In 1954 my old friend died; presumably the then powers that be carefully considered the records and saw the reversal that had been made, but in the event the Chiroma became Emir of Kano, and not only Emir for he was later knighted. That, however, was not the end of the story, as in April 1963 *The Times* carried the news that following an inquiry into the affairs of the Kano Native

Administration where large sums of money were said to have disappeared, the Emir, Alhaji Sir Muhammadu Sanusi, had resigned and the Governor had confirmed the appointment of his uncle, Alhaji Muhammadu Inuwa, Galadima of Kano, as the new Emir.

With the end of the war in Europe first plans for development in the post-war period began to be seen. First we had Walter Elliott and his Commission on Higher Education, one member of which, Mr Creech-Jones, got his first look on the spot at the problems he later dealt with as Colonial Secretary. Lord Swinton, the Resident Cabinet Minister in West Africa, had been a frequent visitor; now his staff included an Adviser on Development and the first incumbent, Mr Noel Hall, visited us. The Oil Seeds Commission sent to investigate the possibilities of boosting production to feed the starving peoples of Europe arrived; they were shown an area near Allaguerno in Bornu where, after the clearing of a little light bush, if the ploughs left at dawn, they must stop their furrows at noon in order to be back by nightfall. They agreed that the site was perfect and that groundnuts were a natural product of the area; they objected, however, that the single track Nigerian Railway and the congested ports could scarcely deal with the crop we already raised. Instead of sending for the men who had laid 'Pluto', who had conceived the artificial ports which made invasion possible, instead of sending for an engineer to advise on what could be done, they wrote us off and left for Tanganyika.

At half the cost of that scheme—of which nothing now remains —parts of the Nigerian railway could have been double-tracked, and the port extensions which were carried out in the next few years at least started; had this been done the Nigerian crop could have been raised in one year from 350,000 to 600,000 tons; moreover the use of chemical fertilizers was shown a few years later to double the yield in favourable conditions.

The Government Station in Kano was to the east of the great city, at a place called Nassarawa, where before the European occupation there had been a summer house of the Emir and others belonging to members of his Court. That of the Emir was still used by him; the others that had been in a better state of repair had been taken over by the early administration. Later, well-built cement houses had been built, but the District Officer, the District Office Finance and some of the other Government Officers still occupied the old mud palaces.

Margaret and I lived in Gidan dan Hausa, which contained a magnificent dining-hall, a small sitting-room and little else, and above two bedrooms and a doubtful bathroom. The walls were six feet or more thick, and even in the height of the hot season, the house was delightfully cool.

Missions of experts now started to come thick and fast, and we would be called upon, in the absence of any hotel, to accommodate a member. The Registrar of Oxford came with instructions to consult especially the younger members of the Administration, to obtain their views on the year's course which we had all taken at Oxford or Cambridge, on the wide range of subjects to which I referred earlier. These courses were to be restarted—for no one knew at that time that Independence was only fifteen years away. He slept in our guest wing with another junior District Officer.

Next came Elspeth Huxley, *en route* to East Africa to advise, after studying our efforts, on a translation and literature bureau. Gidan dan Hausa and the city of Kano appeared in her next book.

Meat mission, cotton mission, missions on this, that and the other: expert advice, but largely from well-meaning men who knew nothing about the country and who did not stay long enough to learn. It would be difficult to find any permanent memorial of their efforts and the money—and ink—spent on them.

Kano was a wonderful place in which to serve and we were lucky in our Resident, Commander Carrow, who had joined the Administrative Service after a distinguished naval career. He was respected by all, but was not noted for great patience or for sufferings fools gladly. There was a good social life, in that we could play polo and tennis; there was even a cinema and a club, and race meetings, where Njaro and I won one race. It was a good start for a newly arrived wife, and Margaret enjoyed life to the full.

With no prior warning, the phone rang one morning just before nine: I was to catch the midday train for Zaria and take over the Translation Bureau; the officer who would hand over was going on leave and I was to replace him for six months. 'And by the way,' came from the other end of the line, 'you will then go on leave and return for two tours to the Secretariat.'

Sorrowfully I wrote to Mr, now Sir, Douglas Veale, at Oxford, to tell him of the fate that had overtaken me. A week later, having returned to Kano to pack, we parted with High Force, a dun pony who had partnered Njaro at polo, sent off Garuba and Njaro by road, and finally, with many people at the station to say good-bye, left by train for Zaria.

Birnin Kebbi

Punishment Posting

Lugard had promised, when installing each Emir way back in 1903, that there would be no interference with the Moslem religion. That promise had been kept, and no mission station had been allowed in any part of the Moslem areas until, a few years before the war, a few medical centres were allowed, on the understanding that there would be no proselytizing. One result was that the missions had no schools, and that therefore all education was in the hands of the Native Administrations and the Nigerian Government; a further result of this was that there was no urge to teach the English language, and the local vernacular—Kanuri in Bornu, Hausa in Kano and in much of the rest of the North—was the language of instruction. This was probably a mistake in view of the sudden march to Independence for there was no possibility of translating the modern knowledge of the West into these vernaculars.

A small translation and literature bureau had been running for some years in Zaria, producing a weekly Hausa newspaper and a few simple school books. Now a grandiose scheme had been launched, costing well over £100,000, with the help of funds voted by the British Government under the Colonial Welfare and Development Act. I found half a dozen magnificent new stone and cement houses being built, a vast printing-works and so on.

Just before we left Kano, the first member of that Native Administration was sent, with the help of the British Council, to spend a period with the Penzance Council, where incidentally he made many friends and impressed all who met him with his ability. But the representative of the British Council in Lagos protested that no attempt had been made to introduce this Hausa to the elementary facts of English life; he had been taught nothing about our meals or such matters as push-and-pull sanitation. In Zaria we found a member of the staff of the Bureau preparing to go to London for a year to teach Hausa at the London School of

African and Oriental Languages; he too had had no instruction. Margaret and I therefore started a crash course for all members of the staff, inviting them in turn to dinner, where we served European food, and put as many knives, forks and spoons in as many different combinations as possible to give instruction and confidence.

Njaro and I now completed the second leg of the double recorded in the pages of *The Field*, by winning the event at the Victory Meeting in which we had been second at the Outbreak of War Meeting.

I was unhappy with what I found at the Gaskiya Corporation; to my mind, bearing in mind the almost complete absence of medical and other amenities in the greater part of the country, it was being started on much too grandiose a scale. It seemed to me a waste of money to install six monotype casting machines for a couple of weekly papers and for the very small number of books and pamphlets then available in Hausa. The cart was being put before the horse, and I had seen, in a new Hausa Dictionary produced by a member of the Administrative Service, a new and cheap method of reproducing typed matter by a photographic process. The Gaskiya Corporation was top-heavy on the printing side with expensive plant and methods which could not be justified for many years, and hopelessly weak on the preparation of books side. I wrote a report saying so, which was regarded as so important by the Administration of the Northern Region, that it was on the desk of the Chief Secretary in Lagos within ten days—an unheard-of record.

I received no acknowledgment or any other communication about this report—nor have I ever done so—and on leave, meeting my local Member of Parliament on matters unconnected with Nigeria, I incautiously told him of the gist of the report. Without telling me he was going to do so, he asked a question in Parliament, with the not unnatural result, that when I descended from the plane in Kano, the first person I met greeted me with, 'My God, you're in for it.' I was, at least by Secretariat standards.

The then Governor of Nigeria was Sir Arthur Richards, now Lord Milverton; a year or so earlier he had disturbed the entire Administrative Service by sending out a circular telling us that we must realize that promotion to the higher posts lay only through the Secretariats; the ability to deal with paper was apparently of much greater importance than the ability to deal with men. Two of us in Kano had asked that it be recorded in our files that neither of us wanted to be posted to the Secretariats, no matter what might be the effect on our careers. I had dared to speak to a Member of Parliament; I had dared to criticize what was one of Sir Arthur's pet schemes; I had shown myself unsuited for a Secretariat career; I must also be punished.

To Sir Arthur, it appeared, nothing could be worse than a posting to Gwandu Division in Sokoto Province, so to Gwandu I was to go. When I arrived in Sokoto, the Administrative Officers there were considering a protest to Kaduna, for Gwandu was the plum posting in Sokoto. Wherever it was, it suited me; like Brer Rabbit in the fable, a fable which sprang from bush in West Africa, I felt like singing: 'Born and bred in a briar patch, born and bred in bush Brer Richards.'

Birnin Kebbi was the administrative headquarters of the Gwandu Division, which consisted of the Gwandu Emirate, whose Emir resided at Birnin Kebbi, and the Yauri Emirate, a much smaller and older chiefdom with its headquarters at Yelwa on the River Niger, 130 miles to the south. The ruler of Yauri, although a follower of Gwandu, was not a Fulani, but the descendant of a sister of Queen Amina, the legendary ruler of Zaria some hundreds of years before. In Northern Nigeria, things are not 'as old as the hills' but 'from the time of the walled cities of Queen Amina'; and any old city wall is said to mark the site of one of the towns of this great Queen—a near contemporary of Queen Elizabeth I.

The Hausa word for Chief is Sarki, so the Emir of Gwandu's title is 'Sarkin Gwandu', but his capital is not the town of Gwandu after which he takes this title, but Birnin Kebbi, the 'Capital of the State of Kebbi'. Sarkin Gwandu, however, is not Sarkin Kebbi: there are several chiefs bearing the title 'Sarkin Kebbi' that is 'Chief of the Kebbi people', and in order that one may know of whom one is speaking, one refers to Sarkin Kebbi Argungu or Sarkin Kebbi Jega or some other town. The reason for all this apparent confusion—for of course none exists to the inhabitants themselves of this part of Nigeria—lies in the history of the Kebbi people.

The Kebbawa, to give them their true name, are Hausa-speaking and are claimed by some to be the original Hausa. Their origin is uncertain but is probably connected with the arrival in Bornu of the Kanuri in about A.D. 1000; the displacement they caused of other tribes, in a general southerly and westerly direction, has been referred to in earlier chapters, and the arrival of the Kebbawa into the area that now lies astride the boundary of Nigeria and Niger appears to have occurred about the end of the thirteenth century. As in other areas, they in turn caused the southward movement of the aboriginal people and from the hill called Duku which lies immediately to the south of Birnin Kebbi, they drove away farther south the inhabitants thereof; the descendants of the aboriginals, still called the Dukawa, are to be found on the borders of Yauri.

At the foot of Duku hill the Kebbawa built a new town: their capital, Birnin Kebbi. To the west of the town lies the wide valley of the river which runs from far to the east of Sokoto, in a great circle round that town and then southwards to join the Niger. This is now dry for much of the year, but during the rainy season it again fills, and canoes float and ply upon its surface; all the year round, at the foot of Duku hill, lies a deep pool, in which it is said lies the golden bark of one of the Kantas, the great chiefs of the Kebbawa. Here one of my predecessors as District Officer had kept a boat which he himself had built, in a small boathouse, in which he was able to submerge his treasure in order to prevent its timbers opening in the scorching sun. On one occasion, in company with the Emir of Gwandu, I was visiting one of the schools in the town; on such occasions I would try to excite an interest in their past, by asking the children about the history of their ancestors. I asked some such question, so did the Emir; I asked another, so did he, and the children delighted to answer us. 'And to whom did the boat belong which tradition says lies in the pool of Duku?' I asked; there was a moment's silence and then one of the brightest boys waved his answer: 'To Mr Weatherhead,' he said. The Emir and I carefully avoided each other's eyes but thereafter whenever we referred to this distinguished predecessor of mine, we always gave him his new honorific, 'Kanta Weatherhead'.

During the holy war of the Fulani led by Shehu Uthman dan

Fodio, against the Hausa, the warfare with Kebbi was bitter in the extreme, but the Kebbawa, although defeated on many occasions, retained their independence. Their capital was lost to Abdullahi, founder of the Gwandu dynasty, brother of Shehu Uthman dan Fodio, and has remained ever since the capital of the Emir of Gwandu. Until recently, when time had healed the scars of a hundred and fifty years ago, the Kebbi Emir of Argungu, to which place the capital of the independent Kebbi State was removed, would never sleep nor eat a meal in the old capital of his forebears. Some of those who take the title 'Sarkin Kebbi' are the descendants of Kebbi chiefs who, tiring at last of the long war, gave in and were confirmed in their posts by the Fulani; others, such as Sarkin Kebbi Jega, are descendants of Fulani war chiefs who killed one or other of the Kebbi chiefs and were rewarded with the title.

By 1817, when Uthman dan Fodio died, he was head of a great empire which, by Fulani custom, should next have been ruled by his younger brother, Abdullahi. But the dying leader had made a will, leaving the greater part of the empire, those emirates in the east, to his son Bello, and only a smaller part in the west to his brother. When these two next met, their followers prepared for war, but the elder man, Abdullahi, dismounted and greeted his nephew as his leader. Civil war had been averted, and since that date the Fulani inheritance has been that whilst most of the Emirs follow Sokoto directly, others follow Gwandu, the Emirate of Abdullahi, and through Gwandu, Sokoto.

The most famous of the descendants of Shehu Uthman dan Fodio was the late Prime Minister of Northern Nigeria, Alhaji Sir Ahmadu Bello, K.B.E., who gave in his book *My Life* not only the genealogical tree of the descendants of the Shehu, but also showed how the latter was descended from the Prophet himself.

The British occupation of the western part of Northern Nigeria was based on treaties concluded with the rulers of Gwandu and Sokoto. The first were signed by Mr Joseph Thomson, better known for his exploration of parts of East Africa, who in 1885 ascended the Niger and obtained his treaties without difficulty. By them the whole of the dual empire was placed, as far as relations with European powers were concerned, under the protection of Great Britain. In 1894, further treaties were signed between the

201

two states and the Royal Niger Company; that with Gando, as Gwandu was generally known, confirmed the earlier treaty; it stated that the Gwandu section of the empire included 'Ilorin and Gurma as far as Libtako'. Gurma is the country about 300 miles away to the south-west, south of the River Niger, immediately to the north of Ghana, and it became part of the French Colony of the Upper Volta. One District Head in Gwandu is still called 'Sarkin Dendi', Lord of the land of Dendi—that is the country on either side of the Niger west of the present Nigeria.

The coming of the British Administration brought peace at last to this part of the country, and the rulers of Sokoto and Gwandu, the senior and junior leaders of all the Fulani Emirs, are good friends of the descendant of their ancestor's enemy, Sarkin Kebbi Argungu. The Kebbawa were at last freed from the threat of constant war, but the treaties between France and Britain had split their country between Nigeria and Niger Colony. The inhabitants of the latter along the Nigerian border still recognize Sarkin Kebbi Argungu as their Chief, and, at any rate when I was in charge of the two divisions, still sent their customary gifts as a token of their fealty. Gwandu still claim that Gurma is theirs: this is yet another of the nonsensical boundaries which should be corrected, at least as far as the area north of the River Niger is concerned.

To be District Officer in charge of the Gwandu Division was one of the most pleasant posts to which any member of the Administration could be sent. Not from the point of view of climate or living conditions, however, and it was this perhaps which impressed Sir Arthur Richards. Birnin Kebbi is not only very hot, but, because of the presence of the old river, has also a very high humidity and a plague of mosquitoes. The District Officer's house had been condemned pre-1914, but no one had ever got around to making funds available for its replacement. Instead, some small additions had been made, and the dining-room had been mosquito-proofed; in the garden had been erected a framed room covered with mosquito gauze, and with a corrugated iron roof. In the dry season we slept on camp beds in the garden, in the open air under the stars; at dawn Margaret and I would arise, and armed with flit-guns adjourn to the bathroom and lavatory, using the flit-guns as required to have undisputed control of wherever we sat; she then spent most of the rest of the day in the dining-room, flit-gun to hand, and in the evening we and our guests sat in the cage in the garden until we came in to dinner, then out to the cage again and finally, after another visit to the 'usual offices' with our flit-guns, to bed under the stars.

Barth has written of these mosquitoes and tells how the inhabitants of this region prepared a *rudu*, a light hut on tall posts, into which they retired after lighting a smoky fire below; entering the hut through a hole in the floor, they sealed this by laying a mat over it and sleeping on top of it. Hermetically sealed, and with the smoke discouraging mosquitoes, they slept in comfort. Now the *rudu* has largely disappeared, for many have their own mosquito-nets, not to ward off malaria but simply to get a night's sleep; *rudus* are still to be seen, however, in every riverain village.

At the edge of the river-bed was a small garden and a pool of water about two and a half feet deep in which from time to time the small European community swam; during my sojourn none of us suffered any ill-effects from this pleasure but a year or two later all the Europeans in the station went down with bilharzia, a most unpleasant disease the cause of which spends its life partly in man and partly in a particular type of water snail. From the small irrigated patch we got each day a few vegetables and some fruit, which went far to vary our rather monotonous diet. I introduced a number of date trees from Bornu to test my theory that they should do well here and add to the food supply of the area.

The members of the Emir's Council were all intelligent, keen, and anxious to see the area developed. They and the Emir were frequent guests at our house for lunch or dinner, and on the rare occasions when a head of department or some other Government notable visited us, some of the Council would meet him over a meal. The Emir too introduced a cook, and from time to time we had delightful dinner-parties with him under the stars in the courtyard of his palace. For the junior staff of the Native Administration we had regular tea-parties held every fortnight under a shady tree in the compound.

In the Chiefly hierarchy of Northern Nigeria, the Sultan of Sokoto and the Shehu of Bornu are generally accepted as equals, though in recognition of the fact that most of the other Emirs recognize the Sultan as their superior, Sokoto takes some slight precedence over Bornu. Third in the list is the Emir of Gwandu as Head of the western section of the Fulani Empire. Inevitably however Kano, as Chief of the greatest trading centre and of the most populous emirate, and one, moreover, only 150 miles or so from Kaduna, the capital, had a place of great importance in the deliberations of the powers that be at the capital; of great importance too was the younger, educated Emir of Katsina. As a result therefore, the Emir of Gwandu, 400 miles away from Kaduna, tended to be forgotten and overlooked, yet it was in his emirate probably more than anywhere else, that the most desirable developments in local government were taking place.

Another factor that told perhaps against due weight being given to the views of the then Emir of Gwandu, was that in his youth he had wanted to become a Christian and had only been persuaded to remain Moslem by appeals to his patriotism on the part not only of his family and the Administration, but also on the part of the particular mission which had been responsible for his potential conversion. As a Christian he would have been unacceptable as Emir of this still fanatically Moslem area and his great talents would then have been lost to the Administration; it would have been impossible for him to stay in the area and his value would have been lost to the mission. From every worldly point of view it was better that he remained a Moslem; but this had erected some barrier, even if only slight, between him and his fellow Fulani Chiefs.

When I arrived in Birnin Kebbi, I was the only European, but in the next two months, not only did Margaret arrive, but also an A.D.O., a doctor, and a Development Officer and his wife. But before they arrived, I set off on a three weeks' trek mounted on Njaro in order to learn about the Division.

A climate such as that of West Africa is not conducive to the keeping of long diaries; by evening one is glad to sit back and rest, and replace some of the pints of liquid lost by sweating during the day. Even if one does keep a diary, there are the natural enemies of mildew, rats and white ants whilst, as much of one's time is spent in thatched buildings of one kind or another, the danger of fire is ever present. The documentation of the early days of British Administration is therefore scanty.

There may well be many private diaries in this country kept by officers in the past; a few, such as Vandeleur and Kisch, have written books about the period 1898–1908 and there are several other books of a later period. There are the quite astonishing annual reports of Lord Lugard for the years 1900–8, and from time to time, as I have related, I was able to locate various early official papers and diaries and put them in places of safety. On taking over the Gwandu Division I found to my surprise that despite the fact that pretty well every senior officer in the administration had at one time or another been in charge, there were no District Notebooks. These are the guide books of the District Officer to each of the districts within an emirate, showing the village units, their history, size, tax collection figures over several years, and details of the village chiefs—whether the appointment is hereditary or not, and, if not, if there is some traditional way of choosing the next one. Where the office is hereditary, there is a family tree of the ruling house, showing the holders in the past, the existing chiefs and possible successors. Their object is both to instruct new officers on taking over and to be the source of information when disputes arise; they were regarded by Lugard as of the utmost importance.

In view of the illustrious names that had preceded mine, the absence of such notebooks was quite astonishing, and I hunted high and low. None were to be found and in the event I prepared a new set, but in the course of my searchings, I did light, in an old store, upon a mass of old files and books of records of various kinds. These were sifted to see if the missing notebooks could be there, but all was junk except for some station diaries, which a cursory inspection showed to be dated from early in the century until 1917 or so. These I rescued from the white ants which were getting the rest and took them on tour with me for a careful study.

Before telling of their contents, however, as the first did not start until 1906, it may be as well to tell the earlier history of our administration of this area.

In 1897 France and England were poised for war along the western border of what later became Nigeria. What had happened was that the French, ignoring both the line drawn back at right-angles to the coast in accordance with the decisions reached in Brussels and Berlin to separate British and French spheres of

influence, and the treaties signed with the various states, had tried
to turn it south of the Niger by occupying places which were well
to the east, including Nikki, Gwamba, Illo and Boussa, the last
three of which are all in Nigeria. Accounts exist of the relations
between the officers of the two forces, entertaining one another
for dinner one night and the next being joined by some fire-eater
—generally French—who cut off all intercourse and by dealing
in insults and threats, made war almost inevitable. Luckily good
sense prevailed, and in August 1898 the French agreed to move
and leave most of the disputed territory to Great Britain. A list
of the garrisons sent to these remote places reads:

KAYAMA	2 officers	40 men
BOUSSA	3 officers	60 men
KISHI	1 officer	20 men
SAKI	2 officers	20 men
ILLO	6 officers	100 men

The casualties in a year of these operations were five officers
and fifteen British N.C.O.s dead, and twelve officers and eighteen
N.C.O.s invalided. Of these only one officer and one N.C.O. had
been killed, and these because of a misunderstanding when they
visited one of the islands above Boussa and were murdered by the
inhabitants, some of whom were probably the grandsons of those
who killed Park. (Fifty years later I met some of the men who had
been involved in the fracas.) The rest had died from disease.

Then in 1903 came the British Administration and the first
Residents were posted to the area; not, however, to Birnin Kebbi
itself but to Jega and Ambursa twenty miles away on either side.

To while away the evenings on my first tour in Gwandu, I put
these old diaries in the office box among the other paraphernalia
which must accompany the administrative officer on tour. They
were read, as much of them was written, sitting in the mud en-
trance-hall to a native compound, while all around the voices of
the women and children of the town, the beating of pestles and
the barking of dogs, gave the same background for the reading as
for the writing.

The first was for 1906 and was incomplete, being endorsed on
the cover, 'DIARY, 1906', and in another hand *'up to 15 February
1906'*, and was kept by the Assistant Resident at Jega.

The name of the writer was not given, but from the delicate, careful hand-writing it could be identified as that of Mr Assistant Resident McAllister, for I found other old papers, bearing his signature, in the easily identifiable script.

The diary starts by recording the usual humdrum daily round. It is 1 January, but not a day of holiday, for the December accounts are dispatched to the Resident in Sokoto and Mr Wright of the telegraph party leaves with £250. The next two days are taken up with routine work, while a homicide case at a place called Kimba leads to a lot of trouble throughout the month with the local native judge, who seems to be stupid and deliberately misunderstands the writer.

The village head of the place where this killing occurred is fined 400,000 cowries; some 69 bulls are received from another Assistant Resident as payment for the cattle-tax of an area to the south. Captain Esmonde of the police hands over to Sergeant Ingham of the West African Frontier Force and proceeds with the pay of the police escort to join Mr Wright. On the 12th appears the entry:

Faji, a woman of Jega, complained that she had been fined by the Alkali; it appears she was accused of stealing some kolas and £2 10s. in cash. She was not allowed to swear that she was innocent because if she did so no one would have to refund the £2 10s. to the man who had lost it. A curious idea of justice!

The same day, a village headman behaves in such a disorderly manner that he is put in the charge of the guard. Later there are visitors; Mr Vertue passes through for Sokoto, and Sergeants O'Donohue and Gosling (going in opposite directions, it appears). The Residency is whitewashed by the townspeople. Sergeant Ingham next leaves for Zungeru with a warrant which should have been signed by the Assistant Resident at Ambursa, but the latter has not done this, so McAllister does it for him. Sergeant Gosling must have had a miserable journey to Sokoto if my experiences are anything to go by, for his transport consisted of one camel, four asses, two bullocks and two carriers, a heterogeneous and strange little caravan riding along in late January 1906, riding into the history of Nigeria, for we shall hear of Sergeant Gosling again.

207

On the 31st we get a glimpse of a still persisting failing in this part of the world:

Sarikin Fada brought up £110 of the Town Tax and said that the Sarikin Jega had been taking the money as it was collected by the headmen and he had spent £40 of it himself, the balance, £10, would be subscribed by Abdu Kadari £9 and Magaji £1.

So next day, 1 February:

I ordered all the headmen to come in (the king is sick) and asked them if this was the truth. They said 'yes'. I then told them to go back and see the king and make arrangements with him as to how the money was to be made up and told them that they should appoint someone to hold the £110 in the meantime. They agreed that Sarikin Fada should take charge of it. I further told them that when they had seen the king they were to send me word as to the earliest date on which they could pay the whole of the money.

Sarikin Fada came in later and told me that it had been agreed that the king should refund the money and that he should call on his sons to help him and that after seeing his sons, a date would be submitted.

It is unfortunate that the king is an imbecile.

This 'king' was the Sarkin Kebbi Jega, the headman of the main market town of this part, whose family still governs the District under the Emir of Gwandu, and whose title records the killing in battle of one of the independent Kebbi chiefs by the ancestor of the 'king'.

On the 5th and 6th 'nothing was done' as the Mohammedan festival was held. Another murder occurs at Kimba, and again the native judge is obtuse, whilst on the 10th, the wife of a soldier complains against the sergeant of the detachment, alleging attempted rape and assault. The colour-sergeant is asked to report.

I turned the last page and saw that the entries ended half-way down the page, whilst the opposite sheet was empty. It is the 11th, and Captain Ruxton with Captain Harbord has arrived from Ambursa; the former is handing over the division, the latter is taking over. On the same day Colour-Sergeant O'Donohue (who apparently has returned to Jega) reports that the woman has no corroborative evidence, so the charge is dismissed. On the 12th

Harbord leaves for his station at Ambursa, and on the 14th Ruxton leaves for Zungeru and home.

Then came the last entry, and a prickle of excitement ran down my spine. The noise of the women was forgotten; the dogs barked on unheeded; here was drama stark and unforgettable, hidden away for forty-one years.

15th. Received a pencilled note from Colour-Sergeant Gosling from Sokoto stating that 'C' Coy Mounted Infantry had been annihilated by Mahdi at Satiru (?) and that Resident Hilary, Assistant Resident Scott and Lieutenant Blackwood had been killed and Dr Ellis severely wounded. He asked that the Jega detachment of W.A.F.F. should proceed to Sokoto at once to relieve Fort Sokoto

Left for Sokoto at 2.30 p.m. with Colour-Sergeant O'Donohue and 30 men. Left Mr Wright, Telegraph Inspector, in charge of the station, and told Sarikin Fada that I held him responsible for the peace of the town.

I was no longer in the world of 1947, but back in the Gwandu before two World Wars had changed history. In my mind's eye I could see the tiny body of men marching north, perhaps to certain death, with their very gallant Resident at their head, thinking perhaps of that other *Mahdi* who had brought fire and sword to the Sudan but a few years before.

I could see the streets of the strangely deserted Jega, with every household humming with the rumours that only Africa can breed, rumours of the imminent end of all Europeans, after this, the first reverse suffered by their armed forces.

I could see Sarkin Jega, thanking God for what had happened; wondering which way to jump; certain that none would return to question him further about the missing forty pounds; I could see Sarkin Fada looking at the hundred and ten pounds in his care with speculative eyes wondering when he could use it for his own purposes.

I turned the other pages of the diary to see if there was a record of the events of the next few weeks, but there was none. When entries recommenced, it was some time later and they were the mundane events of day-to-day administration.

The rest of the story must be found in Lugard's Report for 1905–6.

The Sokoto report opens in a subdued manner. Major Burdon reported that owing to the loyalty, energy and ability of the Sultan and his Waziri, the preliminary assessment had been most successful. The staff had averaged only four British Officers (for 1,500,000 people), 'and has been insufficient.' The harvest was good, except to the north on the French frontier and the Sultan 'had seconded the Resident's efforts to prevent deforestation and to preserve game, though the application of rigid laws on these matters would be premature. The drying up of the streams seems to indicate a progressive dessication of the country in this direction, and an encroachment southwards of the arid area of the Sahara.'

Then: 'The Sokoto annual report from which I have been quoting was dated on February 10th last; on the night of the 15th a telegram arrived to the effect. . . .' The telegram doubtless having been sent off by our Mr Wright on instructions from Mr McAllister on receipt of the pencilled note from Gosling. Steps are immediately taken. The gallant McAllister is joined by 150 African horsemen from Tambawel in Sokoto and instructed over the new telegraph from Jega—again doubtless through Mr Wright —to retire on Argungu, sixty miles or so to the north of Jega, the Kebbi chiefdom which had remained independent of the Fulani rulers of Sokoto, and which would remain loyal even if all Sokoto rose against us.

For six days there is no further news (has Wright, too, scurried off to Argungu, leaving Sarkin Jega more than ever convinced of the righteousness of Allah?) though from Bauchi in the east, the Honourable Oliver Howard reports that he has been taking active and successful steps against another Mahdi who has risen there. A second appears at Bauchi and it appears the small garrison there has more than enough to keep it busy.

The only men available are 75 rank and file at Zungeru, so they march north to be joined by the same number from Kontagora, with orders to fall back on Zaria if they meet the hostile forces moving eastwards. A hundred men are ordered up from Lokoja, and 'marching with great rapidity' the 150 under Major Goodwin, Royal Artillery, reach Sokoto on 1 March, followed by the Lokoja detachment on the 8th. Major Burdon, who had just handed over to Hilary the day before the disaster, has returned to Sokoto;

the Sultan is loyal, and mounted men are pouring in, maintaining a watch between Fort Sokoto and the rebels' headquarters only fourteen miles to the south. Mounted Infantry from Kano arrive, and on the 10th, Major Goodwin, with 573 rifles, 30 Europeans, 70 police 'whose arms however, were almost useless', with a 2·95 gun and several Maxims, advances against the enemy.

The successful rebels had spent the time since the massacre of 14 February, in raiding and burning neighbouring towns, but had left the gathering forces in Sokoto alone. Their prestige was, however, enormous and parties of the Sultan's warriors, numbering over 3,000 men, had refused to face them. They numbered but 2,000, mostly unmounted men, armed for the most part with spears, axes and hoes.

The action started with the Mounted Infantry going forward to draw them on whilst the rest of the column formed square; as the enemy advanced, the Mounted Infantry fell back, clearing the front of the square to let the infantry fire take effect on the charging mass. A Sokoto Chief who had been present at the previous disaster described the action with terse force: 'They came on and the horsemen ran away and went back; no one took any notice. I thought we were all going to be killed as before. Someone gave an order, everybody fired, then a whistle blew, everyone stopped, and there was no one left alive in front.'

The fighting was still not over, however, for several brave charges were made and fierce hand-to-hand fighting took place in the village. But eventually the brave Hausa and Fulani peasantry broke and fled, pursued by the Mounted Infantry and the now reassured warriors of the Sultan. The leader and five of the principal rebels were tried by the Sultan's Court and sentenced to death. The village of Satiru was totally destroyed, and the Sultan laid a curse on whomsoever should again rebuild it or till its fields. On the scene of the disaster were found the bodies of the three officers who had been killed; they were buried with full military honours in the little graveyard at Sokoto where lie the bones of the explorer Clapperton, and several early members of the Administrative Service.

So ended the Satiru revolt, and another page in the history of Nigeria and the Empire had been marked by the graves of the principals who lost their lives in a vain effort to save bloodshed.

Hilary and Scott had ridden forward ahead of the troops to try and harangue the rebels; Lieutenant Blackwood, fearing for their safety, had galloped forward, breaking square to get there in time. Momentarily dispersed they had been attacked by the overwhelming numbers of the enemy and killed. Sergeant Gosling had escaped, and with the wounded doctor had drawn off the survivors to Sokoto, where he found Sergeant Slack, left in charge of the fort, sallying out to their aid.

The remarkable feature of the whole incident had been the loyalty of the Sultan of Sokoto and his chiefs. All had rallied to the help of the Sokoto garrison with their men—and this only three years after the occupation of the area. The Emir of Gwandu, in whose territories lie both Ambursa and Jega, had been passively hostile, however, so before the troops returned to their stations a strong force marched on his capital and arrested him. He was deported to Lokoja, where he shortly afterwards died.

Ambursa and Jega still stand, but no traces now remain of the Residencies where Harbord and McAllister received the news of the disaster.

And what of Mr Wright? Was he present at the second engagement, or was he busy 'under the protection of the Emir of Argungu' pushing the telegraph line northwards, wondering if he would again have to transmit bad tidings to the granite Governor in Zungeru?

We shall never know—though perhaps mouldering away in some Posts and Telegraphs storeroom is the diary with his story of those anxious three weeks.

To some the above story may not appear to warrant further comment. To me, the absence of heroics and the matter of fact way in which McAllister made what might well have been his last entry in this or any other diary, is notable in the extreme; moreover, his leaving at once with his pitifully small body of men to go to the aid of the stricken garrison in Sokoto, is to me a matter of intense pride, and is a small part of the story of the Colonial Administrative Service which surely deserves to be widely known.

The attitude of the Emir of Gwandu was, to say the least, not friendly; before McAllister lay a hundred miles of possibly hostile country; the route lay through dense sand; there were only four hours of daylight left, and once night fell his men's rifles would be in no way superior to the spears and bows and arrows of a brave and hardy peasantry—opponents moreover imbued with a fanatical religious hatred of these Unbelievers. Even as late as 1947, the inhabitants of Koko, a town near Jega, were still hostile to a school set up by the Gwandu Native Administration giving a secular education in their own tongue, because of this intense religious fanaticism.

Is not the story of McAllister, like the stories of other similar members of the early Administrative Service, worth recording? Our children absorb the largely fictitious histories of the trigger-happy ruffians of the Western States of America; is there nothing for them to learn from the example of men like McAllister of Jega, Moloney of Keffi and the others?

'When the power of the city shall seem great to you, consider that it was purchased by valiant men and by men who knew their duty.'

CHAPTER SIXTEEN

Trekking in Gwandu

My first tour in Gwandu, during which time I read these early diaries from cover to cover, took me down the course of the Sokoto River, the great valley of which was dry at that time of the year. During one of the wetter phases of the past, when away to the east in Bornu Lake Chad spread far beyond its present bounds, it had been a great river the whole year round, fed by many tributaries rising far to the north in what is now the Sahara. But now the valley fills only in the rains; for the rest of the year the river flows only in a narrow channel down the last thirty or forty miles of the valley, and above that a chain of cut-off lakes marks the deeper parts of its wet season channel. In January of each year in the Argungu area occurs a remarkable scene when some of these sheets of water are fished on what can only be described as the Archimedean principle; vast crowds collect at a given lake, and at a signal everyone jumps in. The greater part of the water is displaced, and with it the fish, and the thick mud that remains as the water flows back is combed with hand-nets for the survivors. Very few fish survive this mode of fishing and the effect of the catch was so great that the Native Authorities made an order forbidding fishing in one fifth of the lakes each year in rotation. Poachers got away with some monsters from the protected areas, but the plan worked well, and when the rains arrived and the river flowed again, vast numbers of fish moved out of each lake.

North of the Nigerian border the product of the fields is not sufficient to feed the whole year round the people needed to till them. In normal years therefore, as soon as the harvest is in, the young men leave and trek south to Yorubaland and to Ghana; I have spoken to men from 200 miles north of Sokoto working as deck-hands on boats on the round-trip between Takoradi and the Congo. In a bad year, everyone must leave, and the whole of Nigeria receives an influx of the '*masu-chin rani*', they 'who must eat the dry season', working as water-carriers, fetchers of firewood, labourers on the roads and so on; March and April come and the first storms in the south, and the roads are thronged with the family groups of man, wife, children and perhaps a donkey making their way back over hundreds of miles to dig up their hidden seed corn and to prepare the fields—generally now with a new covering of wind-blown sand.

In certain years, for reasons as yet unknown, the rain-belt moves farther north, and not only does this northern area revel in floods, but the true desert also receives rain and 'blossoms like a flower'; the dead rivers of the desert again flow with water; the harvests are good in the desert border lands, there is enough food for all for a year, and few of the young men need venture on their usual thousand-mile journey on foot. But the balance is on a knife edge; little is needed to tip the scale the wrong way and allow desert conditions gradually to replace the farms of today.

My tour coincided with the beginning of the rains and I met many of the later groups returning from the Gold Coast, as it then was, hurrying home forty or fifty miles a day, day after day. I trekked down the length of the valley to near where it joined the Niger; no horse from the north was ever taken into the last few miles fringing the river or across into the country to the south, as here the tsetse ruled and only a few horses of the many taken into these parts survived, acquiring in the process a lifelong immunity to the disease carried by the tsetse.

On my return I was joined in rapid succession by an A.D.O., Margaret, a doctor, and a Development Officer and his wife. Believing with Lugard that a junior could only learn his job on tour, I sent the A.D.O. off to check the cattle-count and, when that was done, to carry out a resident assessment of the Bunza District. My predecessor had drawn up plans to drive wide roads through the warren of houses that formed the old town of Birnin Kebbi, with the necessary drainage and culverts, and for the roads to be lined with shade trees. The Development Officer was here to supervise this work: to accommodate those whose houses were destroyed a new suburb was laid out outside the town after I had given him some lessons in elementary surveying. He marked out the lines of the new roads, then supervised the demolition of the buildings within these lines using paid labour. We then sent the town crier round to tell the townspeople that every man had three days in which to take as much of the demolished mud walls of his own house as he wanted; after that we threw the ruins open to all; an army of men and donkeys moved in and in a few days the main worry was lest they took too much from the streets and turned level roads into gullies. With this work well under way, I could now get out on tour again as I aimed to spend at least ten days a month away from headquarters, including a visit each month to the small emirate 137 miles away to the south, where the Emir of Yauri resided at his headquarters town of Yelwa, visited by Park on his last journey downstream on the Niger.

In order to see the riverain area, Margaret and I went on a long tour down the Niger in my poling barge, one similar to that in which a former Resident of Yola had been drowned when it had overturned in a sudden storm. First we went by lorry some hundred miles to the south of the emirate, where a motor track came close to the river itself, for the Niger in this part of its course has a wide flood plain on its left bank, a flood plain which is of great economic potential. Here my barge awaited us. We went over the Niger and visited the town of Illo and saw the remains of the two forts where British and French troops had so nearly precipitated a European war. We then went upstream to the French boundary, and visited Dole Fransa, so called to distinguish it from Dole Kaina in Nigeria from which it was separated by a single iron post set in concrete; we turned and slept the night at Lolo, the first Nigerian village on the right bank of the river, and were told that Margaret was the first European woman ever to sleep there. Next we voyaged downstream, stopping at the villages on the bank, and riding into Kaojè, some fifteen miles to the south, on 'salted horses'—ones which were now immune to the bite of the tsetse fly. At one village we saw a horse recovering from this horse-sickness in an evil-smelling hut; the unfortunate animal rested on a cradle of timbers under its belly, with its legs hanging down each side; it was covered with sores, was a bag of bones and it appeared a miracle that it could survive. Yet its eyes were bright and it was eating some corn and I was told that it would never again go down with the sickness; one horse in fifteen we were told, recovered, and was then of great value.

One day early in the voyage we spotted a dead cow coming

downstream, all four legs stiff and straight in the air. In a moment we were pushed into the bank and four of our polers were off after this prize in a small canoe; they caught it and brought it to the bank. It had obviously been dead a day or two but was otherwise quite good. We spent the night on shore and the next day came to the river bank to find our crew with distended stomachs, a few of the locals equally gorged and little left of the carcass except the large leg-bones, which with a few strips of meat on them were being dried over a fire. We pushed off and by nightfall those legs were making their presence felt. 'Tell them,' I said to the headman, 'that they must take them ashore tonight and sell them; if I find them on board tomorrow I shall throw them overboard.' Next morning I was assured that they were gone, and we proceeded on our fortnight's voyage downstream; in a day or two both Margaret and I were complaining of the smell and again I gave a long homily to the headman. That evening, walking round the small market of the place where we had tied up, I spotted a member of our crew with two well remembered legs in front of him, which were being turned over in an approving manner by the matrons of the town. Next day we were greeted with great grins by the crew who admitted that they had hidden the bones but that now they had only dried fish which they had bought with the proceeds of the sale. 'Stink fish', as they are called, are not too bad and we tolerated their presence, but from time to time we would remark on the singular pertinacity of the smell of bad meat which hung over the barge; nothing we did seemed to remove it.

'You know,' said Margaret, 'I think it is getting worse, not better.'

'I can't understand it,' I said, 'we've had everything out of the barge twice. They can't have hidden anything else, but at Yelwa tomorrow I'll have it washed from one end to the other before we go on downstream.'

Next morning we reached Yelwa, still of some importance as a port on the Niger, and gateway to southern Sokoto; there on the bank to greet us was the Emir, there to greet their husband were the four wives of our headman; there was an animated conversation between them and then a forepeak which I had not noticed was opened and, as Margaret and I and the Emir fled, we saw the adoring looks the four cast at their spouse as they received the bonne-bouche he had brought them—the slightly smoked head of the long-dead cow.

We stayed two days, not one, whilst the headman and his wives washed out that forepeak, not once but many times.

Two days or so downstream, we turned at the rapids at Boussa where Mungo Park is believed to have died, and made our way back. Staying in the village where, some fifty years before, the unfortunate officer and British N.C.O. had been murdered, we sat in our rest-house not far from the banks of the river. Past us marched a remarkable looking man with a very queer walk and carrying a kettle in one hand and a long horn from some wild animal over his other shoulder; the kettle was not at all out of the way as most of the population carry water in this way before washing for the daily prayers—water can be easily poured from the spout—but the horn was unusual. A few minutes later he passed again; and again; and yet again; this was too much. We sent for the rest-house keeper and learned that our visitor was a harmless lunatic who spent his entire life walking along this strip of ground. But not for the remainder of our stay—I asked the District Head to accommodate him in his own compound for the night. When we pushed off next day we could only hope that this interruption in his usual perambulation had in no way worsened his affliction.

But as the Victorian novelist would have said, what would you, gentle reader, have done if, in a place where two of your countrymen had been murdered in error, a madman with a limp, carrying a kettle and a long horn, had passed you and passed you and passed you every few minutes?

We next came across another example of a rift between elders and the younger generation such as I have described amongst the Tiv. Ascending the river back to Yelwa, we stopped at a large village of the Pagan tribe which inhabits the north bank of the Niger in this area, and with my Emir's representative and my messenger I went into the village square to meet the elders and to chat with them. My arrival was unannounced, but the square was packed with the entire population. On one side were the village head and the elders, old men bent with years of toil, with rheumy eyes, straggling beards and bad teeth, dressed either in a few filthy rags which would have disintegrated had they been placed in water, or in hairless goatskins, brown and supple from years of wear. On the other side sat the younger men and youths, clean and washed, in spotless white robes, trousers and skull-caps; behind them sat the women, also decently and cleanly dressed; at their head was a rather sleek and oily *Mallam*, or Moslem teacher, of rather Chadbandy appearance.

I sat and asked what was happening and was told that the *Mallam* had come from Boussa six months previously to convert the village to Islam; the younger generation had 'repented' as conversion is called, and were now all strict Moslems. (The Christian Mission at Yelwa working amongst these people, whilst respected and liked for its medical work, had had no such success in conversion.) The young men had stopped drinking beer and whilst their conversion to Islam was not opposed by their elders, their refusal to give the traditional corn with which their future fathers-in-law might brew beer for the wedding-feast had appeared to be less a matter of their new religion than a deliberate rebuff to their elders and betters. To the younger men, beer was *Haram*, forbidden by the Prophet; they respected their fathers and their elders, but they refused to follow a custom, no matter how hallowed by time, which was unlawful. The women gave their full support to the younger generation.

At first the meeting was orderly and the two sides put their cases more in sorrow than anger; suddenly tempers flared, everyone began to shout at once, and in a moment a deafening uproar broke out.

Back on the barge, Margaret sat doing some embroidery whilst the boys engaged in their household chores, and the polers fished or washed their clothes. On this idyllic scene, there suddenly burst an appalling noise of many voices raised in sudden and violent anger. The polers dropped their fishing lines and grabbed their long poles; my boys grabbed the paddles and leaving Margaret to fend for herself, rushed *en masse* to save me, or, as they told me later, if they were too late, to save my corpse from indignity and to carry it to safety.

No one had moved from where they sat in orderly rows when this sudden gale of anger swept through the village; I was still seated in their midst when my gallant crew poured into the square.

A moment's silence on all sides and then a great burst of laughter as everyone realized what had happened; back on the barge the embroidery was resumed as the roars of continuing laughter came over the roof-tops; almost helpless with laughter my crew drifted back to the barge, and after urging Mr. Chadband to allow his flock to hand over the necessary corn—for as I pointed out, corn is not *haram*, and none can say whether or not it will be used for brewing—I and the others followed them. What the end of the argument was I never heard, but we pushed off with a laughing, cheering crowd bandying jests with my crew. The laughter lasted for many hours.

On our return the work of clearing the new roads was almost complete, trees were being planted, and the only flaw in the plan was that people did not want to live in the new suburb, though well content to build houses to fill up any spaces in the existing pattern of houses in the old town. In a short time the Emir told me that every District Head in the place was asking for similar action in the larger towns in the emirate. Birnin Kebbi had had the full treatment; a proposal had been put up to Kaduna; it had been approved subject to the approval of a town plan by the Director of Public Works; this had been done. If now we were to wait for similar steps in every case demanding action, we would wait for ever; so we dealt with each town on an *ad hoc* basis.

The Emir and I, with the Development Officer, the District Head, the village head and his elders would walk all over a town. We would decide on the general line of the new roads; in Birnin Kebbi these had been straight but I saw no merit in straightness, and was prepared to accept a winding road; width to allow access and to act as a firebreak was what was wanted. We would agree on an outline plan; then the Development Officer was left to place pairs of bamboos, each topped with a piece of cloth, along the two sides of each new road. Again the committee examined the proposal, and if we approved, strings were attached to the poles to mark either side of the road, and with a hoe a line drawn across compounds and over buildings, so that every householder could see what was proposed. A little compensation was assessed in those cases where a house was completely destroyed, and paid labour drove a line through each wall that stood in the way along the hoe marks. The people of the town were then left to salvage the building material in the walls to be demolished, and in a few days we would return to find everything removed. In went the trees, the nearest householder was instructed to water the one in front of his house and to maintain the goat-proof fence with which we ringed each tree, and we could move on to the next town.

We had plans for the construction of new schools, two dispensaries, a new rest-house, new roads and so on. My Resident had once been District Officer Gwandu, and at Kaduna so had the Development Secretary, the Chief Secretary, and the Chief Commissioner. When therefore I put anything on paper, it was well minuted upon, as each in turn remembered what he had proposed for the area. I arrived to find plans for a new European reservation and for new housing; I ventured to criticize these and to put forward other suggestions. The final minute, I was told, was one from the Chief Commissioner, which read: 'We have argued over the proposals for Birnin Kebbi since 1914; after 33 years we get agreement; now the present District Officer wants to start again; we cannot wait another 33 years.'

The work was done after I had left, and in later years the new European station in Birnin Kebbi was described as the worst Senior Service slum in Africa.

I wasted no more time in writing.

We were at last beginning to do something for the development of the area; we read of the great schemes which were lauded in the Press and in the English Parliament; we heard of the millions that were to be spent on the groundnut scheme and on the Gambia egg scheme; we read of the shortage of dollars. I suggested that we could earn plenty of the latter by advertising in the American Press: 'Come and see Unchanged Africa, the Africa of a Thousand Years Ago'—for south of the Niger there were two small schools and one dispensary after nearly fifty years of our rule. There were no roads, no bridges, nothing different, except for these three small buildings, from what had been the case when the garrisons at Illo and Gwamba were withdrawn in 1898. 'The only marked difference,' I wrote, 'is the absence of slave-raiding, but if that should prove an extra dollar-earner, it could be resuscitated in a week or so.' I received a measured rebuke.

The Division had had its share of jesters in the past; in one file was the copy of a circular telegram from Kaduna: WIRE EARLIEST NUMBER OF CASES RAPE IN NATIVE COURTS YOUR DIVISION LAST YEAR and the classic reply: NONE STOP THEY ALL RAPE ELSEWHERE.

On the banks of the Niger was a one-man mission station, the incumbent of which had been, at one period in his youth, a fisherman on the Grand Banks of Newfoundland, and had later 'seen the light' as he said, and become a missionary. Fish were in his blood, however, and also in the Niger; in the years of shortage at the end of the war, he wrote in proposing to establish a fish-curing station on his mission plot. In forwarding the proposal to the Secretariat, one of my predecessors had written to the effect that he could not recommend the application as he felt that 'the cure of souls and the cure of fish should not be carried out on the same plot'. After the letter had been written, however, he had had second thoughts and across the duplicate in the file was written: '*Not sent*'. No doubt it was this flair for discretion which led to his eventual promotion to the post of Deputy Governor and a richly merited knighthood.

Birnin Kebbi was a happy station. To us and to many of the others who had known him, the Emir was the finest man of his generation in Nigeria. As he was a person free from all trace of humbug himself, he was not sufficiently courtier to ingratiate himself with those in high office who like, before they recognize merit, to know that their generosity will be both recognized and welcomed. The relations between the Emir of Gwandu and his District Officer had become similar to those of a chairman of a county council and the clerk to the council. I was his right-hand man; I was his chief executive; but it was the Emir and his Council with myself present as Chief Executive that planned. I would not think of going on tour until I had agreed my route with the Emir and he would tell me of matters into which he wanted me to inquire; he would tell me that he proposed to visit such and such a place so that I would not duplicate his efforts. Together we would go to watch the progress of some new road, and together I and the Emir and members of his Council went out duck-shooting on the flooded plain of the usually dry river.

Although there was no sign at this time of the sudden approach of Independence, we often discussed the future organization of

Government in Nigeria and the place therein of the Native Administrations. 'What will you do when I am replaced by a Nigerian District Officer?' I asked the Emir on one occasion. 'As long as I am alive and Emir,' he replied, 'no Nigerian will come to Birnin Kebbi as District Officer, be he Hausa or Fulani or Ibo or Yoruba. When we Nigerians are able to run our own affairs, the need for District Officers and Residents will have passed. I and my Council will be the sole agent of the Central Government in Gwandu. We shall have our own medical staff, and our own engineer and our own agricultural officers, and we shall want a highly trained and capable man to run the central offices, and whether they are black or white or even Indians like the men that Lugard brought in the early days, does not matter. But when the day comes when it is said that no European District Officer need be sent here, I and my Council replace him.' The Council nodded their assent and our argument ranged back and forth over the place of a District Officer *vis-à-vis* a Native Administration. The position that had been reached in Gwandu was, we felt, the first and correct step; in due course the District Officer must cease to be responsible to the Resident and must become the employee of the Gwandu Native Administration, and when that stage was reached, he could, as the Emir said, be black, white or brown; colour did not matter. That was surely the goal and we District Officers—at any rate as part of a Provincial Administration separate from the Native Administrations—were merely a stage in the evolution of the latter, a stage which ended when its efforts had reached success. It is sad to read of African Residents and District Officers today; their continued existence is a confession of failure on our part to develop strong Local Administrations before we handed over to an independent Nigeria.

For a number of years, the Emir had been in the habit of presenting those District Officers of whom he approved with a small imported prayer-rug which could be bought at the canteens in the larger towns for a few shillings. Not all District Officers received this present which had become known unofficially as 'the Order of the Carpet' and it was therefore a matter of some pride when in due course we received ours.

It was formerly the custom in Nigeria to greet a visiting potentate with a whole series of presents—horses, slaves, corn, food and so on—and despite every effort to the contrary District Heads, particularly those with uneasy consciences, would greet visiting Administrative Officers with quite substantial presents: corn, chickens, perhaps a lion-skin or something of that nature; by Government regulation whilst we might accept them, we must give the bearer a return present—generally of money—equal in value to that received; in most parts of the country, by 1930, such presents had become very nominal; in Gwandu under the leadership of the very enlightened Emir, they were little more than token —perhaps two miserable old hens and three eggs of doubtful age.

On one occasion the Emir himself sent such a present to a visiting Resident, and the Emir's messenger had scarcely disappeared from view when I was summoned to the Resident's resthouse; the great man was perturbed: perhaps he had visions of another Satiru. I was questioned long and thoroughly as to whether the sending of such a miserable present was or was not a studied insult, not of course to my interrogator personally—who cared nothing for such matters—but to the British Administration. For half an hour a very agitated Resident strode up and down; in due course I had a word in private with the Emir and when next the Resident visited us all his previous fears were banished; it was in the rainy season and the river was full of fish; a huge Nile perch—called in Hausa 'the elephant of the water'—had been caught; one donkey could scarce carry it, but at last it was triumphantly handed over to the Resident as the customary present from the Emir. The Resident was delighted and Margaret, the Doctor (who was a bachelor), and the wife of the Development Officer, each received an enormous cut of fish; we had no fridges, so we and our boys ate fish for a day at each meal.

The Resident departed and we had our weekly dinner-party.

'What,' said the Emir as the joint appeared for me to carve, 'no fish?'

We did not always get fish to vary our diet of chickens, but on one occasion, towards the end of the dry season, Margaret and I were trekking back on horseback from a short tour to Gwandu town; our return route lay along one of the dead or dying rivers, tributary to the main stream through Birnin Kebbi, which had been followed by Barth ninety years before. Our cook obtained some fish for our dinner, but when evening came the number of flying ants which congregated round the lamp meant that we had to place it some distance away and eat our dinner almost in darkness. The fish was good; the cook was told that we would eat up the remainder for breakfast. Next day we rode on our way and in due course stopped at our destination and sat down to breakfast. In a short time, Margaret pushed her fish over to me for me to inspect; curled up in the flesh was a worm of some kind and it did not take long to discover that there were others. They were placed in an emptied aspirin bottle and covered with gin, and on our return to Birnin Kebbi I consulted the doctor. He was perturbed and the specimens were sent off post-haste by airmail to some laboratory in London. A week passed, a week during which time the Emir told us that he and the other Fulani in the area never ate fish from this particular river as to do so gave the eater leprosy. In due course the report of the laboratory arrived: the worms were nematodes of some kind, probably new to science; similar ones had been placed subcutaneously in various birds and experimental animals which in due course had died, apparently raving mad, as the worms reached and penetrated the brain. 'In this case, however,' said the laboratory cheerfully, 'the fact that the worms had been cooked before being eaten and the attack of the gastric fluids should mean that any that escaped mastication would be unable to penetrate from the stomach into the flesh of your patients; it is therefore only remotely possible that any harm can come to them though of course the possibility cannot be ruled out entirely.'

Had greater notice been taken of the Emir of Gwandu and the way in which relations between his Administration and the District Officers had developed over several years, Gwandu might have become the model for many other places, and the whole system of local administration be on a much sounder basis than it now is.

On only one occasion did I see the Emir in a rage: this was when, in 1948, we found that certain District Heads were extorting money from their peasantry by a very mean trick based on the repayments of some thousands of Savings Certificates bought some years earlier as part of the war effort in the area. Amongst those involved was one of his close kinsmen who he had hoped was as honest and as devoted to the well-being of his people as he was himself. This particular man was due to go on a visit to Great Britain, and if the Emir had had his way that visit would have been cancelled, but the Resident of the Province ruled otherwise. The Emir vented his wrath on his Councillors, then dismissed them and sat alone with me in his Council Chamber, almost heartbroken. Such petty, miserable offences were only too common in certain parts of Northern Nigeria; that they should have occurred in his Emirate was almost more than the Emir could bear. He spoke bitterly of his relative and of resignation from the post of Emir and a retirement into private life where he could divest himself of the cares of state.

In later years, when I was a Head of Department in Kaduna, our house became the nodal point for many of our friends when the meeting of the House of Chiefs took place, and the drive of our house would be almost choked with the large cars of Emirs, whilst their retainers sat around under the trees. On some of these occasions, which coincided with school holidays in England, they met my two sons and to their delight a photograph was taken of the Emir of Gwandu and some of his Council and the two small boys. It was a bitter personal blow, and a great loss to Nigeria as a whole, when the Emir died in 1954. To whichever heaven he has gone, whether that of the Christians whom he liked and admired and whose religion he had wanted to follow, or that of the Faithful, of one thing I am certain: he will have brought distinction to it. The words of the late Prime Minister of Northern Nigeria to the House of Assembly in 1954 are a sufficient epitaph . . .

'He died as he lived, in the course of serving his people.'

CHAPTER SEVENTEEN

'Previous Occupation—Slave'

I have told of the usual Friday morning inspection of the local Prison by the District Officer, with either the Emir, or, in the very biggest Native Administrations, the Chief Alkali. When a man had been tried for murder, and sentenced to death by an Emir's Court, it was also the duty of the District Officer to ensure that the condemned man was fully aware of his right of appeal. Should his appeal be dismissed there was next a whole drill to be followed with regard to informing the prisoner of when he would die, the repeating back of telegraphed instructions to ensure that no mistake occurred, then the grisly business of arranging the execution, perhaps fixing the noose on the man's neck, and finally the inquest which law demands.

In 1947, in Birnin Kebbi, an old man was brought in under arrest charged with murder, and in due course he was tried by the Emir and his Court. After the trial he was brought into my office by the Galadima—the Emir's right-hand man—and squatted on the floor. Three peasants in dirty gowns followed him and, with rather anxious salutations to me, also squatted down, carefully tucking their legs away under their gowns as they did so. Behind the prisoner stood two Native Administration policemen; the Galadima waited till all were settled, then turned to me and said:

'We have concluded the case; here are the minutes of the hearing; these men here are the principal witnesses as to the actual assault on the old woman, and there are of course the dispensary attendant and the nurse from the hospital who looked after her wounds until she died, but I haven't brought them along. We have found the prisoner guilty of murder; the dead woman had no relatives whatsoever. Had there been blood relatives we should have urged them to accept blood-money and let the prisoner suffer the Koranic punishment of a hundred lashes and a year's imprisonment; but we can find none. The Chief Alkali has searched all his legal authorities for a similar case to see if there is a ruling as to whether the Emir or anyone else can assume the position of the blood relatives, but there is no precedent to guide us. We feel the man should not die but should suffer some lesser punishment, but there are no relatives to agree to this. Therefore the law must take its course and the man, subject to the Governor's consent, is condemned to death.'

Throughout the proceedings the policemen looked at me; the witnesses sat with downcast faces, whilst the prisoner looked straight at me with practically no expression to show whether or not he cared what happened to him. I looked at the minutes in Hausa which the Galadima had given me; the facts of the case were well known to me as I had seen the prisoner several times whilst he was awaiting trial, during my weekly inspections, and the doctor had told me of the injuries inflicted on his victim. The case was concluded, and it now remained for me to send forward the necessary translations, certificates, and other forms on which the Governor and his Executive Council would determine whether or not the law should take its course or whether the death-sentence should be commuted; I must also confirm that the accused did not wish to appeal.

I read the minutes through; they were simple and to the point. The prisoner had lived for some years in a small remote village with his two sons. Some months before, his elder son had sickened and died; two or three days before the murder, his second son had died similarly. The old man had brooded on the bitter fate which had befallen him—to die childless with no one to mourn him—and in his sorrow had decided that an old woman in a neighbouring hamlet was responsible. She too was childless; what more natural than for her jealously to kill his two fine sons by witchcraft? The old man had brooded for a couple of days and had then taken his axe and gone to the old woman's house. Witnesses had seen him enter; they had heard her screams and seen her run out to collapse in a pool of blood; they had found the old man with a bloody axe in his hand inside her house and he had owned to the assault, saying that he intended to kill her.

In court he confessed that he had done his victim to death to avenge the death of his sons. The summing up gave the legal position with regard to the blood relatives and stated the Moslem authorities for the court's view that in their absence the only punishment that that law allowed was death.

I came to the end, and flicked the pages over again; everything was in order; there remained only the question of translation and whether or not the prisoner wished to appeal to the Supreme Court against the verdict. One thing struck me that I had not noticed before; the court had entered the age of the old man as eighty; he was certainly old, but could not be more than sixty-eight or seventy.

'Galadima,' I said, 'you state here that his age is eighty. Do you really think so?'

'Not really,' replied the shrewd old man, 'but the Emir said it was to be entered thus so that perhaps the Governor's heart would be touched.'

Not for the first time I cursed the unbending Moslem Law which allowed no mercy, and marvelled—as I found myself doing every day—at the subtlety of the Fulani rulers of the land; bound by an unbending law, and unable to show mercy as they wished, they did all they could to make certain that the Governor or Supreme Court would do so.

'Umoru,' I said in Hausa to the prisoner, 'you have been tried and found guilty of the crime of murder. Do you agree that you received a fair trial?'

The old man looked down at the hem of his gown which he was twisting in his fingers. 'Yes,' he replied.

'You have been condemned to death. That sentence is liable to confirmation by the Governor, the Great White Man who is the representative of the King of the White Men. But apart from that if you do not agree with the justice of the sentence passed on you you can appeal to the Court of the White Man's Judges. Do you understand?'

The old man was still playing with his gown. One of the witnesses sat back on his heels and looked at him; the others still looked at the floor.

'Do you understand?' I repeated.

'Do you understand?' said the Galadima. 'You know that the Emir explained to you how you could appeal if you so wished, but you said that you wished only to die. Think again, Umoru, and tell the District Officer if you wish to appeal.'

The old man said nothing.

'Umoru,' I said, 'you have been condemned to death. You do not say if you wish to appeal. I cannot tell what the Governor and his advisers will say, but I shall point out to them that the Emir thinks you are very old; that had there been blood relatives the Emir and his Council would have urged them to accept blood-money and let you suffer only the Hadi punishment—that laid down by the Koran. I cannot speak for the Governor: who am I to put words into his mouth? But I think that perhaps he will ponder well on these things and on the death of your sons, and that perhaps you will not be hanged.'

The old man looked up at me. 'I wish to appeal,' he said.

'Good,' said the Galadima, 'he may yet get off.' The policemen looked pleased and the witnesses relieved.

'Take him away,' I said; 'I will send off the necessary telegrams at once,' and he was led out into the glaring heat of the sun.

In due course his appeal was heard in Zaria, but dismissed, and Umoru returned to us after his first journey for many years in the great world away from Birnin Kebbi. In due course I received a telegram direct from the Clerk of the Executive Council to say that His Excellency had decided to exercise the Royal Prerogative and that the sentence was to be commuted to life imprisonment. Again Umoru appeared before me, looking more alert after his long journey to Zaria for his appeal and a little fatter for his sojourn in prison.

'Umoru,' I said, 'the Governor has seen fit to exercise clemency. You are not to die, but you will be imprisoned till the day of your death. Do you understand, and have you anything to say?'

'Yes,' he replied. 'I want you to thank the Governor for his decision and I want you to give me a tin in which to keep these papers;' he handed over to me a clean white paper, and a filthy old one which was in two parts. The first was the formal notice of his appeal handed to him in accordance with law, the other was a discharge certificate from the West African Frontier Force, and I read it with some surprise. It was old, very old, and he had been allowed to retain it in his possession when he was first brought in to the prison, so that I had not previously seen it.

'This is to certify,' I read, 'that Umoru Kebbi enlisted at Lokoja on 1 April 1897, was discharged on 31 March 1907 with the rank of Corporal. Character: Good. War Service: Raha and Kalgo 1900; Sokoto 1903; Satiru 1906. Previous occupation: slave.' It was signed by some indecipherable name, 'Captain "B" Company, Mounted Infantry Battalion, Northern Nigeria Regiment.'

'You were once a soldier?' I asked.

'Yessah,' said the old man and tried to stand stiffly at attention; 'I was for ten years.'

So Umoru was taken back to prison and became our special prisoner—allowed to keep a flat cigarette-tin in which he kept his precious papers, and, quite against all prison rules, the Emir allowed him to spend a little of his small private savings—the result of the sale of his few belongings and harvest—on extra food and snuff. The old man was happy and became quite a familiar of the Galadima who had many questions to ask about the attack on Raha from which the Galadima had fled as a youth, those long years before.

Umoru was not talkative; indeed, his great sorrow was still with him; for there is no end more dreaded than to die childless. In any case it was only when I visited the prison that I saw him to speak to, and perhaps he did not always feel talkative on every such occasion, but little by little I got the story of his life.

Born in about 1880 in a Kebbi village to the north-west of Birnin Kebbi he had been captured whilst only a child of three or four, when his village was burnt to the ground in a Fulani raid from Gwandu. Reared as a household slave in the house of one of the many sons of the then ruling Emir at Birnin Kebbi he had grown to near-manhood working in the house and fields. But once he had struck his master in the course of some long-forgotten quarrel, and had been beaten almost to death.

Then one day the customary presents had been brought to the Gwandu Court from the subsidiary Emir of Bida, away to the south near the Niger, and because of his obstreperous spirit Umoru had been handed over to the Bida emissaries as part of the return present which is customarily given on such occasions. At Bida he had been further ill-treated and had been threatened with castration if he did not mend his ways, to become a court eunuch either there or at one of the other courts.

But Bida in those days was full of rumours: of the presence of many white men at a new town downstream called Lokoja, of great canoes on the river which needed no hands to pole or paddle, but which consumed great quantities of wood and which beat the water with great wheels. Beaten and ill-treated, he fled at last with a companion to the banks of the Niger. A canoe was found and stolen; the fugitives were lucky, and one of the white man's boats seen the next day.

And so to Lokoja, the then capital of the area soon to become Northern Nigeria, where a small military force was being welded from diverse elements, many of them like him, ex-slaves. Umoru had joined them and learnt to use the rifle. Too late in joining to take part in the expeditions against Bida and Ilorin, he was later with a small party which burnt Raha and Kalgo to the ground for slave-raiding. Then the final advance to Sokoto and the founding of the new British Colony of Northern Nigeria.

Three years afterwards came his last active service, for in 1906 he had ridden out of Sokoto with his company of the mounted infantry against the inhabitants of a small village called Satiru, where a holy war against the white unbeliever had been declared. He had seen the two white Political Officers ride forward to parley with the insurgents; he had formed square with his companions and they had then ridden forward, losing order and line as they did so in a futile attempt to save the lives of the two men. He had seen his own officer killed with them, and also many of his companions, and then with the remainder, a white sergeant and a badly wounded doctor, had withdrawn to Sokoto. Help had come and the insurrection ended and peace had come to the land. He left the army when time expired, returned to his old village to find that in the wars and the boundary settlement with the French all had fled and he had no relatives left. He had wandered about for some years, working as a labourer when he could get work; then he had married and settled down some way to the south of the site of his native village. The years passed and Umoru had prospered; he had in time three wives. But always his children died: except two, born late in his life. His wives left him or died, and he was left alone with his sons, who were not yet old enough to marry. Over the years, too, his prosperity had decreased and then with his old age had come the two disasters which had brought him to trial for his life.

So ended his saga.

Umoru had fought a cruel fate. No placid slave, he had fought and fled; then in later years he had fought against less tangible enemies: jealousy and the witchcraft of the woman he killed. Revenged, as far as man can be revenged on this earth, he had accepted with Moslem resignation the punishment which the law had ordained for killing. And then, something I had said or done that day in my office had reignited the old proud spirit; the old rebel came to life again.

Unbeaten and philosophical as ever, Umoru sat with his little box in the prison, waiting for the final act of his drama. 'Previous occupation: slave'—perhaps; but a rebel at heart, one of the undefeated.

PART FIVE

Idoma

CHAPTER EIGHTEEN

Stirrings of Democracy

Whilst we were busy opening up Birnin Kebbi and the other towns of Gwandu, building drains, stopping erosion, planting many thousands of trees, building schools and dispensaries and new roads, considerable publicity (including the preparation of a film) was given to similar developments at Udi in the Eastern Provinces; the chief difference from our campaign appeared to be the concentration on communal, unpaid work which, in view of the difference of social organization between the two areas, was not surprising. Amongst the Ibo, Native Treasuries and taxation were at an embryo stage as compared with the Northern Emirates, and the people of the Udi area were still in the extended family stage of social organization with its possibilities for communal work. This had died out in the Gwandu area hundreds of years before.

The Emir and his Council read of the Udi experiment in our local papers and we had long discussions about it; it appeared that an exchange of visits might be of mutual benefit by comparing what was being done. My leave was approaching and the date of my return would coincide with a meeting of the House of Representatives in Lagos; to save travelling expenses, we thought that a party of four or five from Gwandu could proceed from Lagos to Udi where I would join them after travelling there direct from leave. Udi confirmed that they would be pleased to see us and that the proposed date was convenient. My Resident was then informed of the position and his authority was sought to go ahead with our plans and to spend the thirty or forty pounds needed for the extra travelling expenses, but to our surprise, the reply was far from enthusiastic, and whilst neither agreeing to nor forbidding the visit, said, to the great disappointment of the Emir, that the matter should be left until the date of my return was known.

We went on leave, leaving all our loads and my car and Njaro at Birnin Kebbi; a fortnight before the date of my return there arrived a letter from my Resident saying that the Udi trip must be postponed, and that before returning to Birnin Kebbi to take over the Gwandu Division again, I was to do a special investigation in Sokoto itself. Five days later arrived a letter from the Secretariat to say that I had been posted to the Benue Province and that my Resident had been instructed to send loads, car and boys to Makurdi; the following day arrived a letter from a friend, half-apologizing for this posting, which was apparently his fault. After a long spell in the Secretariat, he had been told that he would be posted elsewhere, and that it was proposed that he should go to Benue. He paid a hurried visit to his doctor, who issued a medical certificate that he must not serve in any Province other than Zaria or Plateau—the two most temperate in climate and with most amenities. Accordingly, the usual game of general post that followed the posting of an officer to or from the Secretariat had become even more involved than usual, and the next officer of suitable seniority due from leave had been posted to Benue; this was because 'it was essential that the chronic shortage of staff in Benue should be relieved at once', and I was the next to return.

This question of postings had always been a vexed one: it had been axiomatic for years that plans for officers to serve in the Secretariat must be made well ahead and that nothing must be allowed to interfere with them, no matter how many others must ensue as a consequence to fill each resultant vacancy made necessary by the first. It was held that, whilst the Secretariat had no 'slack' in the way of officers extra to the establishment, every Province had a certain number of touring officers who in the last event could be drawn upon for office posts until the shortage passed. The system was neither new nor confined to Nigeria; Leakey in his book *Kenya*, published in 1936, took a number of officers and showed the postings each had had over a number of years, and took certain posts and showed who had filled each over the same period.

Had any colony been homogeneous, there would have been less objection to this senseless moving about of officers, but there were very many ethnic and linguistic groups in Northern Nigeria. Changes from tour to tour meant that an officer never had time to learn an extra language; in Bornu I had the utmost difficulty in passing my Hausa examinations; at various times I started to learn Shuwa Arabic, Tiv and Fulani but in every case before I got far, I was moved elsewhere. Even this posting to Benue did not mean that my knowledge of the Tiv and their language would be of value, as I was posted to the Idoma Division.

The frequent changes brought about in order to fill posts which could otherwise have been left vacant for a month or two, were disliked both by the Administrative Service and by the people for whom they worked, and the Emir of Gwandu protested at my being moved, but to no avail.

A few years afterwards, when I had become the head of a Department, I visited the Yambio area of the Sudan with my Northern Nigerian Cabinet Minister; this was the headquarters of the Zande people very similar to, and probably relations of, the Tiv; to our astonishment we learnt that in forty years this Division had had two District Commissioners—and Yambio was neither a healthy nor a coveted posting, deep in the Congo forests.

This policy had been introduced into Nigeria soon after the First World War; up till that date, there had been in effect two services, the one staffing the Secretariats and the other, the old Political Service, in the field. Indeed up to the time of the amalgamation of the two, the complaints had been to the other extreme, that officers spent too long in one Division. The preface to an official publication, *Notes on the Tribes, Provinces, Emirates and States of the Northern Provinces*, by Temple, the Lieutenant-Governor of the North, published in 1922, read:

Though a political officer may have the completest knowledge of the Province in which he is working, it has been in the past extremely difficult for him to obtain knowledge of other Provinces. Thus a man may work for many years—an official lifetime even—in Sokoto, and yet have no knowledge of Yola or Bornu. Indeed his knowledge may very well be restricted for many years to the affairs connected with the district in which he is stationed.

In Kano, in one of the old files I found, dating from the beginning of the century, was a minute concerning a later eminent Governor: 'This officer has for too long been the sole pebble on the beach of Katsina; it would be good for him to be transferred to where he would be but one amongst the other grains of sand on some southern river bank.'

239

I protested at this posting; after all, I had been sent to Gwandu as a punishment; it was unhealthy and the housing was dreadful; it was not as if I was protesting at being posted away from one of the much sought after Divisions in Zaria or Plateau Provinces; in any case, the ostensible reason was exactly the same as had held in Kano when the Northern Division was left for some months without a District Officer, and the same as had occurred during the time I was in charge of Gwandu when for several weeks I took over Argungu Division as well.

But again I got into serious trouble for daring to protest at action by the Secretariat, and I was accused of persuading the Emir of Gwandu to register his protest. For two months, therefore, I served in the Secretariat at Lagos whilst the powers that be decided what to do with me, during which time, mounted on two of the oldest and worst screws owned by the Lagos Polo Club I helped the Red Tape Worms to win the Merchants' Cup, playing No. 3 to the Back of Sir Hugh Foot.

1 January 1950 would be the anniversary of fifty years of British rule in Northern Nigeria. During my sojourn in the Secretariat, my schedule included such matters as Posts and Telegraphs, and I therefore suggested that this coming anniversary should be marked by a special issue of stamps; not only would this bring in a quite considerable sum from stamp-collectors all over the world, but it could be made the occasion for making a permanent record of the various explorers of the country. Each stamp, I suggested, should be the size of the higher values in this country; each, in addition to bearing the head of His Majesty, should also bear a portrait of one of the explorers and a map showing his route. That for Mungo Park for example would show Africa from near the present Dakar to Nigeria at Boussa; the next value would show Clapperton and Denham and their route across the desert to Bornu and Sokoto; then Clapperton to Sokoto; the Lander brothers and their route down the Niger from Boussa to the sea, and so on. But the idea was unacceptable; as usual every obstacle to a new idea was put forward, and the benefits were discounted. I commend the idea to the present Postmaster-General in Lagos.

But despite the long delay in filling the vacancy which was the ostensible reason for the switch in my posting, discipline had to be maintained, particularly with such an obstreperous individual as I was proving to be, so in due course I took over the Idoma Division. From a material point of view, particularly after Margaret had joined me, we scored; instead of a miserable cement box, condemned pre-1914, we had a new two-storied Lagos-type house, with its own guest wing; it stood on a ridge about seventy feet above the plains at its feet, amongst large trees; we had a lawn and a rose garden, and in the rains we looked across about sixty miles to where the 6,000-foot peaks of the Sonkwalla Hills, which I had climbed in 1941, stood against the eastern sky. We were only eighty miles by rail from Enugu, capital of the Eastern Region, with its many European-type shops; three times a week we could get cold store 'chop', fresh butter, sausages, pork, kippers, bacon and ham; we had pineapples and guavas, mangoes and even coconuts. I had three A.D.O.s, a well-digger, there was a railway official and his wife whom we still number amongst our close friends, a Catholic Mission with a Bishop Apostolic, half a dozen Fathers and four Brothers; and a Methodist mission; we did not lack for company.

Before Margaret arrived, following my old maxim that a District Officer must spend the first few weeks on trek, I set off for a three weeks' tour on foot and bicycle round the high rain-forest of the south of the Division, accompanied for part of the way by the Chief of the Idoma.

Discounting the Bushmen and Pygmies, the earliest inhabitants of Africa south of the Sahara were the true Negroes. At various times there have been the invasions from the north and east of other peoples, as I have described earlier, followed by inter-marriage between the latest arrivals and the earlier peoples. The result is that the true Negro is confined very largely to the high rain-forest along the shores of the Bights of Biafra and Benin, never reached by the invaders.

Idoma Division is another of the great meeting-places of different peoples, and whilst the Idoma clans recognize that they are interrelated in some way, this is not by descent from a common ancestor as amongst their neighbours the Tiv, but by conquest by a small force of invaders and marriage with the women of the conquered. Over the border to the south is the country of the Ibos, true Negroes, and two or three of the Idoma clans along that border recognize that some of their kindreds are not descended from the same tribe as the rest, but are whole kindreds of Ibos which have been adopted and assimilated; they are, whilst of Ibo descent, 'Idoma' and do not regard themselves as Ibo.

In the north of the Division are the purest 'Idoma', the Agatu clan who claim to be an offshoot of the Jukon invasion, if not of the Jukon tribe itself; they had migrated down the Benue and occupied an area across the river on both banks. Slave-raids from Keffi and Nassarawa had driven the bulk of the clan to the south bank, whilst the arrival of the Tiv had driven them more miles westwards to their present site. In the south-east, the elders of the Igumalè clan wear remarkable cocked hats which are said by some experts to be a remnant of Portuguese influence some centuries before. One of these cock-hatted elders had been Lugard's cook for many years.

The Idomas are therefore a mixture of peoples of varied origin with a common bond of marriage with some immigrant race from the north-east; some clans, those nearest the Benue, were more 'Jukon' than the others, but in all Negro blood predominated. They had been head-hunters until recent years, and whilst not imbued to the same extent as the true Negro with secret societies (the Leopard Society existed over my southern border), they had many of the southern customs; amongst these was the ceremonial beating to death of a horse over several days, and, on occasion in the past, human sacrifice at the New Yam Festival. As with the Tiv, the British Administration had organized them on the basis of their clans with the elders of each clan forming both the local court and the Native Authority; like their neighbours to the east, they too had been impressed with the virtues of a paramount chief and they had asked Government to recognize one of the elders of one of the central clans as Chief of the Idoma. This had been done some eighteen months before I arrived in Oturkpo, but to the chagrin of the Chief, there had so far been no formal installation.

During the long tour I made of the southern clans, with the Chief, the Och'Idoma, we tried to meet representatives of an Ibo clan who were infiltrating over the border and occupying farm-land belonging to the southernmost Idoma clan, that of Agala, where the Ibos had built a hamlet. Land pressure in the Ibo country, the first rumblings of the population explosion in this part of the world, had recently become acute whilst there was as yet no similar population pressure amongst the Idoma. The first incursion by these particular immigrants had occurred several years before; as the best way out of the impasse that then occurred as they refused to recognize the authority of the Agala elders, they had been left in possession. They had in time built a small village and the newest trouble was due to the fact that they were now taking a second bite at the cherry, as it were, and moving out of their bridgehead.

This was a serious incursion, so the Och'Idoma and I, with representatives of Agala, arranged to meet the District Officer from the south with his elders on the boundary. Whilst on our way, we met a messenger who said that my opposite number had been summoned to his Provincial Headquarters and could not meet us; he had however urged the Ibo elders to meet me to discuss the matter. We arrived at the boundary of the old farmland, marked by a line of tall earthen cairns, and we sat and waited. No one appeared but we could see from time to time almost naked figures flitting through the bush. One of those on our side who could speak the local Ibo dialect shouted out to tell the other side that we awaited their elders but there came no reply. We next sent a very reluctant emissary along the path that led to where the Ibo hamlet was sited, but after a few paces, shouts were heard, which, I was told, announced that if he persisted, he would be killed. We were unarmed but we could see that the other side were carrying Dane guns—long-barrelled flint-lock guns made from a variety of iron and steel tubes, charged with black powder and broken pieces of iron pot capable of inflicting terrible wounds at the close ranges which the thick bush allowed, as can be seen in Boisragon's account *The Benin Massacre*. Our shouted attempts at intercourse continued, but some of our entourage became alarmed when it was apparent that some of the other side were making their way through the bush to cut off our retreat. Then a voice called that we must go at once as their young men were threatening to kill us. This was no idle boast, for no one in this part of the world was particularly law-abiding. Lugard's first attempt to control Idoma had ended in disaster: Captain O'Riordan, an officer of long experience in Southern Nigeria, had entered the area with a newly appointed police officer, Mr Amyatt-Burney, 15 soldiers, 38 police and 40 carriers; they had been attacked and Burney killed.

243

O'Riordan was first wounded then killed and the entire party either killed or taken as slaves, of whom 56 were eventually released, after a long and expensive punitive expedition. If my demise were the cause of another, I should get little sympathy, so after shouting that we should tell their District Officer, we slunk, like small boys who threaten the other side that they will tell their mother, back through the bush to the north.

Back in Oturkpo the daily round continued until we received word that the Acting Chief Commissioner would visit Benue Province in November to install the Paramount Chief of the Idoma. In law his recognition had taken place eighteen months or so before, when, after a great deal of careful investigation, it had been decided to accede to the requests of the Idoma and recognize one of their elders as their first paramount chief, but in the eyes of the local population, it had not yet occurred as he had not had the ceremony of installation. In the meantime we had entered the new age of Nigerian constitution-making, and the superiority of the ballot-box over traditional methods of electing or selecting leaders, was being actively canvassed, particularly by the younger generation. Some of the younger Idoma, perhaps a couple of dozen in all, were convinced that much needed changing in their country and that only a young, educated man could do it.

One had every sympathy with them but the fact remained that the vast majority of the tribe still clung to their old ways. At Igumalè the clan was in the throes of selecting a new leader, and the nominee of the younger generation seemed infinitely preferable to the rather horrible old grey-beard favoured by the majority; but no matter what I could say or urge, the younger man was rejected. The activities of one of the Oturkpo educated young men became so outrageous at Igumalè following this rebuff that I sent full details of them to the Crown Counsel and sought advice as to the possibility of charging him with an offence against the relevant section of the Criminal Code. The reply was to the effect that, on the facts stated, a charge would certainly lie, but that it was doubtful if a Court would convict in view of the types of witness we could expect on both sides. I put this advice away and thought hard.

News of the approaching installation triggered off overt opposition to the Chief on the part of the younger generation; it was useless to tell them that the only step that mattered had been taken eighteen months before and that this coming installation was merely to give publicity to the fact. Indeed, as I told them, as the Idoma had never had a paramount chief in the past, there was no recognized ceremony of turbaning or stooling or lifting on a buffalo hide as was the custom in Bornu; I had had the task of designing a 'traditional' ceremony, including the giving and taking of oaths. I told them that Kaduna had only agreed to the appointment of a paramount chief after everyone had been consulted; as far as Government was concerned the time was long past for objection. But they were unconvinced. 'He has not been installed; he is no true paramount chief; we will not have him.'

In fact the Idoma were very lucky in their choice; they had chosen a man in the prime of life who, whilst not literate, could write a little; he was not out of sympathy with the younger generation and was accepted by the elders.

The Idoma, as I have shown above, had no close ties other than those within the clan; they are an independent and a truculent people and there were thousands of Dane guns in the area; the Chief's own clan would be there on the day in the greatest numbers and if a disturbance occurred, they might be supported by the representatives of all the northern clans, and take a bloody revenge for the cancellation of the ceremony if that was forced upon us. In any case, any interruption would be deplorable, and any, probably distorted, account in the Press might set back Idoma's political development for many years. The only factor to my mind that must guide the Administration was, what was best for the Idoma people? A further period of argument and division, or a chance to have a period during which they could learn to live as a unit? The Och'Idoma was doing a very fine job; he was gaining the confidence of the various elders; he must be given a chance to prove himself further.

Now a new factor entered into the picture; out of the blue I was told that I was to proceed forthwith to Kaduna to assume control of a new development scheme; there was no one to replace me, so I was to hand over to the most senior of my A.D.O.s—a second-year Cadet. This was ironic; I had been sent to Idoma as no time could be allowed for anyone else to return from leave, nor could any A.D.O. be allowed to take over. But it seemed to me that it would be monstrous to leave the problems of the installation to a very junior officer in this way, and I therefore said that I must stay until after the ceremony.

The Och'Idoma and his Council were very upset at my posting, and yet again a letter was sent to Kaduna protesting at my being posted away; I had been accused of putting the Emir of Gwandu up to such a protest, but I was not accused a second time.

I had told the Resident what I feared and we had a long meeting, as a result of which a plain-clothes constable of the Nigeria Police was sent to Oturkpo to gain the confidence of the young plotters. A fortnight before the great day, we had another meeting in Makurdi at which my worst fears were more than confirmed. The ringleader was the same man who had caused trouble at Igumalè; it was apparently proposed that he and a small band of supporters should interrupt the Installation Ceremony, and whilst one gave the Chief Commissioner a protest in English setting out the reasons why no paramount chief was wanted, others would read out translations to the assembled crowds; some of the elders of some of the southern clans were said to have agreed that if this was done, they would get up and leave the ceremony. Fighting would immediately break out, and perhaps lives would be lost. I urged that the ringleader be arrested and charged with the offence at Igumalè, and that bail be refused in order to remove him from the scene. The Resident refused to countenance such a plan; he would arrange for another dozen unarmed police to be present to control the crowds; I must try and persuade the trouble-makers not to cause a commotion on the day.

Finally I lost patience; I pointed out that I was staying at my own suggestion as it was little short of scandalous to leave a second-tour officer to handle serious trouble; I could leave and wash my hands of the whole affair if I so wished, at once; was he, the Resident, prepared to assume responsibility and allow me to go? There was more hesitating, and I left saying that if I was in charge I would act as I thought necessary to prevent rioting and bloodshed.

Two nights before the ceremony I received word that emissaries were going from clan to clan stirring up feeling against the chief. His own clan were threatening to take action against anyone who interfered in any way. They were bringing even more men than we expected to the installation and were ripe for a fight. At 3 p.m.

the following day I issued a warrant for the arrest of the ring-leader and he was put in gaol on a charge arising from the Igumalè episode. Within half an hour his friends arrived demanding his release on bail; this I refused and they withdrew making threats. The Sergeant of the Nigeria Police unit next arrived to say that he feared an attack on my house; an attempt might be made to shoot Margaret or myself from the shelter of the garden. We brought four of his men to sit in dark shade around the house.

The next day dawned clear and fine, and vast crowds were soon assembling on the football field where we were having the ceremony; soon the elders of the many clans were seated in a half-circle facing the dais. Wearing full dress uniform, I made my way to the station to meet the Chief Commissioner's special train; on the platform was a deputation of the trouble-makers. The train drew in and I climbed on board, greeted the Chief Commissioner and told him and the Resident what I had done. The latter pro-tested that I had not consulted him; I told them of the waiting deputation and a letter was accepted asking for my immediate removal; I said that I accepted full responsibility for whatever might occur, peaceful or bloody.

We reached the field and the ceremony I had invented started in the presence of a vast crowd, and with all the Europeans in the station present. The cadet to whom I was handing over immedi-ately after the ceremony stood close to me at the side of the dais on which we three senior officials sat; I saw a youth crawl across the open space between the elders and the crowd; he spoke to one from a southern clan, and I saw the latter turn and make a sign which was repeated by someone in the crowd. I spoke urgently to the cadet and told him to take a couple of police and seize who-ever it was; he made his way slowly round the back of the crowd whilst I sat on tenterhooks and the messenger crawled back to the crowd. I saw him reach the place at last, lean over and tap a man on the shoulder, saw the latter stand up and be grabbed by the police and taken off to the guardroom. No one else stirred, but I saw the elder in the middle of the ground hastily stuffing a paper down the front of his gown and trying to appear inconspicuous. The protest was ended; no one else moved; the Chief was in-stalled, and surrounded by dancing and singing crowds he went back to his house.

Changing from uniform to lounge suit, I accompanied the Chief Commissioner on a tour of the Central Office, dispensary and so on. An hour later, having handed over, Margaret and I left for Kaduna.

The Resident gave me an hour's start and then, quite rightly, released the ringleader on bail; in due course I received a letter from him to say that he had been charged and stood his trial, but that a man with a better brain than mine had found him not guilty. He gloated at my confusion and called me rude names. I would probably have done the same had our positions been reversed.

But by now my career as a Bush D.O. was at an end; at last that half-sexed desk-bound life that I loathed had caught up with me. The Och'Idoma, now fifteen years in office, still sends us a Christmas card each year.

NOTE: Sir Hugh Foot, at that time the Chief Secretary to the Government of Nigeria, had actively intervened in my case. In his book *A Start in Freedom* he writes:

'Take a young man with only a few years' experience in the territory to which he has been sent. Put him in charge of a District. Make him responsible for everything in that District. He may have a few technical officers, one or two doctors, engineers, policemen, agricultural officers to help him but he is responsible to higher authority for all the varied activities of the government in his district.

'Leave him there for say five years; to get to know the people and work with them and for them and learn their language and share their difficulties and disappointments and their aims and hopes. At the end of this time—there is no question of credit or merit in this, it is automatic and inevitable—he becomes wholly devoted to the people of his District. And he spends much of his effort fighting higher authority to get for his people what he thinks they need and deserve.'

'The few technical officers' must relate to his early service in Palestine for none but the largest Divisions (as we called Districts in Nigeria) had any such staff. As for posting anyone for even two tours—that is, about three years—this too was almost unknown in Nigeria. I had two tours in Bornu Province, not however in one Division, and one full and two half tours at either end, in Kano Province, again in a multiplicity of jobs. I know of no officer in my time in Nigeria who spent five consecutive years in one Division.

Postscript

'The woolly-minded people will use the woolly word;
And when they find a good one they leave it foul and furred.
"Exploiting" is a noble term of enterprise and toil;
It rides the world on rubber, and it drives the world on oil.
Where would the coloured people be, and where would be Detroit,
If we had sat at home and said, "Oh dear, don't let's exploit".'
From 'Exploitation' by
Sir Alan Herbert.

It is the prerogative of the young to believe that they alone are idealists and that no previous generation had any ideals; with increasing years not only does one recognize the existence of youthful idealists in all generations but on occasion one is left wondering at their astonishing blindness to reality. What is one to think now of the generation which gladly immolated itself in the years 1914–16, and of the Oxford generation which vowed never to fight for King and Country? To most of the world today, particularly the younger generation, the words *Colony* and *Colonial* are pejorative, yet perhaps in another twenty-five years, it will be recognized that the first fifty years of this century were the Golden Age in most of the underdeveloped countries of the world, and that we who served there did more for our charges than do the idealists in the Voluntary Services of today. Ignorant no longer of the problems which face Africa, many of the people of this country now wag their heads and sagely opine that we did not do much for our former colonies; they and the Government of this country certainly did not, but history will surely laud the efforts of the men on the spot dealing with ignorance and superstition, as yet unaffected by any wind of change.

It is idle talk, too, to suggest that the politicians in the years 1945–64, have followed a carefully thought-out plan for Africa; as Heussler shows, as late as 1948 the Colonial Office was still planning the training of future generations of Administrative Officers. In *Britain's Moment in the Middle East, 1914–1956* the author argues that the desire for Empire, like the changing cut of fashion, is partly dictated by economic reasons. By 1946 confidence about Empire as a mission and ideal, and confidence about Empire as part of the order of things, had decayed. As the tasks of Empire became more exacting and more thankless, the confidence that Empire was the right thing to pursue—in itself but a short-lived concept in Britain—crumbled. Perhaps the Welfare State and full employment have made a lifetime spent in bush, despite the idealism they show at Easter weekends, no longer acceptable to the youth of today?

Whether the sudden change was due to a different mental attitude or to other factors will be for history to assess. One politician has hinted that it was American pressure, almost one might say, American subversion, that made us give way. Was it because when the control of the Indian Army passed from our hands, we no longer had the man-power to underwrite the risks that call from time to time for military intervention? Perhaps our politicians, exposed to the carefully planned questioning of television personalities, are no longer sufficiently robust to face the odium of ill-informed world opinion when subversion and 'freedom' movements, inspired from outside, make them appear reactionary? 'No Roy,' said Duncan Sandys to Sir Roy Welensky. 'You see, we British have lost the will to govern.'

Whatever the reasons, and they must be complex, the results of the sudden *volte-face*, or the rapid speeding-up of existing plans—call it what you will—are not wholly disappointing; there is much of which we can all be proud, the present rulers of the new states and their one-time teachers. The short time during which this country was responsible for much of Africa included two World Wars and the longest economic depression ever known; nothing was possible during those periods but to maintain law and order.

To those who were on the spot, no hindsight is required to know that little thought was given in Whitehall to the future of the colonies; plenty of time was spent by lawyers drafting out constitutions—many of them unworkable—but no attempt seems to have been made to assess the needs of trained manpower: no one seems to have realized that if the men of our Colonial Services were withdrawn, others must take their places, and would be willingly supplied by other interested powers, for trade has never followed the flag, but the nationality of the adviser on the spot. The Colonial Services were largely brought to an end with the maximum cost and disturbance to the one-time Colonies when in fact they should, in most cases, have been vastly expanded. What was required was not large gratuities which to many Africans appear as large bribes to their European Officers to leave them in the lurch, but a system of guarantees to the members of the Services, underwritten by the Home Government, which would have persuaded them to stay as long as there was work for them. Perhaps in the same way as British troops now don the blue berets of the United Nations, the Colonial Services, as Heussler suggests, should have donned a United Nations badge.

Reduced to its simplest terms: there are four major fields in which help is required in Nigeria and the other Colonies, for years after independence. The first, now past, was in the field of Cabinet Government and the organization of the Central Departments which stem therefrom; in Nigeria some 100 officers at most were required for this work, but instead of this relatively small number being seconded from the Home Civil Service, Bush D.O.s like myself were drawn in; none of us had any knowledge of Cabinet Government; most of us had joined the Colonial Administrative Service to avoid a Civil Service existence; we were worse than the blind leading the blind as few of us had any faith in the organization which we were supposed to be creating. It also seems to have been accepted too easily in Whitehall that what Africa wanted, and what was best for Africa, was Cabinet Government on the British model. Its rapid collapse in Ghana and the Sudan—to mention the obvious examples—casts some doubt on the correctness of the axiom.

In *The Times* in December 1963, Professor Bauer of the London School of Economics wrote: '. . . reports in your columns on Ghana should enlighten opinion on the situation there. But they do not discuss the responsibility of the West, and particularly of Britain, for its emergence and development. Ghana is not only a dictatorship but largely a totalitarian state. . .' and he goes on to show that our creation and perpetuation of vast state trading monopolies for the major export crops and the use of their surpluses to set up state-controlled industries was the best foundation possible on which to build a totalitarian state. Did any of the economic experts who advised the Colonial Office ever foresee or warn those in power of these dangers?

In the second field, that of Local Government, in Nigeria little thought had been given to how it should develop or the time necessary for its development. There were so many differing native structures; the strong Emirates of the North were the worst material possible if the ultimate goal was elected bodies similar to those in this country, whilst the seemingly more backward Ibo were much more suitable; between lay tribes like the Idoma and Tiv, which, as I have shown, surprised everyone by their sudden demand for paramount chiefs, demands which were agreed to, though in both cases if the ultimate goal is a one-man one-vote 'democracy', it was probably a retrogressive step in the long run. The Colonial Office and its successor has one Adviser on Local Government; can it be seriously suggested that he has a sufficient knowledge of the many differing needs throughout even one single colony to be in a position adequately to advise? In this country since 1945 more and more power has been taken from the local Councils to new bodies such as now run our hospitals and transport, or to the Central Government; are we certain that something on the lines of the American town-manager system is not what is best for Africa? None of the Bush D.O.s, the men most concerned with the problem, were ever given any training or education in this matter; in 1949 some eight members of the Native Administrations in the North were sent for two months to this country to study Local Government; can it be seriously contended that such a subject can be adequately studied in such a short time, the more so as at that time the eight neophytes had never been to England before, so that much of their time went in learning about a new mode of life, climate and the rest, leaving little time or mental capacity to study this subject when suffering from the mental indigestion which followed their sudden transfer to a whole new environment. Was this the best we could do, or was this merely the small amount of whitewash judged sufficient to hide what we had not done?

After Idoma, I became the Head of a Department dealing with major economic development—the third area where outside help

is required. Unused, unlike all good Secretariat Officers, to be-
coming an expert on anything in a very short time, I wrote that
we should stop kidding ourselves, and get the advice of real
experts. I suggested Professor Arthur Lewis, later chosen by
President Nkrumah as his adviser, but this suggestion was unacceptable; I then suggested the World Bank. Presumably this
sounded sufficiently impressive, and the World Bank came, saw
and advised.

In any case, much of this major development is being under-
taken by private organizations; it is they who spent £45,000,000
on prospecting for oil in Nigeria before a drop was found; had
it been left to any of us, more ink than oil would have flowed
once £4,500 was spent. The World Bank Survey stimulated
other schemes: I had pleaded for urgent consideration of a
£2,000,000 hydro-electric scheme at Shiroro but no one dared
act; fifteen years later the Nigerian Government is undertaking
the £100,000,000 Niger Barrage scheme, of which Shiroro forms
a small part which could have been built first instead of last as is
now planned.

Many of the problems of these new states stem from the arti-
ficiality of their creation, which ignored all the facts of geography
and economics. Much of the former French Chad and Niger
Colonies are parts of the Nigerian economic and transport hinterland and should be persuaded in the interests of us all to join an
enlarged Nigerian Federation. The great Niger–Benue River system needs an International River Authority if the destruction of
timber in the forests of Sierra Leone is not to affect the new Niger
Barrage and if the capture of the Chari-Logona system by the
tributaries of the River Benue is to be stopped (if that occurs,
Chad will dry up and the effects on the climate of this part of the
world are unforseeable).

There remains the fourth—the field of local development,
forestry, agriculture, veterinary, education, roads, dams, fisheries
and so on, where the need is so great; but this is a roll-call of the
old Colonial Services which were wound up with such haste. Again
to quote *The Times*; in January 1964 Professor Hollingsworth
wrote of the mounting help being given by other States at the
time when ours is ending. 'Scores of Russians in Mali, twenty-five
Geologists from the States in Pakistan, are random examples of

such activities which have recently come to my notice,' he wrote. An editorial in *World Crops* in September 1963 was more specific:

It is relatively easy for a developed nation to assist in medical aid schemes by seconding medical practitioners to an area of need. With little or no experience of local conditions the medico can produce dramatic results saving many lives and thereby markedly stimulating population growth. Comparable dramatic results can rarely be achieved in terms of food production in these areas. It is indeed much easier to succour a peasant family dying from the effects of malnutrition than it is to persuade them to alter their system of farming in order to overcome the causes of malnutrition . . . the technologist fresh from the Canadian prairies or a Danish Agricultural community can in fact do more harm than good in fields other than research. The volunteer organisations such as the Peace Corps and Voluntary Service Overseas are, by their very nature, worse than useless for purposes of agricultural extension. The irony of the situation is that at the present time the experience and know-how required is being disposed of at an unprecedented rate. Branded with the politically expedient term 'colonialism' experienced expatriate agricultural and research workers are being packed off home. In their place far less effective and much more expensive FAO advice is sought. . . . As a sequel the experienced expatriate agricultural officer returning to his homeland is an unwanted technician in a land of plenty; one who ends up as the Secretary of a Golf Club.

One might also quote the findings of President Kennedy's Committee on the 'Older American', which lamented the loss to the community of their skills and knowledge; 'it is an incredible waste not to find some way to put this vast reservoir of ability into action'. Many of us were half their age when our service ended.

Those coming direct from the Western World hope to deal with ignorance with a fine missionary zeal; they little realize that ignorance is easy to deal with. It is a clean slate ready to take the new knowledge. But instead of ignorance they find anti-knowledge, a mountain which must be first cleared away before the ignorance which exists below can be dealt with.

The mistakes of the past twenty years are not dead and buried; rather we have sown a crop, the harvest of which no man can foresee and for which we can only wait.

But recrimination is useless and only fools learn not from their folly. We must all, white and black, look forward to a happier state of mutual respect, as citizens of that world community which we cannot flee. The need in Africa is not for hundreds of untrained youthful volunteers; when all their expenses have been paid, the cost in many cases will be found to be out of all proportion to the benefits conferred on those they went to help. Indeed, the chief value of much of this effort lies not in concrete results but in the better understanding that stems therefrom, between the citizens of tomorrow of the countries of Africa and Europe. Enthusiasm for short periods is not enough; knowledge, dogged determination, a capacity to learn, sympathy and time to learn are all necessary.

But the rewards are great. Not in the bloated capitals; not in the Departments of Government, in the clubs and the bars of the big hotels, not on the golf courses and beaches, but out in the bush amongst the hard-working, lovable, estimable men and women of Africa; men like my friends: the ex-slave Umoru Kebbi; Agapalawa, leader of his people and trustee for them as part of the greater unit of those on earth and those still to be born; Yahaya, Emir of Gwandu; Abdullahi Bayero, Emir of Kano; the Emirs of Yauri and Zaria; Yerima Boyi and Moman Biyu; Bukar Maroua; Kamkura and Garuba my horse-boys; Musa Shuwa, Karimu and Ibi, some of my boys; hundreds of others from prisoners to Prime Ministers; the old Pagan whose name I have long forgotten who told me that each night if he looked down on Gwoza and saw a light in my house, he too lit a fire that I might know that he, my friend, was watching over me.

It is not a Service that the Start in Freedom has destroyed, but a way of Service, without which no Start would have been possible.

'I am a Berliner,' said President Kennedy to underline the indivisibility of Freedom.

I was a Bush D.O.

L'Envoi

In Northern Nigeria under our rule, visitors to the Emirs were always accompanied by a member of the Administrative Service, partly to interpret, partly to ensure that nothing went on of which the Administration was unaware.

A year or so after the events described in this book, as Director of a Government department, I accompanied two important visitors from England on a tour of part of Northern Nigeria. In Zaria we saw the Resident, and my charges asked if they might meet the Emir; in response to a phone call, the Emir suggested an immediate visit, and added that, since I was with them, no other interpreter was required: *'Mr Wayit dan gari ne'* – I was no stranger to the town.

We were received, and the Emir showed his guests round before we retired to the audience chamber, where the usual platitudes were exchanged through me. Tiring of his guests, the Emir ignored them, and, speaking to me in Hausa, asked if I had heard of the recent rebuff he and some of the other Emirs had received. I had not, so the Emir continued in anger:

'We went to the Governor; we told him that since the time of Lugard we have been an integral part of the Administration, for we are the Fathers of our people; now we are ignored; our advice is unwelcome, but these clerks, these lawyers from the south, are listened to in our place. They run to England, and all listen to them, even in the seats of power. Then the Governor here is told what to do, based on what these clerks have said. We too want to go and see the men in England who wield authority—for the Government is not listened to. But we have been told that, if we go, we go at our peril; we shall not be accompanied, we shall not be helped, we have even been refused an interpreter. We may go, but we shall not be received. The clerks go and are received like chiefs; we chiefs ask to go, and are told that we shall be treated like criminals who have exhausted every appeal.'

But no matter what the fears of the Emirs and of the Administration, the march to Independence could not be stayed. Nigeria had a plethora of barristers, for, in countries emerging from illiteracy, memory still fills the place of knowledge stored in books, and legal examinations require only memory, not practical knowledge. There were also a few doctors, but, as far as I am aware, representatives of other professions could be counted on the fingers of both hands. In Northern Nigeria there were no barristers, for the Moslem religion includes a legal code, and, in 1954, only one locally born doctor. In the absence of any others, the first leaders to replace the British Administration came perforce from the ranks of the teachers and of the members of the Native Administrations.

Sir Abubakar Tafawa Balewa was a teacher; we were fellow members of the Northern Regional Development Board, and after accompanying me to one of the development schemes of which I was in charge, he moved that a vote of appreciation of my efforts should be included in the Board's minutes. A year or two later, I accompanied him on part of a tour of this country. Before he became Prime Minister of Nigeria he was a constant visitor to our house, and it was because of this old friendship that I asked him to write a foreword for our book. It is said that he was assassinated because the young leaders of the Army wished to rid Nigeria of corruption. I do not believe that Sir Abubakar was ever corrupt. He died as one might have expected; a devout Moslem, he asked only to be allowed to say the early prayer; he was then shot, pleading, I am certain, for no mercy, but treating his murderers with the proud disdain that his faith taught.

Sir Ahmadu Bello, the late Prime Minister of Northern Nigeria, was the Sardauna of Sokoto when I was at Birnin Kebbi. He was our guest there on several occasions, and when we were posted to Kaduna he was a frequent visitor to our house. When I resigned in 1954 he, with the members of his cabinet, gave a farewell reception in my honour; twice since he has asked me to return to Nigeria to head the department I founded. He was shot without mercy by men who would not have dared face him by daylight, alone and unarmed.

Faults the Sardauna may have had; but that was no reason brutally to murder his five police guards, or to shoot his wife, who, hearing the noise of shooting, ran to shield his body with her own. No mercy was shown.

What of the future? These murders are not the end of the chapter but the opening of a long history of trouble. In the past two years, probably more people have been murdered in the name of politics in Nigeria, particularly in the Western Region, than died in all the 60 years of British rule, including the original campaigns of annexation. To end corruption, three Prime Ministers and another leading politician have been done to death. Yet corruption is the evil that consumes not only Nigeria but the whole of Africa; the evil is not ended by removing a few of those who may have benefited from it.

Now the rule of force has taken the place of the rule of law; now he who can rely, momentarily perhaps, on the guns at the disposal of the company commanders, rules; when the company commanders are tired of him, he will go. The rulers of other parts of Africa must now all be looking over their shoulders, wondering if they will be allowed to die in their beds. And if they do, what guarantee have they that their successors will not be chosen at gunpoint?

Sir Abubakar is dead; it will be long before the name of Nigeria is again strong and respected in the councils of the world.

Index